South of France with Kids

Kathryn Tomasetti

To my favourite kids: Isabella,
Ted, William, Myles & Isla.

Villefrance Bay on
the Riviera.

Lounging snugly along the Mediterranean, the South of France is as exotic as it is exciting. This region is synonymous with action-packed adventure and year-round fun in the sun, whether you're travelling with tots, teens or kids of any age in between.

The entire Riviera is beautiful beach territory. Stretches of sand race from the Estérel's crimson-coloured inlets, past Nice's 5-km seafront to the parasol-dotted promenade on Italy's frontier. St-Tropez teeters on the tip of a luscious peninsula, around the corner from a sprinkling of sub-tropical islands. Inland, Haute-Provence is home to the Gorges du Verdon, an adventure sport haven. Gentler is the Luberon, the Provence of movie sets: fields of lavender and sunflowers, criss-crossed with cycling routes and hiking trails.

Marseille is flanked by kilometres of limestone *calanques* and some of the coastline's most brilliantly turquoise waters. While in the wild Camargue, cowboys and girls can saddle up, steal a peek at black bulls and spot flamingos on the flatlands. And at the end of the day? Dine in terraced restaurants or plump for beachside, sand-in-your-toes tables; stay up late telling stories in a treehouse or snooze out under the stars.

Introduction

Kathryn Tomasetti formed a crush on the South of France during an InterRail trip in the early '90s, and in 2005 she made a permanent move to an apartment in Nice. Her favourite sights in the area are the Pont du Gard bridge (see page 154), the Iles de Lérins (see page 40) off the coast at Cannes and the Roussillon ochre walking trail (see page 134). Kathryn is also the author of Footprint's *Provence & Côte d'Azur*.

About the book

South of France with Kids is a handy, selective guide to help your family plan your holiday in advance and make the most of your time while you're abroad. Dreaming of days in the sun? Browse through the book for vacation inspiration. Its small size makes it perfect for referrals on the road too. All of the guide's listings include postcodes to help you track them down with satnav, although do remember that a French *code postal* can be quite general, more similar to a US zip code than a street-specific postcode in the UK.

South of France with Kids covers the Mediterranean coastline from Menton, on the Italian border, to the Camargue, west of Marseille. Inland, this region sweeps north, encompassing the Luberon, the Provençal (Southern) Alps and the Parc du Mercantour. It takes in major cities from Montpellier to Nice, as well as the islands scattered off these shores.

We couldn't list all of the South of France's family-friendly activities, restaurants and places to stay. We've chosen our favourites, but if we've missed yours, drop us a line so we can check it out for the next edition.

Below you will find some background information to help you get the most out of the book and out of your holiday.

Bienvenue!

In most places in France – and in all places in this guide – your family will be welcomed with open arms. In restaurants, kids have their own menu, and in many bigger or more casual establishments, an outdoor play area. Hotels usually offer large or interconnected family rooms, and almost always allow one child under 12 years old per double room to stay free of charge. Trains, buses, boat trips and sights have reduced fares for under 18s, and are frequently free for tots and kids of primary school age.

Blue Flag awards

Blue Flag eco-awards are given out to beaches all over the world on a yearly basis. Check blueflag.org before you travel for an up-to-date annual list.

Tourist boards

The official, multi-lingual website of the Comité Régional de Tourisme Provence-Alpes-Côte d'Azur (Regional Tourist Board for Provence, the Alps and the Côte d'Azur) is decouverte-paca. fr. For the Comité Départemental du Tourisme des Bouches-du-Rhône (Departmental Tourist Board for the Bouches-du-Rhône – Provence, Marseille and the Camargue) it's visitprovence. com. Details for local Tourist Offices are given in Grown-ups Stuff (page 172) or within each specific chapter.

Symbol key

Beaches
- Blue Flag award
- Café/pub/restaurant
- Beach shop
- Deckchairs for hire
- Beach huts for hire
- Water sports for hire
- Amusement arcade
- Lifeguards (summer)
- Dogs allowed year round
- Toilets nearby
- Car park nearby
- Warning!

Campsites
- Tents
- Caravans
- Shop
- Playground
- Picnic area
- Disabled facilities
- Dogs welcome
- Walk to beach
- Electric hook-up
- Family bathroom
- Baby-care area
- Bikes for hire
- Café or takeaway van
- Campfires allowed

It is up to parents to assess whether the ideas and suggestions in *South of France with Kids* are suitable or appropriate for their children. While the author and publisher have made every effort to ensure accuracy of information on activities, accommodation and food, they cannot be held responsible for any loss, injury or illness resulting from advice or information given in this book.

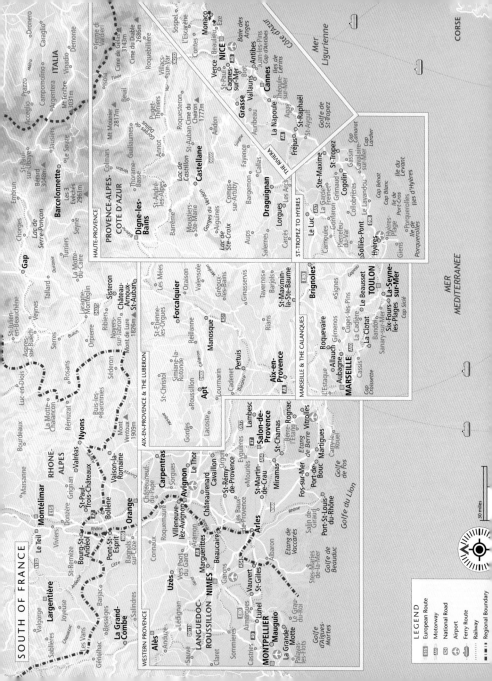

Contents

Adorable animal parks

Alpha Wolf Park St-Martin-Vésubie 92
La Ferme du Far West Antibes Marineland, Antibes 41
Musée Océanographique Monaco 42
Parc Ornithologique de Pont de Gau Stes-Maries-de-la-Mer 164
Parc Zoologique Fréjus 42
Réserve des Monts d'Azur Thorenc 92
Seaquarium Le Grau-du-Roi 165
Village des Tortues Gonfaron 69
Zoo de la Barben La Barben 132

Adrenaline rushes

Aboard Rafting Castellane 88
Aerogliss Parapente St-André-les-Alpes 88
Base Sport & Nature Entrevaux 88
Colorado Adventures Rustrel 130
Downhill skiing at one of Haute-Provence's four ski resorts 90
Inter Racing Kart Fréjus 38
Les Montgolfières du Sud Uzès 150
Montgolfière Vol-Terre St-Saturnin-d'Apt 134
Nature Elléments Roquebrune-Cap-Marin 39
Via Ferrata du Rocher de Neuf Heures Digne-les-Bains 87

Beautiful beaches

L'Aiguille Théoule-sur-Mer 49
Les Belles Rives Juan-les-Pins 36
Calanques Figuerolles La Ciotat 107
Le Canadel Rayol-Canadel-sur-Mer 64
L'Espiguette Le Grau-du-Roi 163
L'Estagnol Bormes-les-Mimosas 65
Gigaro La Croix-Valmer 64
Hi Beach Nice 46
La Mala Cap d'Ail 34
Les Marinières Villefranche-sur-Mer 35

Big days out

Les arènes Nîmes 152
Azur Park Gassin 68
Château des Baux Les Baux-de-Provence 152
Labyrinthe des Sens Cogolin 69
Parfumerie Molinard Grasse 41
Musée du Bonbon Haribo Uzès 153
Palais des Papes Avignon 158
Petit Train des Plages Le Lavandou 69
Les remparts Aigues-Mortes 162
Train des Pignes Nice to Digne-les-Bains 93

Cool spots to snooze

Airotel la Sorguette L'Isle-sur-la-Sorgue 167
Canvas Chic Labastide de Virac 167
Château de Valmer Gigaro, La Croix-Valmer 77
Le Domaine des Grands Prés Dieulefit 141
Old Creek Camp Cuges-les-Pins 120
Orion B&B St-Paul-de-Vence 50
Péniche QI Avignon 168
Réserve des Monts d'Azur Eco-Lodges Thorenc 97
Terre d'Arômes Séranon 97
Tiki Hutte Ramatuelle 77

Dazzling drives

Bormes-les-Mimosas to Col du Canadel (Route des Crêtes no 1) 61
Corniche de l'Estérel
D543 between Aix-en-Provence and Rognes 48
D6 through the Plateau de Valensole 129
D7n between Sénas and St-Cannat 128
D71 along the Gorges du Verdon's *rive gauche* (left bank) 95
D943 between Lourmarin and Apt 128
La Ciotat to Cassis (Route des Crêtes no 3) 105
La Palud-sur-Verdon loop above the Gorges du Verdon (Route des Crêtes no 2) 95
The Riviera's three *corniches*: the *grande* (high), *moyenne* (middle) and *basse* (low) 31

Fun & free

Catch the **changing of the guards in Monaco** 32
Float over to **Ile de la Barthelasse** on Avignon's free shuttle boat 157
Follow your nose to the **Luberon's** *lavande* (lavender) fields 129
Hike the **sentier du littoral**, the South of France's coastal walking path 60
Look out for flamingos at the Camargue's **Domaine de Méjanes** 163
Play around at Nice's hilltop **Colline du Château** park 45
Take in the cartoony artworks at **Musée d'Art Naïf Anatole Jakovsky** in Nice 45

Top 10

Chaudeyrac Châteauneuf-de-Randon
St-Étienne-de-Lugdarès
le Tanargue 1458m
Aubenas
Marsanne
Montboucher
La-Bégude-de-Mazenc
Bouvières
La Motte-Chalancon

N102
Valgorge
Voquë
Le Teïl
Montélimar

Bagnols-les-Bains
Largentière
Villeneuve-de-Berg
E15

RHONE-ALPES

Le Bleymard
Sablières
Joyeuse
Viviers
Donzère
Rémuzat
Rosans

Mont Lozère 1699m
Villefort
Les Vans
Ruoms
St-Remèze
Grignan
Valréas
Nyons
Montjay

le-Pont-de-Montvert
Génolhac
St-Paul-le-Jeune
Ardèche
Chassezac
Bourg-St-Andéol
Pierrelatte
St-Paul-Trois-Châteaux
Tulette
Buis-les-Baronnies
Montauban-sur-l'Ouvèze
Séderon

N106
St-Germain-de-Calberte
Bessèges
Barjac
Orgnac-l'Aven
Pont-St-Esprit
Bollène
Vaison-la-Romaine
Mollans-sur-Ouvèze

La Grand-Combe
N86
Mondragón
Malaucène

Vallée-Française
St-Martin-de-Valgalgues
Salindres
Bagnols-sur-Cèze
Orange
Malaucène
Mont Ventoux 1909m
Revest-du-Bion

St-Jean-du-Gard
Mialet
Alès
St-Quentin-la-Poterie
L'Ardoise
Courthezon
Jonquières
Bédoin
Sault

Vallerauque
Anduze
Vézénobres
Connaux
Laudun
Châteauneuf-du-Pape
Mormoiron
St-Christol
Bano

Lasalle
Monoblèt
Musée du Bonbon
Pouzilhac
Roquemaure
Carpentras
Monteux
St-Saturnin-les-Apt
Simiane-la-Rotonde

Sumène
St-Hippolyte-du-Fort
Lédignan
Uzès
Vers Pont du Gard
Tavel
Bédarrides
Sorgues
Nesque

Ganges
Sauve
St-Chaptes
Pont du Gard
Villeneuve-lèz-Avignon
Le Pontet
Cave Thouzon
L'Isle-sur-la-Sorgue
Roussillon
Rustrel

Laroque
D6110
Gard
Remoulins
Avignon
Le Thor
Gördes
Apt
D900
Colavo

St-Bauzille-de-Putois
Claret
Marguerittes
Aramon
Caumont-sur-Durance
Lacoste
Bonnieux

LANGUEDOC-ROUSSILLON
NIMES
Beaucaire
Châteaurenard
Cavaillon
Lourmarin

Le Pic St-Loup 644m
Sommières
Garons
Tarascon
Plan d'Orgon
St-Rémy-de-Provence
Orgon
Durance
Cadenet
Pertuis

St-Martin-de-Londres
Beaulieu
Nages-et-Solorgues
Bellegarde
Les Baux-de-Provence
Château des Baux-de-Provence
Sénas
D572

Les Matelles
Castries
Aimargues
A9
Garons
A54
Maussane-les-Alpilles
Mouriès
Eyguières
Salon-de-Provence
Lambesc
Peyrolles-en-Provence

Castelnau-le-Lez
Lunel
Vauvert
St-Gilles
Arles
St-Martin-de-Crau
La Barben
Parc Zoologique de la Barben

MONTPELLIER
Mauguio
A54
Aix-en-Provence

Villeneuve-lès-Maguelone
La Grande-Motte
Aigues-Mortes
Albaron
N568
Miramas
Istres
Berre-l'Étang
Rognac
Vitrolles
Gardanne

Gigean
E80
Palavas-les-Flots
Le Grau-du-Roi
Mas Thibert
Les Pennes-Mirabeau

Bouzigues
Frontignan
Etang de Vaccarès
Rhône
Fos-sur-Mer
Etang de Berre
Marignane
Châteauneuf-les-Martigues
Allauch

Sète
Golfe d'Aigues-Mortes
Stes-Maries-de-la-Mer
Salin de Giraud
Port-de-Bouc
Martigues
Carry-le-Rouet
L'Estaque
Aubagne

Golfe de Beauduc
Port-St-Louis-du-Rhône
MARSEILLE
La Penne-s-Huveaune

Golfe de Fos
Cap Croissette
Cassis

LEGEND

E15	European Route
A84	Motorway
N24	National Road
✈	Airport
⏥	Ferry Route
⋯⋯	Railway
▪━▪━	Regional Boundary
▪▪▪▪	International Boundary

30 miles
30 km
Approximate Scale

Algérie, Tunisie ▾
Corse, Sardegna ↘

Aspres-
sur-Buëch
Aspremont
Serres
Tallard
Barcillonnette
Turriers
La Motte-
du-Caire
Laragne-
Montéglin
Orpierre
Ribiers
Noyers-
sur-Jabron
Mont de
Lure
1826m
Sisteron
Château-
Arnoux-
St-Auban
Peyruis
St-Étienne-
les-Orgues
Forcalquier
Reillanne
Volx
Manosque
Ste-Tulle
St-Paul-
lès-Durance
Rians
Vauvenargues
Pourcieux
Trets
Auriol
Roquevaire
Gémenos
Cuges-les-Pins
La Cadière
La Ciotat
Bandol
Sanary-sur-Mer
Six-Fours-
les-Plages
Cap Sicié

Durance
Authon
Malijai
Les Mées
Oraison
Valensole
Gréoux-
les-Bains
Vinon-sur-
Verdon
Ginasservis
La Verdière
Tavernes
Barjols
St-Maximin-
la-Ste-Baume
La Roquebrussanne
Signes
Cuers
Le Castellet
Le Beausset
Ollioules
TOULON
La Seyne-
sur-Mer
La Garde
Giens
Hyères-
Plage

St-Paul-
sur-Ubaye
Lac de
Serre-Ponçon
Le Lauzet-
Ubaye
Barcelonnette
Les 3
Evêchés
2961m
Seyne
Verdaches
Allos
Colmars
Thorame-
Basse
Thorame-
Barrême
Senez
Bérard
3048m
Jausiers
Le Sauze
PROVENCE-ALPES-
COTE D'AZUR
Digne-les-
Bains
Train
Vapeur
Bisone
Mézel
Barrême
St-André-
les-Alpes
Moustiers-
Ste-Marie
Lac de
Castillon
Riez
Lac de
Ste-Croix
Aiguines
Gorges du Verdon
Castellane
Comps-
sur-Artuby
Bargemon
Seillans
Fayence
Callas
Aups
Salernes
Cotignac
Carcès
Lorgues
Le Thoronet
Draguignan
Le Luc
Besse-
sur-Issole
Gonfaron
La Garde-
Freinet
Grimaud
Cogolin
Collobrières
Pierrefeu-
du-Var
Solliès-Pont
Hyères
Bormes-les-
Mimosas
Le Lavandou
Train
Vapeur
Cap Bénat
Cap Blanc
Île de
Port-Cros
Île de
Porquerolles
Porquerolles
Îles d'Hyères

Prazzo
Acceglio
Campomolino
Larche
Argentera
ITALIA
Mt Tenibre
3031m
Vinadio
St-Étienne-
de-Tinée
Auron
Isola
Mt Pelat
3051m
Mt Mounier
2817m
Valberg
Beuil
Guillaumes
St-Sauveur-
sur-Tinée
Verdon
Annot
Entrevaux
Puget-
Théniers
Roquesteron
St-Auban
Cime du
Cheiron
1777m
Coursegoules
Andon
St-Vallier-
de-Thiey
Grasse
Auribeau
Mandelieu-
la Napoule
La Napoule
Cannes
Théoule-
sur-Mer
Îles de
Lérins
Côte d'Azur
Mer
Ligurienne
Mëira
Dronero
Caraglio
Cuneo
Borgo S
Dalmazzo
Demonte
Entracque
Terme di
Valdieri
Cime
de Gélas
3143m
Tende
Alpha Parc
des Loups
St-Martin-
Vésubie
Cime du Diable
2686m
Saorge
Roquebillière
Lantosque
Villars-
sur-Var
Peira
Cava
Breil-
sur-Roya
Sospel
Levens
Contes
L'Escarène
Vence
St-Paul
Cagnes-sur-Mer
Biot
Vallauris
NICE
La Trinité
Èze
Villefranche-
sur-Mer
Cap Ferrat
Roquebrune-
Cap-Martin
Menton
Monaco
Beaulieu
Baie des Anges
Espace
Marineland
Antibes
Juan-les-Pins
Cap d'Antibes

Gros
Gorges
Roquesteron
Var
Siagne
Puget-sur-
Argens
Le Muy
Les Arcs
Roquebrune-
sur-Argens
Vidauban
Zoo Fréjus
Agay
Fréjus
St-Raphaël
St-Aygulf
Ste-Maxime
Golfe de
St-Tropez
St-Tropez
Plage de
Pampelonne
Gassin
Cavalaire-
sur-Mer
Cap Camarat
Cap
Lardier
Argens
Cagou
Mer
Méditerranée
Calvi,
l'Île Rousse,
Ajaccio
Bastia
Cap Corse
CORSE
Rogliano
Parc
d'Attractions

Family favourites

La Platane.

Baby-Friendly Boltholes

Catch yourself reminiscing fondly about long weekends away (pre-kids) in boutique hotels? Blanching at the thought of dashing after your beloved babies, whisking breakables out of reach? Holiday booking agency Baby-Friendly Boltholes (BFB) pairs stylish accommodation with total family-friendliness, and might just be your dream come true. With loads of welcoming places to stay on their books worldwide, their stamp of approval is a green light for style-savvy parents travelling with young children.

BFB offers three great self-catering spots in the South of France. Each one is stocked with high chairs, cots, changing tables and play mats, as well as kids' cups, plastic plates and cutlery; all three also have Wi-Fi throughout. Additional specific nursery gear can be reserved when booking. For families looking for a little more luxury, meal deliveries, pre-arrival shopping services, daily cleaning and babysitting can also be arranged.

Mas du Luberon, Bonnieux, Aix-en-Provence & the Luberon. £4808-10,962/week, sleeps 14 adults plus infants. In the heart of Provence's lavender fields and rolling vineyards, Mas du Luberon is a six-bedroom villa broken up into three independent sections, each with their own eating and sleeping areas. Outside in the 20-ha gardens, tall cypress trees ring the heated saltwater swimming pool.

Le Platane, L'Isle-sur-la-Sorgue, Western Provence. £4808-9423/week, sleeps 10 adults plus infants. This renovated French farmhouse is truly sumptuous, its style a mix of Provençal architecture and North African decor. It sits directly on the Sorgue River, which means the fearless can grab a canoe and paddle into town; the less adventurous can splash around in the pool.

Wide Open Space Villa, Montauroux, Haute-Provence. £1500-2950/week, sleeps seven adults plus infants. Four-bedroom villa near Fayence, with a heated outdoor pool and a separate paddling pool and loads of toys. Golf-loving grown-ups may find nipping away to the nearby Four Seasons Provence (fourseasons.com/provence) 18-hole course irresistible.

babyfriendlyboltholes.co.uk

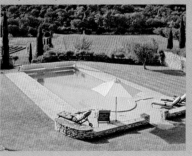

Boat trips

Wind in your hair, the sun sparking off the waves … who doesn't love a boat trip? If you're travelling with tots, there's no minimum age and their passage is usually free.

The Riviera
Capitaine Nemo, bateauxsaintraphael.com, Apr-Aug. 'Underwater vision' trips from Agay along the Estérel's coastline.
To Îles de Lérins: Trans Côte d'Azur trans-cote-azur.com. Ferries to Île Ste-Marguerite from Cannes (year round) and Nice (Jun to mid-Sep).
Riviera Lines riviera-lines.com, Apr-Oct. Ferries to Île Ste-Marguerite from Juan-les-Pins and Golfe-Juan. **Planaria** cannes-ilesdelerins.com. Ferries from Cannes to Île St-Honorat year round.

St-Tropez to Hyères
Les Bateaux Verts bateauxverts.com. Year-round ferries from Ste-Maxime to St-Tropez and Port-Grimaud.
Brigantin II lebrigantin.com. Sightseeing trips from St-Tropez to the Baie des Canoubiers.
Seascope vedettesilesdor.fr. Year-round 'underwater vision' trips around the Îles d'Or, from Le Lavandou.
To the Iles d'Or: TLV tlv-tvm.com. Year-round trips to Porquerolles, and from Hyères's port to Port-Cros or Levant.
Vedettes Iles d'Or vedettesilesdor.fr. Year-round crossings from Le Lavandou to Port-Cros, Levant and Porquerolles.
Trans Côte d'Azur trans-cote-azur.com. Longer ferry rides from St-Tropez to Cannes and Nice (Jun-Sep).

Marseille & the Calanques
Frioul If Express Ferry Service frioul.cityway.fr. Ferries to the Frioul Islands.
Île de Bendor bendor.com. Daily crossings between Bandol and Île de Bendor.
Île des Embiez les-embiez.com. Daily ferries from Port du Brusc, Six-Fours, to the island.
Île Verte laciotat-ileverte.com. Daily runs from La Ciotat to Île Verte.

Western Provence
Croisieres en Camargue croisieres-camargue.com and Péniches Isles de Stel islesdestel.fr, both Apr-Oct. Excursions from Aigues-Mortes along the canals.
Croisières Mireio mireio.net, Apr-Sep. Daily cruises from Avignon along the Rhône.
Île de la Barthelasse A free shuttle boat (mid-Feb to Dec) every 10 minutes between Avignon's quai de la Ligne and Île de la Barthelasse.
Tiki III tiki3.fr, Mar-Oct. Tours along the Petit-Rhône from Stes-Maries.

Kayaking excursions

With endless coastline and loads of placid rivers and lakes, the South of France is tailor-made for kayaking. You can rent your own, but joining a group excursion can double the fun. Whether you pile into a four-person floater or opt to skim the surface alone, there are a variety of kayaking companies that can get you paddling. Here's a round-up of our favourite local outfits (see individual chapters for more details). Remember, all participants must know how to swim.

The Riviera
Base du Rocher, D7, 83520 Roquebrune-sur-Argens, T06 61 41 75 74, basedurocher.fr. April to September. Minimum age four. Kayak along the calm River Argens to nearby Lac du Noirel or south to the Mediterranean shores.

Marseilles & The *Calanques*
New Evasion Provence Canoe, strade Deferrari, Base Mer, 83150 Bandol, T04 94 29 52 48, provence-canoe.fr. Minimum age 11. Loop around Ile de Bendor (half day) or explore the nearby calanques (full day).

Provence Kayak Mer, 3 rue Rompicul, 83870 Signes, T06 12 95 20 12, provencekayakmer.fr. May to September. Minimum age 12. Guided expeditions all along the calanques, plus enchanting sunset tours along the coast.

Western Provence
Alpha Bateaux, route des Gorges de l'Ardèche, 07150 Vallon-Pont-d'Arc, T04 75 88 08 29, canoeardeche.com. Easter to September. Minimum age seven. Paddle your way through

Randoxygène walking guides

A must for any family keen to get out and explore the South of France on foot. Both an info-packed website and a printed series of walking guides (distributed for free at most tourist offices), Randoxygène charts all of the waymarked footpaths in the Alpes-Maritimes region. They stretch from the Italian frontier in the east to the Estérel's russet landscape in the west, and from the Provençal Alps in the north to the *sentier du littoral* on the coast, which runs along the Mediterranean's shore.

Walks are divided into three general categories: *Pays Côtier* (along or near the coast), *Moyen Pays* (inland) and *Haut Pays* ('highlands' or walks at high altitudes). Each walk is then marked with loads of specifics. It's prudent to check these details closely before you set off, including *durée* (an average of how long the walk will take), *dénivelée* (increase and decrease in altitude over the course of the walk), *période conseillée* (recommended season) and level of difficulty: *facile* (easy), *moyenne* (medium), *sportive* (sporty, ie difficult) or *alpine* (Alpine, 1000 m above sea level or higher).

Randoxygène guides also cover cycle tracks, canyoning routes, Via Ferrata Alpine climbs and snowshoe paths throughout the region.

The only downside to this wonderful resource? It's only available in French. But with advance planning and a little help from a French friend (or possibly a few rounds on Google Translate), you should be able to glean all the information you need for a great day out.

randoxygene.org

Spacebetween adventure holidays

If your family is dreaming of pony-trekking, canyoning, rock climbing, snowshoeing, hiking and bedtime stories under the stars, Spacebetween has the getaway for you.

Seven years ago, affable British owners Mel Jones and Liz Lord set up this small, personalized outfit offering family adventures in the Mercantour National Park, an hour's drive north of Nice. Choose to get on the trail of the park's wild wolves, herd horses, squeeze in some serious snow time or try their popular Thrills & Spills week, which mixes loads of different outdoor activities together.

The week-long holidays offer plenty of opportunities for family bonding, as groups are usually limited to 10. But there's a chance to take a break from your nearest and dearest too. Spacebetween organizes exciting afternoons out, where kids can try mountain biking, canyoning, saddling up Mel and Liz's horse or even braving the precipitous Via Ferrata Alpine climbs. Parents can join in, or simply take a little personal time. Accommodation runs the gamut from self-catering (in Spacebetween's Berthemont-les-Bains *gîte*, La Zourcière) to *chambres d'hôtes* (breakfast included) and half- or full-board hotels. Your location, in the pristine heart of the Provençal Alps, means you'll probably spot chamois, ibex, golden eagles and loads of other wild animals.

Spacebetween's website has a handy online calendar, so you can see which of their programmes are upcoming and have availability – but if you don't find one that suits, make a special request!

Spacebetween takes a proudly responsible approach to travel. They are environmentally aware, support local businesses and buy organic local produce. They encourage families who book with them to do the same. La Zourcière, Berthemont-les-Bains, 06450 Roquebillière, T04 93 03 48 57 (UK +44 (0)870 243 0667), space-between.co.uk. From £560pp/week self-catering to £810pp/week all-inclusive. Minimum age 10.

Hungry hands: how to make salade Niçoise

Crunchy salade Niçoise is served everywhere in the South of France, not just in Nice. The real local recipe uses only raw seasonal veggies (no cooked potatoes or green beans), making it a cinch to put together at home or on holiday. You can pick up all the ingredients you need from any of the region's marvellous markets.
Serves 4

You will need:
4 medium bowls
1 fork
1 small bowl
1 tablespoon
1 teaspoon
1 cutting board (optional)
1 sharp knife (optional)

Necessary ingredients:
Mesclun salad leaves
1 tin of tuna, drained
2 hard-boiled eggs, each one shelled and cut in half

Choose at least four of these optional ingredients:
Radishes
Cherry tomatoes
Peas
Broad beans
Raw artichokes
Niçois olives
Fresh basil leaves
Spring onions or a shallot, chopped
Celery, chopped
1 red pepper, chopped
Cucumber, chopped

Dressing:
2 tablespoons olive oil
1 tablespoon red wine vinegar or ½ lemon
Salt
Black pepper (optional)
1 teaspoon Dijon mustard (optional)

Salad dressing: Squeeze the lemon or measure out the red wine vinegar into the small bowl. Add a few shakes of salt, then stir in a little black pepper and the mustard, if you're using it. Add the olive oil, and mix everything together well.

Salade Niçoise: Place one handful of mesclun leaves in each medium bowl. Top each one with your choice of the optional ingredients. The neat thing about this salad is that it can be as simple or as extravagant as you like. Find chopping a chore? Use bite-sized veggies, like peas, cherry tomatoes and radishes. Hate peppers? Skip them.

Feeling fancy? Add the artichokes – it's fun! Pull off the outside leaves: you'll be left with the artichoke's heart. Chop off the tips and the stem, then cut it into quarters. Use a spoon to scoop out the fuzzy 'choke' from each quarter (see photo), then in they go!

Use a fork to break up the tuna into smaller chunks, then place roughly ¼ of the tuna onto each salad. Top the salads with one half of a hard-boiled egg. Drizzle a little dressing over each one, then serve up with a fork and a napkin apiece. And voilà – you're ready to dig in!

If you're heading to the beach, why not turn your salad into a *pan bagnat* instead? It's essentially salad in a bun, and is also one of Nice's culinary staples. You'll need one bread roll per person. Slice (or tear) it in half. Pile the salade Niçoise on one half. Drizzle a little dressing over it. Top with the other half of the roll and press down to squeeze all the ingredients together. Wrap in a napkin or a plastic bag, making sure the sandwich sits snugly inside and no bits will fall out en route to your picnic.

Making memories

One wonderful way of remembering a great holiday is to create a treasure box, filling it with items you've collected during your travels. The beach is perfect for sourcing shimmery rocks, special shells, feathers or smooth sea-worn glass. On a forest walk, keep your eyes peeled for twisty twigs, colourful flowers or whatever takes your fancy! If you're collecting just one type of item, such as cool-shaped leaves, why not bring a book along to help you identify the ones you've found? Or if your family is travelling with a laptop or iPhone, you can cross-reference your finds online. Take your treasures one step further: by packing paper, coloured pens and glue, you can use your finds to create some French-inspired collage artworks!

Boredom busters

Brainteasers
Maths: The person in the front seat reads out the last two digits on the number plates of a passing car. See who can add up the numbers the quickest, or take turns trying.

Trivia: Choose a quizmaster and a theme. As he or she asks a question, competitors have to buzz in (shout out 'bzzz') if they know the answer. The first person to answer five questions correctly wins.

Spot the shape
Choose a shape, such as a circle, square or triangle. Take turns looking around the car, train or out the window and try to spot that shape.

Choose a colour to look out for instead:
Find the entire alphabet, one letter at a time from A to Z, on number plates, shop fronts and roadside signs.

Scavenger hunts:
Make a list (in advance, in-car or on the train) of items to spot based on where you're travelling. In the countryside these items could include a cow, a tractor or a *chambres d'hôtes* sign. In town, look out for a dog, a policeman or a *boulangerie*.

Test your memory
One person begins by saying 'I'm going on holiday and in my suitcase I packed a... (toothbrush, teddy, banana…). The next person repeats 'I'm going on holiday and in my suitcase I packed a... (whatever the first person packed)', then adds an item. Go around in a circle, each person adding an item. If you forget anything, you're out!

Holiday read

The Man who Planted Trees
by Jean Giono
Once upon a time in Provence, there was a desolate valley with no trees and no water. This book is the story of an old shepherd who transforms the barren land into a lush green paradise, thick with trees. A great 'to be continued' bedtime story to read on holiday.

5 activities to try in the South of France

Hop aboard a boat: Whether a quick ferry ride or a long-distance tour, on board a boat is one of the best ways to get around.

Visit an island: The South of France is dotted with postcard-sized paradises, all of them car-free. Spend a day splashing around, looking for treasure or building sand castles in the sun.

Play *pétanque*: Challenge your family to a game of French boules, a favourite pastime all along the French coast. You can rent or borrow a *pétanque* set from lots of local cafés and bars – just ask! For *pétanque's* rules, see page 71.

Go snorkelling: See what life's really like beneath the waves. Tip: it sounds gross, but a little bit of spit on the inside of the mask, then a dunk in the water, helps prevent the mask from fogging up.

Hire a bike: Pedal along city cycling tracks such as Nice's Promenade des Anglais, or whizz down steep hills out in the countryside.

Stargaze

The sea breezes and lack of light pollution make the South of France great for spotting constellations. You'll need a map of the night-time sky, so it's best to buy one before you set off on your travels. *Zoo In The Sky: A Book of Animal Constellations* by Jacqueline Mitton and *Find the Constellations* by H A Rey are both fun, clear and practical guides. Online, Astroviewer (astroviewer.com) is also a handy resource: you can plug in your exact location and the time, and this website will give you an accurate picture of the constellations you can see at that very moment in the night sky.

When you're ready to start stargazing, find a comfortable place to stretch out on the ground. You could lie down on a blanket outside your tent if you're camping, or find a good spot on a soft and sandy beach. Skies in southern France are normally very clear, but ensure there are no lights nearby as they can make seeing the stars more difficult. The simplest constellations to find are Ursa Major and Minor (the big and little bears, also called the big and little ploughs). Look out for super-bright Polaris (the North Star), in Ursa Minor. Too easy? Try to spot Leo (the lion) or Aquila (the eagle) instead.

Contents

The Riviera

Life's a beach at Cap d'Ail.

Russian Orthodox
church, Nice.

The French Riviera sprinkles a touch of glamour over its sublime beaches, *villages perchés* (hilltop villages) and happening seaside resorts. Thanks to its well-developed tourism industry, it can satisfy the whim of any visitor, from teens to tots to grown-ups.

Cap d'Ail.

The eastern Riviera around Nice, Cannes and Monaco is the most action-packed: try paragliding and pony rides, or bobbing along underwater with a snorkel and fins. **Antibes** has one of the world's biggest **oceanariums**, where you can get up close to dolphins, killer whales and polar bears. In the far west of the region lie the Estérel hills – a tranquil area of mountains, inlets and beachside coves.

The South of France's entire coastline – from the Italian border all the way to Marseille – is edged by a *sentier du littoral*, or coastal footpath. Some sections merge with bustling seaside promenades while others link fishing villages and quiet beaches. Along the Riviera, this trail is almost continuous, weaving its way under the shade of Aleppo pines and through lunar-like landscapes. Take your pick of places to go to try hiking a portion of it.

Too action-packed? The *grande* (high), *moyenne* (middle) and *basse* (low) *corniches* are coastal roads that climb and saunter their way along the 40 km or so from Nice to the Italian border. Each one is a delight to drive, passing pretty towns and panoramic picnic spots. Or get away from it all by heading offshore. Just a few kilometres from Cannes, the **Îles de Lérins** are two heaven-sent islands, laced with flat, shady walking paths and dotted by sheltered beaches, each one ideal for an afternoon of simply splashing around. Both are completely car-free.

Off season, the Riviera hosts festivals and parades: try **Nice's Carnival** (nicecarnaval.com, Feb-Mar), **Grasse's** sweet-smelling **Expo Rose** (ville-grasse.fr, May) or **Menton's Fête du Citron** (Citrus Festival, feteducitron.com, Feb-Mar), where ginormous sculptures are constructed out of lemons and oranges. And although July and August do attract the biggest crowds, squeal-worthy fireworks displays (Cannes, Cagnes-sur-Mer, Nice, Monaco and Antibes, cotedazur-tourisme.com, Jul-Aug) light up the summer skies every other night.

Perhaps best of all, no matter how you choose to fill your sunny holiday days here, frequent, inexpensive buses, trains or ferries zip around pretty much everywhere.

You must

- Be brave: visit the Man in the Iron Mask's spooky prison cell.
- Concoct your own personal perfume in Grasse.
- Dance to the beat of a musical fountain on Cap Ferrat.
- Get wet: try windsurfing or sea-kayaking at nearly any seaside town.
- Hike a stretch of the *sentier du littoral*, or coastal footpath.
- Meet dolphins, penguins and polar bears at Marineland.
- Roll, cycle or skate along Nice's 5-km Promenade des Anglais.

Play in the park

Fréjus's former airfields have been transformed into **Base Nature François Léotard** (1196 blvd de la Mer, 83600 Fréjus, T04 94 51 91 10, frejus.fr, daily mid-Jun to mid-Sep 0800-2000, mid-Sep to mid-Jun 0800-2300), a giant (85-ha) outdoor park with playgrounds, cycle tracks and four waymarked hiking trails. There's also a mini skate park (8-12 years), tennis courts, a rollerblading route and 1.5 km of sandy beaches, plus a restaurant (Apr-Oct), picnic areas and a snack bar. On cooler days, there's an indoor pool (€3 adult, €2 under 16s).

Spread a blanket in the shade and spend a few hours revelling in the (free) gardens at **Musée Renoir** (Chemin des Collettes, T04 93 20 61 07, Wed-Mon 1000-1200 and 1400-1700 (until 1800 Jun-Aug)). Auguste Renoir purchased the Domaine des Collettes, including 1.5 hectares of olive trees, in 1907. And while the gardens are not a park per se, the citrus groves, lavender-scented grassy fields and the views up to the village of Haut-de-Cagnes are a delight, particularly with tiny tots. The museum (€4 adult, under 18s free) itself is Renoir's former house and studio space: although a must for art fans, it's less likely to enchant the kids.

Cap Ferrat is filled to the brim with walking... and scooting opportunities.

Watch the guards

A vision of both flamboyant footwork and military precision, the changing of the Monegasque guard (Prince's Palace, Palace Hill, 98000 Monaco, daily 1155) takes place in front of the royal family's *grands appartements*. The hill as a vantage point itself affords awesome views. To the east, racing fans have an aerial view over the 'swimming pool', the Principality's port and the start point of the Monaco Grand Prix circuit.

Take a hike

The best place to give this region's *sentier du littoral*, or coastal footpath, a whirl is along one of the region's four lovely *caps*: Cap Martin, Cap d'Ail, Cap

Ferrat or Cap d'Antibes. It's no drawback that these peninsulas are dotted with some of the wealthiest homes in the world – think of it as cultural sightseeing.

Cap Martin, just west of Menton, is the quietest of the *caps*. The moderately difficult trail on this peninsula takes around two hours to complete, with a couple of hairy, scary stretches for younger kids, such as a walkway over the sea (guardrails on both sides).

Accessed via a flight of stairs from **Cap d'Ail's** train station (av de la Gare, 06320), this coastal trail twists right in the direction of Mala Plage (see page 34). Pack a snorkel and head left instead, following the paved pathway to miniscule rocky beaches lapped by crystal-clear waters.

Hiking around the whole of **Cap Ferrat** will take around four hours, passing palms, Aleppo pines, Nellcote (Rolling Stones' Keith Richards' former pad), a lighthouse, Lo Scoglietto (Charlie Chaplin's long-ago home), and on the cap's tip, some of the weirdest moon-like rocky outcrops you've ever seen. This route is only for the sure-footed, although sections, such as the loop around Pointe de St-Hospice (beyond Paloma Plage, see page 34), are suitable for younger children.

Small chunks of coastal pathway ring the millionaire's paradise **Cap d'Antibes**: best is the section starting at Plage de la Garoupe (see page 34) and swinging round this promontory westwards. The narrow residential roads that criss-cross this peninsula are equally enticing to explore.

More details about all of these walks can be found in the Randoxygène guides (randoxygene.org, see also Family Favourites page 20).

The pushchair option: unfortunately the *sentier du littoral* is rarely kind to those with wheels. However, it's still possible to stroll along certain portions. Easiest is promenade Maurice Rouvier, which stretches from Villa Grecque Kerylos (see page 42) in Beaulieu-sur-Mer, along the seafront to the Hotel Royal Riviera (3 av Jean Monnet, 06230), then skirts the

Visit Corsica

Why? With kilometres of sandy beaches, lip-smacking local cuisine and prices that are far, far lower than those on the mainland, the better question is: why not visit Corsica? Bastia, Cap Corse, Calvi and the northern coast all have heaps of campgrounds, castles, water sports and coastal hikes.

Where? Ferries make the three- to five-hour journey to the Corsican ports of Calvi, Ajaccio, Ile Rousse and Bastia year-round from Nice. However, it's best to visit between Easter and September, as most hotels and restaurants shut down during the winter season.

How? Corsica Ferries: port de Commerce, 06300, T08 25 09 50 95, corsicaferries.com. Advance tickets can be booked from as little as €30 per single journey, covering the passage of two adults, two children and a vehicle.

eastern edge of Cap Ferrat to the village of St-Jean.

The *village perché* option: So you're not really a trekking kind of family? Go for a walk around one of the Riviera's *villages perchés* (hilltop villages) instead. Oh-so-pretty **Eze** is balanced on an outcrop of rock 430 m above the sea. A former Saracen stronghold, the golden stone village has views over Cap Ferrat and the Corniche. Tour **St-Paul-**

de-Vence's smooth ramparts (great for pushchairs) from Porte de Vence around to Porte de Nice, where a magnificent panorama overlooks the cemetery (including the tomb of artist Marc Chagall) and the Mediterranean beyond.

Note that both Eze and St-Paul-de-Vence are on the beaten track. Visit early, late or out of season if you want their winding streets to yourselves.

Out & about The Riviera

Over the next few pages, the Riviera's beaches are grouped together geographically, beginning at the Italian frontier and moving westwards to Fréjus. Within each geographical area, the beaches are listed in alphabetical order.

Note that the sea's depth drops off steeply on most of the beaches in this region – parents with young children or cautious swimmers should seek out the shallow beaches specified below. For general beach safety, see box page 179.

Promenade du Soleil
06500 Menton.

Along Menton's seafront promenade, separate sections of public and private beaches meld into one long sandy strip. There's a submerged breakwater off the shore, smoothing waves down to gentle bumps, and there's pushchair access (via a few steps) from the wide pavement.

Les Sablettes
Promenade de la Mer,
06500 Menton.

Backed by the Old Town, this picturesque shingle beach to the east of town has a very gradual increase in water depth and is suited to young children.

La Buse
Av de la Gare, 06190 Roquebrune-Cap-Martin.

A wild beach at the western end of Cap Martin's coastal footpath, La Buse is seconds away from Roquebrune's train station (via a flight of twisty stairs). The beach is a sandy, pebbly mix, with huge submerged rocks for kids to scramble up and jump off.

Le Golfe Bleu
Av Louis Laurens, 06190 Roquebrune-Cap-Martin.

This shingle beach is one of the area's largest. Over cooler months, the sky is dotted with paragliders (see page 39). Access is via a long set of steps.

Lavrotto
Av Princesse Grace,
98000 Monaco.

This mix of private and public beaches stretches along Monaco's city centre. Bathers have a great view of the yachts chugging in and out of the Principality's port. Even better, there are children's playgrounds, a summertime kids' club (3-10 years) and a net to protect against any stray jellyfish.

La Mala
Av du 3 septembre,
06320 Cap d'Ail.

Follow the Plage Mala signage from Cap d'Ail's town centre down, down and downhill some more. You'll hit around 100 steps, then the beach – eventually. But oh how it's worth it: a heavenly little cove with two beach bars, kayaks and pedalos for hire, ideal for a day in the sun. A coastal walkway loops back eastwards to Monaco's Fontvieille harbour.

La Grande Plage
Av de la Liberté,
06360 Eze-sur-Mer.

A long pebbly stretch far below the hilltop village of Eze, this pretty beach is backed by a few lucky villas – including one at the eastern end owned by U2's lead singer Bono.

Petite Afrique
Port de Plaisance, blvd Général Leclerc, 06310 Beaulieu-sur-Mer.

Ideal for tots, this warm lagoon is backed by Aleppo pines (arrive early if you're keen to snag some shade). At the northeast end of Beaulieu's port.

Paloma
Chemin de St-Hospice, 06230 St-Jean-Cap-Ferrat.

A small beach that's part super trendy and private (paloma-beach.com), part totally laid-back and public. Head to the beach's eastern end, where rocks submerged in the shallows make protected pools for tots. Celeb-seekers can keep an eye out for the restaurant's private

speedboat zipping over to pick up diners from offshore yachts. Access via one flight of stairs; shade creeps onto the beach by late afternoon. Too crowded? Both Les Fossettes (no facilities) and Les Fosses (no facilities), two beaches just west around the cap's headland, make great, more rugged alternatives.

Passable

Av Denis Séméria, 06230 St-Jean-Cap-Ferrat.

This sand and shingle beach overlooks Villefranche's Old Town from its location at the foot of Cap Ferrat.

Darse

Quai de la Corderie, 06230 Villefranche-sur-Mer.

This pebbly beach is south of Villefranche's Old Town and citadel, with blue water and snorkelling along the western shores of this protected bay.

Les Marinières

Promenade des Marinières, 06230 Villefranche-sur-Mer.

At the back of Villefranche's perfect bay, this long sandy strip is perfect for little ones. The water is shallow, waves are either gentle or non-existent, and for kids who are Thomas the Tank Engine-crazy, frequent trains shuttle past on the elevated tracks behind the beach. There's no shade at all, so be sure to pack a beach parasol. An easy pushchair amble away from Villefranche Old Town.

For beaches in and around **Nice**, see page 45.

La Gravette

Quai Henri Rambaud, 06600 Antibes.

La Gravette is Antibes' sheltered, shallow and easy-to-reach beach. Just east of here, Port Vauban is the largest pleasure harbour in Europe: when the sun gets too hot, take a stroll along Billionaires' Quay, where some of the biggest private boats in the world are berthed.

Le Ponteil & La Salis

Blvd James Wyllie,
06160 Cap d'Antibes.

These two long beaches, southwest of Antibes' Old Town, are split by a small port with windsurfers and small boats to hire. Both have flat, easy pushchair access, and the pavements are dotted with tempting ice cream vans.

La Garoupe

Blvd de la Garoupe, 06160 Cap d'Antibes.

If you've had enough of roughing it, make a beeline for this beach. There's a small public section, but it's private clubs that occupy most of the beach, renting spacious loungers (read plenty of kids' play space) and giant sun parasols by the half-day (around €15). A favourite with models, the local yacht set and Cap d'Antibes' super-rich.

Les Ondes

Blvd du Maréchal Juin,
06160 Cap d'Antibes.

A skinny sandy strip on the Cap's western side. Shallow and sheltered, but you'll need to arrive very early to stake out a coveted spot. Ever popular with local families.

Les Belles Rives

Blvd du Maréchal Juin,
06160 Juan-les-Pins.

Slightly to the east of Juan-les-Pins' famous Belles Rives Hotel, this almost hidden beach is heaven for tots. Seek it out for its warm water and sandy shores. Ideal for lapping up a little of JLP's famous microclimate; easy pushchair access from the port's central entrance.

Port Crouton

Blvd du Maréchal Juin,
06160 Juan-les-Pins.

Just in front of Juan-les-Pins' fishing harbour, this almost entirely public sandy arc is as carefree as they come. Be aware that this beach can sometimes be windy.

Promenade du Midi

Blvd du Littoral,
06160 Juan-les-Pins.

This long palm-tree-backed sweep of sand connects Juan-les-Pins and Golfe-Juan, and is home to both private clubs and acres of public beach. Easy pushchair access.

For beaches on the **Iles de Lérins**, see page 40.

La Croisette

Blvd du Midi, 06400 Cannes.

Along Cannes' main drag, it's no surprise to find beach clubs to suit all tastes, from those that cater to the stars o patches of public sand. During July and August, many of the hotels and private beaches organize kids' clubs (see page 178).

Le Midi

Blvd Jean Hibert, 06400 Cannes.

At the eastern end of La Croisette, the tail end of this beach curls around, making a shallow, sheltered lagoon. A great spot for small children.

For beaches in and around the **Massif de l'Estérel**, see page 48.

St-Aygulf

D1098 St-Aygulf, 83370 Fréjus.

A haven for windy water sports, particularly kite- and windsurfing. Just behind the beach, 240 species of migrating birds (Mar-May and Aug-Oct) stop to feed at the Etangs de Villepey, inland lakes formed from the Argens River's delta. The 260-ha site is criss-crossed with discovery trails to hike and bike. A few kilometres south of Fréjus town.

Juan Les Pins.

Out & about The Riviera

Action stations

Adventure courses
Canyon Forest
26 route de Grasse, 06270 Villeneuve-Loubet, T04 92 02 88 88, canyonforest. com. Jul-Aug daily 0900-1930, mid-Apr to Jun and Sep-Oct Wed 1300-1900, Sat-Sun 0900-1900, mid-Feb to mid-Apr Sat-Sun 0900-1800, first 2 weeks Nov Wed 1300-1730, Sat-Sun 0930-1730; last departure 3 hrs before closing. Minimum age 8. €24 adult, €21 child (8-17).

Four elaborate adventure courses (each one around 3 hrs), with trapeze lines and giant jungle gyms for little and big kids alike. Tiny climbers can head over to try the four new adventure courses at nearby **Pitchoun Forest** (2559 route de Grasse, 06270 Villeneuve Loubet, T04 92 02 06 06, azur-labyrinthe.com, Jul-Aug daily 1000-1700, Feb-Jun and Sep to mid-Nov Wed 1300-1600, Sat-Sun and school holidays 1000-1600, 3-10 years, height 1-1.50 m, €14).

Go-karting
Inter Racing Kart
Av 8 Mai 1845, 83600 Fréjus, T04 94 97 50 97, interracingkart.com. Jul-Aug daily 1600-0100, Sep-Dec and Feb-Jun Wed-Sun 1400-2000, also open Tue during school holidays. €15/8 mins adult (minimum height 1.50 m), €12/8 mins mini-karts (7-14 years, minimum height 1.25 m). Burn rubber at one of these two racetracks (600 m and 130 m), just opposite Fréjus's seafront.

Kayaking
Base du Rocher
D7, 83520 Roquebrune-sur-Argens, T06 61 41 75 74, basedurocher.fr. Daily mid-Jun to Aug, by reservation Apr to mid-Jun and Sep. Minimum age 4, ability to swim essential. 1-person kayak €7/hr, €18/half day, 2-person kayak €11/hr, €29/half day, 4-person kayak (2 adults plus 2 under 10s) €13/hr, €36/half day. Kayak along the River Argens, following one of the three Base du Rocher itineraries: the 6-km Lac du Noirel loop, the more challenging 8-km Verteil route, or a full-day excursion (14 km) south to the Mediterranean shores. Free bus transport is provided for longer itineraries. Mountain bikes (€8/half day adult, €5/half day child) also available for hire.

Get Karter... Older kids and adults too will love a whizz around the track.

Paragliding
Nature Elléments
06190 Roquebrune-Cap-Martin, T06 29 33 23 15, naturelements.com. Oct-Apr. Minimum weight 20 kg. €80 tandem baptism flight.

Paragliding for beginners launching above Roquebrune village, to beach below. Between May and September, Nature Elléments paraglides from their base at Thorame-Basse (04170). Canyoning (Jul-Sep, from €35/1½ hrs) and horse riding (from €20/ hr) also organized.

Going wild at Paloma Plage, Cap Ferrat.

Horse riding
Centre Hippique de Mougins
909 Chemin de Font de Currault, T04 93 45 75 81, chmougins.e-monsite. com. Minimum age 4. €10/30-min pony ride (daily 0930-1130 and 1400-1730), €12/30-min riding lesson (Wed, Sat-Sun).

Friendly local outfit with 30 years' experience, set in the hills behind Cannes. Excursions on horseback also available.

Water sports
Cannes Jeunesse
Two locations: Midi, 108 blvd du Midi, Jul-Aug daily 0930-1800; Mourre Rouge, Port du Mourre Rouge, daily Jul-Aug 1000-1830, Jun and Sep 1100-1800. Both 06400 Cannes, T04 92 18 88 88, cannes-jeunesse.fr. Minimum age 7. Catamaran €36-45/hr, 2-person sailing dinghy €36/hr, 1-person kayak €12/hr, 2-person kayak €16/ hr, paddleboard €12/hr, windsurfer €16-24/hr.

Cannes Jeunesse also runs sailing and windsurfing classes that range from private tuition by the hour to five-day group classes.

Cap Ferrat Water Sports
Paloma Plage, 06230 St-Jean-Cap-Ferrat, T06 16 67 78 28, capferratwatersports.com. Minimum age 5. Waterskiing, wakeboarding and wakesurfing €30/10 mins or €45/15-min lesson. Tubing €20/ person, minimum 2 people per tour, 10 mins.

An expensive hit of adrenaline, just off one of the Riviera's most glamorous beaches.

Club Nautique
Blvd d'Alger, Fréjus Plage, 83600 Fréjus, T04 94 51 40 47. Jul-Aug Mon-Sat 1000-1700, Sun 1200-1700, Sep-Jun Tue-Sat 1000-1200 and 1330-1700. Catamaran €35/hr, 2-3-person kayak €15/hr, paddleboard €15/hr, windsurfer €16/hr.

Scuba-diving
Nice Diving
14 quai des Docks, 06300 Nice, T04 93 89 42 44, nicediving.com. Closed Jan. €45 baptism dive, minimum age 8. CMAS 1* €300 adult group tuition, €450 12-15 years semi-private Junior tuition, 5 dives per course, minimum age 12. Open Water courses €420 adult group tuition, €625 12-15 years semi-private Junior tuition, 7 dives per course, minimum age 12.

Undersea explorations and qualifications in English and French. Dives take place along the coastline east of Nice and around the rich depths that surround Cap Ferrat.

Out & about The Riviera

Iles de Lérins

If you've flown into Nice Airport, little fingers may well have pointed out the **Iles de Lérins**: surprisingly simple to reach yet seldom visited (especially outside summer), these two islands are protected parklands. Each one is criss-crossed with shady walkways, dotted with scores of tiny sunbathing coves and lapped by crystal clear waters. They're also both entirely car-free.

On Ile Ste-Marguerite, the larger of the two islands, the **Musée de la Mer** (T04 93 38 55 26, Jun-Sep daily 1000-1745, Apr-May Tue-Sun 1030-1315 and 1415-1745, Oct-Mar Tue-Sun 1030-1315 and 1415-1645, €3.40, under 18s free) is in the former military bastion of rambling Fort Royal, the island's only settlement. The museum traces the history of local trade through displays of shipwreck booty hauled up from the Mediterranean's seabed. But the museum's highlight is definitely the creepy cell that once held the infamous Man in the Iron Mask. Although the prisoner's identity is still unknown today, many people believe he was French king Louis XIV's brother, or maybe even his twin.

Ile St-Honorat is by far the quieter of the two islands. Its only permanent residents are around 25 monks, who make their own island wine and sell it

Getting to Iles de Lérins

Getting to the Ile Ste-Marguerite: Trans **Côte d'Azur** (quai Laubeuf, 06400 Cannes, T04 92 98 71 30, trans-cote-azur.com) runs 11 daily ferries from Cannes to Ile Ste-Marguerite year round (return tickets €11.50 adult, €9.50 student, €6 child (5-10), under 5s free; 15-min journey). Regular daily departures run from Nice from June to mid-September (also trans-cote-azur.com) and from Juan-les-Pins and Golfe-Juan from April to October (riviera-lines.com).

Ile St-Honorat: Planaria (quai Laubeuf, 06400 Cannes, T04 92 98 71 38, cannes-ilesdelerins.com) operates the sole service (return tickets €12 adult, €6 child (5-10), under 5s free) from the western end of Cannes' harbour to Ile St-Honorat. It departs eight to 10 times daily between May and September, seven to eight times daily from October to April.

in the abbey's small shop (T04 92 99 54 30, abbayedelerins.com, daily 0900-1230 and 1330-1630), along with lavender honey and home-made jams. Just beyond here, an abandoned 11th-century monastery (free) pokes four storeys skyward, perched on its own rocky plinth.

Espace Marineland

306 av Mozart, La Beague, 06600 Antibes, T08 92 30 06 06, marineland. fr. **Marineland**: daily Jul-Aug 1000-2300, mid-Apr to Jun and Sep 1000-1900, Oct-Dec and Feb-Mar 1000-1800. €36 adult, €32 student, €28 child (3-12). **Aquasplash**: mid Jun-1st week Sep daily 1000-1900. €25 adult, €22 student, €20 child (3-12). **La Ferme du Far West**: Jul-Aug daily 1000-1900, Apr-Jun and Sep Wed,

Sat-Sun and holidays 1000-1900, Oct-Dec and Feb-Mar Wed, Sat-Sun and holidays 1000-1800. €13 adult, €10 student/child (3-12). **Adventure Golf**: Jul-Aug daily 1200-2400, mid-Apr to Jun and Sep daily 1200-1900, Oct-Dec and Feb-Mar Wed, Sat-Sun and holidays 1200-1800. €11 adult, €9 child (3-12). Under 3s free.

This cluster of four head-spinning amusement parks, all located just inland from Biot-sur-Mer train station, has an irresistible pull on most kids visiting the Riviera. Hideously expensive combination tickets are available for visitors brave enough to sample more than one of them in a day.

Marineland is the main attraction. There are aquariums, leaping displays of dolphins and killer whales, plus lots of seals, sea lions, penguins and even polar bears. The bold can saunter through the 'Shark Tunnel', new in 2010, a transparent 30-m passageway that passes through giant tanks of sharks and stingrays.

Marineland is surrounded by **Aquasplash**, the Riviera's largest water park, boasting a mammoth 2 km of vertiginous slides and 2010's new 'Shark River' ride, **La Ferme du Far West** (Far West children's theme park), best suited for younger children, with a labyrinth, pony rides, a petting zoo and loads of climbing frames, and **Adventure Golf**, three 18-hole crazy golf courses that wind their way through dinosaurs.

The mega roller coasters of **Antibes Land** (azurpark.com) are also just over the road.

Parfumerie Molinard

60 blvd Victor Hugo, 06130 Grasse, T04 92 42 33 21, molinard.com. €40 1½-hr workshop for adults, €25 30-min workshop for children (5-10, minimum age 5). Mon-Fri, advance reservation required.

Sniff, whiff and learn all about life as a 'nose' (a perfumer) at a

Shark tunnel at Marineland.

Out & about The Riviera

major French fragrance house. Make your own perfume at one of Parfumerie Molinard's workshops in Grasse, the region's capital of sweet-smelling scents, where hundreds of tons of roses and jasmine flowers are crushed annually for Chanel and other top perfume-makers worldwide. As an apprentice perfumer, during the workshop you'll be steeped in aromas, base notes and essential oils, and will leave with your own unique perfume.

Musée Océanographique de Monaco

Av St-Martin, 98000 Monaco, T00 377 93 15 36 00, oceano.org. Apr-Sep 0930-1900 (Jul and Aug until 1930), Oct-Mar 1000-1800. €13 adult, €6.50 child (4-18), under 4s free.
Part museum, part century-old aquarium, this elegant, high-ceilinged mansion's collections come from both Mediterranean and tropical waters. The ground floor is reserved for excellent temporary shows, highlighting the Med's biodiversity (home to 10% of the world's marine species), or exhibiting model ships from around the world. The aquarium showcases 6000 undersea creatures, and has been a pioneer in breeding endangered coral. Upstairs are scores of intact underwater skeletons, including those of a blue whale. Be sure to head to the top floor, for views over the sea and its coastline from the museum's café.

Villa Grecque Kerylos

Impasse Gustave Eiffel, 06310 Beaulieu-sur-Mer, T04 93 01 01 44, villa-kerylos.com. Mar-Oct daily 1000-1800 (Jul and Aug until 1900), Nov-Feb Mon-Fri 1400-1800, Sat-Sun and school holidays 1000-1800. €8.50 adult, €6.30 child (7-17), 2nd child and under 7s free.
Théodore Reinach was ancient-Greece obsessed. So what if he was German and living more than 2000 years after the civilization's heyday? Between 1902 and 1908, Reinach made his dream world a reality, building this faithful replica of a second-century BC luxury Grecian villa. He lived in his faux-Greek world for 20 years, strolling around the *peristyle*, or colonnaded central courtyard, surrounded by pomegranates and vines set against whitewashed walls. The interior of the villa is specially constructed to let in natural light and sea breezes, and features Greek mythical mosaics, a throne room, a marble bathroom with sunken *balaneion* and copies of famous Greek statues.

More family favourites

Fondation Maeght

623 chemin des Gardettes, 06570 St-Paul-de-Vence, T04 93 32 81 63, fondation-maeght.com. Daily Jul-Sep 1000-1900, Oct-Jun 1000-1800. €14 adult, €9 child (10-18), under 10s free.

The Riviera's premier modern art museum; its bright gardens are dotted with colourful Joan Miró sculptures.

Monaco Open-air Cinema

Parking du Chemin des Pecheurs, 98000 Monaco, T08 92 68 00 72, cinemasporting.com. €10 adult, €7 under 20s.
Summer-long al fresco auditorium with English-language blockbusters.

Parc Zoologique de Fréjus

Zone du Capitou, 83600 Fréjus, T04 98 11 37 37, zoo-frejus.com. Daily Jun-Aug 1000-1800, Mar-May and Sep-Oct 1000-1700, Nov-Feb 1030-1630. €14 adult, €9.50 child (3-9), under 3s free.
Visit the zoo's elephants, kangaroos, iguanas and emus on foot, or opt to cruise through the 16 hectares of parkland in your car.

Visiobulle

Ponton Courbet, 06160 Juan-les-Pins, T04 93 67 02 11. Daily Jul-Aug 0925, 1040, 1155, 1400, 1525, 1650 and 1815, Apr-Jun and Sep 1100, 1330, 1500 and 1630. €13 adult, €6.50 child (2-11), under 2s free.
One-hour glass-bottomed boat trips around Cap d'Antibes.

Wander through a tropical garden

With more than 300 days of sunshine every year, it's no wonder that the Riviera is home to the country's lushest gardens, each one's shade-dappled foliage ideal for investigating. Sun-kissed Menton alone has seven (jardins-menton.fr). Pack up the pushchair and head to **Jardin Exotique du Val Rahmeh** (av St-Jacques, 06500 Menton, T04 93 35 86 72, Apr-Sep Wed-Mon 1000-1230 and 1530-1830, Oct-Mar Wed-Mon 1000-1230 and 1400-1700, €6 adult, €3.50 child (7-18), under 7s free) where a bamboo-banistered walkway leads you through muggy Amazonian corners and along blossom-scented trails, finishing at a giant lily-pad pond: sitting on these, Alice in Wonderland style, is sadly prohibited.

A 10-minute drive over the Italian border, **Giardini Hanbury** (43 corso Montecarlo, 18039 Mortola Inferiore, Italy, T00 39 01 84 22 95 07, giardinihanbury. com; mid-Jun to mid-Sep 0930-1800, Mar to mid-Jun and mid-Sep to mid-Oct 0930-1700, mid-Oct to Feb 0930-1600; Jul to mid-Mar €7.50 adult, €6 child (6-14), €20 family ticket (2 adults plus 2 children 6-14 years); mid-Mar to Jun €9 adult, €7.50 child (6-14), €25 family ticket (2 adults plus 2 children 6-14 years); under 6s free) tumbles from seaside cliffs down to the Mediterranean

Sea. Flora here is an English-Chinese-Mediterranean mix that comes into full technicolour bloom in late spring. Note that the garden's steep descent makes pushchairs unwieldy, although there are paved pathways (as well as staircase routes) throughout.

Girly girls will adore **Villa Ephrussi de Rothschild** (06230 St-Jean-Cap-Ferrat, T04 93 01 33 09, villa-ephrussi.com, Mar-Oct daily 1000-1800 (Jul and Aug until 1900), Nov-Feb Sat-Sun and school holidays 1000-1800, Mon-Fri 1400-1800, €10 adult, €7.50 child (7-17), 2nd child and under 7s free), an over-the-top, entirely pink princess of a mansion built in 1905 for Baroness Ephrussi de Rothschild. The Marie Antoinette-style interiors are fabulously showy, but it's the

villa's nine surrounding gardens that will woo the kids: there's a rose garden (at its peak Apr-Jul), a formal French garden, a Japanese garden, and best of all, a large musical fountain garden that spurts water to the beat of classical tunes.

Villa Ephrussi.

Nice

The fabled queen of the Riviera, action centres around the city's small Old Town (Vieille Ville), a triangular warren of pedestrian alleys and avenues set just back from the sea, and the huge array of museums scattered around town. It's all ringed by Nice's 5-km, beach-lined promenade des Anglais.

Get your bearings

If you've driven into town, follow the street signs to Saleya Marché aux Fleurs underground car park (cours Saleya, 06000 Nice), where you can leave your wheels: hop in one of the lifts that exit directly out onto the cours Saleya, the Old Town's main thoroughfare. Public transport blankets Nice,

although distances around the centre of town are easily walkable. If you're staying elsewhere on the Riviera, arriving by train or bus will save you a lot of traffic hassle (and cash). Nice's *gare routière*, or **bus station** (5 blvd Jean-Jaurès, T04 93 85 61 81, lignesdazur. com) is located just north of the Old Town. The handy bus no 100 (€1 adult or 2 children 5-10 years, under 4s free) departs every 20 minutes, running eastwards along the coast and stopping at every town between Nice and the Italian border. Sitting off the northern end of avenue Jean-Médecin, the city's buzzy shopping street, Nice-Ville **train station** (3 av Thiers, T36 35, voyages-sncf. com) is recommended for

visitors travelling to or from Antibes, Cannes and other points west. It's linked with the bus station by Nice's single **tram** line (€1 adult or 2 children 5-10 years, under 4s free; tickets can be bought at each stop's electronic kiosks), which passes through pedestrianized place Masséna en route. For the Train des Pignes (see page 93) into the mountains, the **Chemins de Fer de Provence** station (4 rue Alfred Binet, T04 97 03 80 80, trainprovence.com) is a 10-minute walk north of Nice-Ville train station.

As well as a kiosk at the airport, Nice has two **Tourist Information Offices**. There's a small one adjacent to Nice-Ville train station (3 av Thiers, Jun-Sep Mon-Sat 0800-2000, Sun

0900-1900, Oct-May Mon-Sat 0800-1900, Sun 1000-1700), while the central office is on the promenade des Anglais (5 promenade des Anglais, daily Jun-Sep 0900-2000, Oct-May 0900-1800, both offices T08 92 70 74 07, nicetourisme.com). Online, the handy interactive map **Plan Nice** (plan-nice.org) is useful for getting oriented.

Fun & free
Simply strolling Nice's 5-km **promenade des Anglais** can occupy hours. Benches and bright blue seating overlook the Mediterranean Sea; they're also a perfect vantage point for watching rollerbladers, mimes and other performing artists who flock to this wide, smooth esplanade. Quai Rauba Capeu, at the prom's eastern end, has a huge sundial at its centre (you cast the shadow) and panoramic views over the city. Head around the corner and you'll hit Nice's port. Wide pavements and cycle tracks loop all the way to the port's southeast corner, where local fishermen berth their traditionally painted boats.

Play in the park
High above the Old Town, the Colline du Château (daily Apr-Aug 0800-2000, Sep 0800-1900, Oct-Mar 0800-1800) was the city's former defensive bastion. You're unlikely to forget it, as an ear-splitting cannon still fires off from the top every day at

noon. Locals come up here to play *pétanque*, jam on guitars and let their children run free in the state-of-the-art playground. There's a tumbling waterfall, and the clutch of cafés have cracking views from Cap Ferrat to Cap d'Antibes. To reach the park, make the steep climb up from the Port, take one of the three staircases dotted around the Old Town or opt for the lift instead, located at the base of Tour Bellanda (place du 8 Mai 1945, 06300).

Museum mania
After Paris, Nice has more museums than any other city in France. Even better, all the municipal ones are completely free. In the Cimiez neighbourhood, the **Musée Matisse** (164 av des Arènes de Cimiez, 06000, T04 93 81 08 08, musee-matisse-nice.org, Wed-Mon 1000-1800, bus no 15) pays tribute to long-time local resident Henri Matisse, with works that range from Tahitian oil paintings to his brilliant blue Jazz cut-outs. Just north of the Old Town, the **Musée d'Art Moderne et d'Art Contemporain** (MAMAC, promenade des Arts, 06300, T04 97 13 42 01, mamac-nice. org, Tue-Sun 1000-1800) has pop-art pieces by Andy Warhol. The **Musée Masséna** (65 rue de France, gardens entrance on promenade des Anglais, 06000, T04 93 91 19 10, Wed-Mon 1000-1800), next door to

“ ”

If they are here for Christmas they have to go to the Christmas village and the Grand Roue (giant Ferris wheel, place Masséna, 06000, daily Dec-Feb; €6 adult, €4 under 7s)! Eat sweet waffles, jump in the giant bouncy castles and slides, then go to the café for *chocolate chaud*!

Lene
7 years old

Nice's pink-domed, landmark Hotel Negresco, catalogues the Riviera's glamorous history, while **Musée International d'Art Naïf Anatole Jakovsky** (Château Ste-Hélène, av de Fabron, 06200, T04 93 71 78 33, Wed-Mon 1000-1800, bus no 8) houses art critic Anatole Jakovsky's collection of *art naïf*, or naive art – vivid, playful images set on canvas or sculpted – as well as giant, equally colourful sculptures in the garden outside.

Let's go to Nice

Best beaches

With a 5-km seafront promenade, it comes as little surprise that Nice is home to an abundance of fabulous beaches. The city's 15 private *plages*, plus innumerable public stretches, are all pebbly.

Cap de Nice

boulevard Franck Pilatte, 06000. ⊘ ℗

East of the port, this sprinkling of sunny coves and jutting rocks is less one coherent beach and more just a gorgeous, if rugged, stretch of coastline. After a good doze in the sun, stretch your legs on the *sentier du littoral*, or seaside footpath that twists around the cap (access via signposted steps near Coco-Beach Restaurant, not suitable for young children).

Castel Plage

quai Rauba-Capeau, 06300, T04 93 85 22 66, castelplage.com. Mid-Mar to mid-Sep daily 0830-2000. Sunloungers €15/half day, €19/day, parasol €5.

⊘ ❍ ⊜ ⊗ ❍ ℗

Frequented by visiting celebs, including Harry Potter star Emma Watson, this cooler-than-thou beach club has buckets of teen appeal. Major plus: its position at the promenade's eastern end means it soaks up the last of the sun's setting rays. Major minus: its expensive beachside restaurant.

Hi Beach

47 promenade des Anglais, 06000, T04 97 14 00 83, hi-beach.net. Easter-Oct daily 0900-2400. Sunloungers €12/half day, €20/day, €8/child, Family House €29/half day, €49/day.

❍ ⊜ ⊗ ⊕ ❍ ℗

Super-trendy offshoot of Nice's Hi Hotel (hi-hotel.net). Its seafront space is divided into three areas: Energy, Relax and Play, the latter offering great canvas 'Family Houses' for shade and soft play. Lounge on swing chairs, hammocks or sunloungers, nibble sushi or try the organic Mediterranean menu. Wi-Fi throughout.

Make new friends

If you're visiting the Riviera for a week or two, **Le Kids Club** (2 rue d'Angleterre, 06000, T04 93 82 44 43, lekidsclub.com, 3-10 years) offers week-long holiday camps. Each five-day camp is themed (Around the World in 80 Days, Indiana Jones) and loads of fun activities (music, yoga, cooking, crafts) centre on that theme. Kids can attend half days (0900-1200 or 1400-1700, €135/week) or full days (0900-1700, €250/week).

Roll around town

Nice's bike-sharing scheme, **Vélo Bleu** (velobleu.org, €1/day, bike rental free for 30 mins, €1/hr thereafter; adult-sized bikes only) has 200 points around Nice, although the system relies on texts to your mobile and can be tricky to use. On the promenade,

Roller Station (49 quai des Etats-Unis, 06300, roller-station.fr, daily Jul-Aug 0930-2400, May-Jun and Sep-Oct 1000-1900, Nov-Apr 1000-1800) rents bikes (€5/hr, €10/half day), skateboards (€3/hr, €6/half day) and rollerblades (€4/hr, €6/half day). For the more adventurous, **Nice Cycle Tours** (T06 19 99 95 22, nicecycletours.com, standard tours minimum age 15, tailored family tours also available) leads guided bike tours around Nice (easy 10 km, 3 hrs, €30) and the Riviera (challenging 25 km, 5 hrs, €50). Too tiny to pedal? Try **Nice Cyclo** (T04 93 81 76 15, nice.cyclopolitain.com, Jul-Aug daily 0900-2100, Apr-Jun and Sep-Oct Tue-Sat 1000-1900, Nov-Mar Tue-Sat 1000-1800, 30-min tour from €15/person), electronic rickshaws that taxi passengers and offer sightseeing tours around town. Nice's *petit-train* (promenade des Anglais at av de Verdun, 06000, T06 08 55 08 30, trainstouristiquesdenice.com, daily Jun-Aug 1000-1900, Apr-May and Sep 1000-1800, Oct-Dec and Feb-Mar 1000-1700, departures every 30 mins, €7 adult, €4 under 9s) also loops around the Old Town and port, with a 10-minute stop for pics from the Colline du Château.

Talk to the animals

West of Nice's city centre, the 7-ha **Parc Phoenix** animal park (405 promenade des Anglais, 06200, T04 92 29 77 00, daily Apr-Sep 0930-1930, Oct-Mar

0930-1800, €2 adult, under 12s free, bus no 23) is home to otters, swans, tortoises and parrots, as well as jungle gyms, a musical fountain and wide grassy expanses. Be sure to check out the large greenhouse: in one section, huge iguanas run free, while another arcs over an enchanting orchid enclosure.

And if it rains?

On Sunday mornings (Sep-Jun), take in a family *matinée musicale* at Opéra de Nice (4 rue St-François-de-Paule, 06300, T04 92 17 40 00, opera-nice.org, Sun 1100, €7 adult, under 18s free). Head just north of Nice-Ville train station for a peek at the city's ornate onion-domed **Russian Church** (av Nicolas II, off blvd Tzarevitch, 06000, T04 93 96 88 02, acor-nice.com, Mon-Sat 0930-1200 and 1430-1730, Sun 1430-1730, closed Orthodox religious holidays, €3), built in 1912. And if you simply need to switch off, newly renovated **Cinéma Mercury** (16 place Garibaldi, 06300, T04 93 55 37 81, allocine.fr) shows original language new release films (with French subtitles); children's booster seats are provided to fit the plush chairs.

Grab a bite

For sweet summer peaches, stuffed *fougasse* bread, multi-coloured Niçois olives and more, Nice has two **markets** bursting with fresh produce: the Old Town's **cours Saleya** market (06300, Tue-Sun 0800-1230) and the larger, more local **Libération** market (place Général de Gaulle and av Malaussena, Tue-Sun 0800-1230) near the train station. Both are a foodie's dream; both also have lots of cafés nearby for resting tired legs.

Stop for a scoop of **Fenocchio's** (2 place Rossetti, 6 rue de la Poissonerie and 28 blvd Jean-Jaurès, T04 93 80 72 52, fenocchio.fr, daily 1000-2400, place Rossetti closed Nov-Feb) revered ice cream. There are 92 flavours to choose from – from unusual picks like jasmine, tomato and basil and orange flower, to sure-fire sugar-highs like cookies and chewing gum crowned with sweets.

In the Old Town, **Oliviera** (8bis rue de Collet, 06300, T04 93 13 06 45, oliviera.com, Tue-Sat 1000-2200) is part olive oil shop, part laid-back local restaurant. Affable owner Nadim sources oils cultivated and pressed in the South of France, then showcases their flavours with market-inspired cuisine (mains €10-20). Follow your nose around the corner to **Rossettisserie** (8 rue Mascoinet, 06300, T04 93 76 18 80, rossettisserie.com, Tue-Sat 1200-1400 and 2000-2200), a former bakery complete with 150-year-old oven at the back. Half chickens (€10), and joints of beef, lamb and pork (all €12), rotate straight from the spit onto plates, and are teamed with a side of mashed potatoes, vegetables or chips. Owner-chef Jean-Michel will box up any main dish as a picnic box for €2 less than the menu price. There are no reservations at **La Voglia** (2 rue St-François-de-Paule, 06300, T04 93 80 99 16, lavoglia. com, daily 1200-1430 and 1900-2300), so show up early to sample their platters of antipasti, crispy baked rigatoni and giant bowls of spaghetti.

In the port, **Les Amoureux** (7 rue Fodéré, 06300, T04 93 07 59 73, les-amoureux.com, Mon-Sat 1930-2300), opened by Neapolitans Ivan and Monica in 2010, is hands-down Nice's best pizzeria (pizzas €8-15). Sublime Italian toppings, like buffalo mozzarella, are shipped up weekly from Naples. Pop along to cheap and cheerful **Chez Pipo** (13 rue Bavastro, 06300, T04 93 55 88 82, chezpipo.fr, Tue-Sun 1800-2230) to taste three classic Niçois recipes: *socca* (a chick-pea pancake) *pissaladière* (a local onion and olive pizza) or *anchoïade* (an anchovy dip). **La Zucca Magica** (4bis quai Papacino, 06300, T04 93 56 25 27, lazuccamagica. com, Tue-Sat 1230-1430 and 1930-2200) is the city's favourite vegetarian spot. The set menu (obligatory; €20 4-course lunch, €29 5-course dinner, under 12s eat free) is a seasonal bonanza; kids will love the zillions of pumpkins that make up the weirdly cosy decor.

The Estérel

To the very west of the Riviera region, the mountainous Massif de l'Estérel sits between Cannes and St Raphaël, encompassing 32,000 ha of purpley-red volcanic rock. Protected Parc Départemental de l'Estérel (the 700-ha Estérel Park) pokes up at its centre, while the coastal road, Corniche de l'Estérel, corkscrews through it for 35 km, squeezed below the crimson cliffs and the sea.

Unusual, rugged and often overlooked (particularly by foreign visitors), the Estérel's glowing terrain is bursting with outdoor adventure. It's criss-crossed with hiking routes and cycling paths, and speckled with russet-tinged beaches.

Mandelieu-la-Napoule, Théoule-sur-Mer & Agay
The towns of Mandelieu-la-Napoule, Théoule-sur-Mer and Agay are all lovely, utterly laid-back and steps from the sea. **Mandelieu-la-Napoule** is home to Château de la Napoule (BP940, 06210, T04 93 49 95 05, chateau-lanapoule.com, daily Feb-Oct 1000-1800, tours at 1130, 1430, 1530, 1630, Nov-Jan 1000-1700 (weekdays from 1400), tours at 1430 and 1530 plus Sat-Sun tours at 1130; château €7 adult, €4 child (7-16), under 7s free; garden €3.50, under 7s free). Kooky Wall Street banker Henry Clews and his wife Marie restored this 14th-century fort in 1918, using it to host fancy-dress parties in their (formerly) flamingo-filled exotic gardens. The pretty gardens now offer panoramic vistas over the water, while inside (by tour only) there are spooky, faux-medieval rooms to root around.

Tourist information offices

Agay 83530, place Giannetti, T04 94 82 01 85, agay.fr. Jul-Aug Mon-Sat 0900-1800, Sep-Jun Mon-Sat 0900-1200 and 1400-1700.

Mandelieu-la-Napoule 06210, 806 av de Cannes, T04 93 93 64 64, ot-mandelieu.fr. Mon-Sat 0930-1230 and 1330-1730.

Théoule-sur-Mer 06590, 1 corniche d'Or, T04 93 49 28 28, theoule-sur-mer.org. Mon-Sat 0900-1900, Sun 0900-1400.

A French Robin Hood?

During the 18th century, master-of-disguise Gaspard de Besse stole from the Riviera's greedy landlords, showering their riches on poor local peasants. His methods of trickery included attending fancy-dress balls in elaborate costume, then sneaking out unnoticed, pockets bulging with snooty guests' gold coins and priceless jewels. De Besse was persecuted, eventually arrested and killed, with his head gruesomely chopped off and nailed to a tree. His remaining treasure – buried somewhere in the Massif de l'Estérel – has never been found, but keep your eyes peeled if you're hiking: he used a cave somewhere on the Estérel's Mont Vinaigre as his hideout!

The area around the tiny town of Théoule-sur-Mer is the start of some of the cutest, most isolated beaches on the coast, such as sandy **L'Aiguille** (🅟 ⊜ ⊕) and wild, hard-to-reach ruddy stretches like **Le Petit Caneiret** (🅟), squeezed between a translucent sea and the Estérel's corniche road. Further along, the protected bay of **Agay** (🅟 ⊜ ⊗ ⊕ ⊕ 🅟) is easy to access with pushchairs and is ideal for little ones.

West of Agay, look out for the private island of Ile d'Or, on the opposite side of Cap du Dramont. The island's mock Saracen castle was built by an oddball physician, Augustus Lutaud, who threw wild parties and declared himself king of the island in 1913. Lutaud and the island inspired the Tintin adventure *L'Ile Noire* (The Black Island), where our blonde hero chases a mad doctor.

Action stations

Enjoy a leisurely **boat trip** with **Capitaine Nemo** (rue de l'Agay, 83530 Agay, T04 94 82 71 45, bateauxsaintraphael.com, Jul-Aug Mon-Fri hourly 1000-1800, Sat-Sun hourly 1500-1800, Jun Tue-Fri 1000, 1100, 1500, 1600,1700, Sun 1500, 1600, 1700, Sep Tue-Fri 1000, 1100, 1400, 1500,1600, Apr-May Tue-Fri and Sun 1500, 1600, 1700, €11 adult, €9 child (2-9), under 2s free), offering 50-minute *sous-marin* outings along the Estérel's coastline, with submerged glass panels to peer underwater.

Alternatively try **Sea Safari** (Bassin A, quai 9, port de Cannes-Marina, 06210 Mandelieu-la-Napoule, T06 21 78 20 54, seasafari.fr; minimum age 8), where you can zip along the Estérel's coast in a 12-person semi-rigid speedboat. Choose between a short sightseeing tour (1½ hrs, €30 adult, €20 child (8-12), no stops en route) or a longer day out (5 hrs, €60 adult, €40 child (8-12)), complete with swims in the Estérel's bays.

The Estérel is home to 100 km of **cycle routes** and 40 km of **hiking trails**. For a downloadable map of eight walks (30 mins-2 hrs each) and cycle paths around the Estérel hills and along the coast surrounding Théoule-sur-Mer, visit the Tourist Office's website (theoule-sur-mer.org, descriptions in French only). It's also possible to purchase a

booklet of more detailed bike paths directly from the Tourist Office (€5). Through an extension of their website (visiocarte.com/Gmap/Mandelieu.html), Mandelieu-la-Napoule's Tourist Office offers a handy interactive map marked with 17 walking itineraries in and around the Estérel. They sell a printed guide of the walks too (€9.80).

The tiny train station of Le Trayas is also a good starting point for jaunts into the park, including the strenuous but stunning hike (8.5-km circuit, not recommended for under 10s) up to the 492-m-high Pic de l'Ours, which is signposted from the station platform.

For a spot of snorkelling, grab your mask and flippers and dip into Théoule-sur-Mer's *sentier de découverte sous-marin* (underwater discovery trail) off the Pointe de l'Aiguille, south of the town centre. Four floating buoys mark Posidonia (or Neptune) seagrass, important for protecting the coastline from erosion, spots where scorpion fish feed, you can see sea anemones and a natural habitat that shelters sea sponges. Lazier family members can splash around on Pointe de l'Aiguille's tropical turquoise shores (see opposite).

Agay's sheltered bay is perfect for a gentle paddle. **Base Nautique Municipale d'Agay** (plage de l'Escale, 83530 Agay, T04 94 82 71 42, ville-saintraphael.fr, Jul-Aug daily, Jun and Sep Sat-Sun) specializes in kayak hire (1-person kayaks €7/hr, 2-person kayaks €12/hr) and guided kayak trips (€15/person) along the Estérel's shores (minimum age 6, all participants must know how to swim). Bat'Ski Club (plage de la Figueirette, BP24, 06590 Théoule-sur-Mer, T04 93 75 02 39, Apr-Sep) provides windsurfers, catamarans, paddleboards and kayaks from €8/hr. During July and August, Bat'Ski also offers baby **waterskiing** lessons (4-8 years, €10/trial lesson, €45/five lessons), as well as adult windsurfing (€28-35/hr) and catamaran (€35-45/hr) lessons.

Getting there

The Estérel can be easily accessed from Théoule-sur-Mer, Le Trayas and Agay. The Riviera's regional trains (ter-sncf.com) stop at all of these stations.

Sleeping The Riviera

Pick of the pitches

Douce Quiétude

3435 blvd Jacques Baudino, 83700 St-Raphaël, T04 94 44 30 00, douce-quietude.com. Apr-Oct. €19.50-28 2 adults, pitch and car, €6-10 extra adult, €5-8 child (3-13), under 3s free; 4-6-person cottage €53-225/night.

🅐 🅞 🅔 🅟 🅕 Wi-Fi

Five kilometres from the beaches of St-Raphaël and Agay, this campground is energetically staffed and packed full of activities. Pick from ping-pong, archery or aerobics, opt for a dip in the pool or try your hand at *pétanque*. There are two kids' clubs (ages 6-11 and 12-16), fireworks and themed evenings.

Les Embruns

63 route de Biot, La Brague, 06600 Antibes, T04 93 33 33 35, campingembruns-antibes.com. Apr-mid Oct. €20-24 2 adults, pitch and car, €6 extra adult, €3 under 5s. 2-3-person studio €400-520/week, 4-5-person studio €450-600, 2-4-person bungalow €320-440, 2-person mobile home €240-320, 4-5-person mobile home €350-550.

🅐 🅞 🅔 🅟 🅒 🅞 🅔 🅕

Tantalizingly close to Aquasplash and Marineland, Les Embruns has a leafy landscape and a laid-back attitude. There's a games room and juice bar, and it's an easy walk to the train station and the beach.

Also recommended: Camping du Pylone (campingdupylone. com), just down the road.

Best of the rest

Riviera Pebbles

20 rue Hôtel des Postes, 06000, Nice, rivierapebbles.com.

Purveyors of 80 magnificent apartments in Nice (plus others in nearby Antibes, Monaco, Cannes, Cap Ferrat, Eze-sur-Mer and St-Paul-de-Vence), all of which can be booked online. These upscale properties (from around €70 per night) are uniformly well located and well equipped. Ranging from one-bedroom modern apartments in the Old Town to three-bedroom villas out of town, be sure to book early, as the entire selection fills up fast.

La Villa sur la Plage

La Grande Plage, 06360 Eze-sur-Mer, T08 72 24 99 24, holidaylettings. co.uk/rentals/eze-village/18357. 4-person apartment £420-1597/ week.

These three self-catering apartments offer what so few in the South of France can claim: a swim in the sea less than 10 m from your front door. Each apartment has its own outdoor space, sunloungers and private parking. Friendly Croatian-French owners Meri, Patrick and their son Shane live next door, and will happily point you towards their favourite restaurants and activities.

Cool & quirky

Orion B&B

Impasse des Peupliers, 2436 chemin du Malvan, 06570 St-Paul-de-Vence, orionbb.com. Jul-Aug 1-week minimum stay, Apr-Jun and Sep-early Nov 3-night minimum stay, mid Nov-Mar 2-night minimum stay. **Shere Khan** 2-3 person treehouse Jul-Aug €1900/week, May-Jun and Sep €850/3 nights (Fri-Sun) or 4 nights (Mon-Thu), Apr, Oct-early Nov €750/3 nights (Fri-Sun) or 4 nights (Mon-Thu), mid Nov-Mar €375/2 nights (Fri-Sat); **King Louie** treehouse 2 adults plus 2 children Jul-Aug €2100/week, May-Jun and Sep €950/3 nights (Fri-Sun) or 4 nights (Mon-Thu), Apr, Oct-early Nov €800/3 nights (Fri-Sun) or 4 nights (Mon-Thu), mid Nov-Mar €450/2 nights (Fri-Sat); **Bagheera** 2-person treehouse Jul-Aug €1800/week, May-Jun and Sep €750/3 nights (Fri-Sun) or 4 nights (Mon-Thu), Apr, Oct-early Nov €650/3 nights (Fri-Sun) or 4 nights (Mon-Thu), mid Nov-Mar €325/2 nights (Fri-Sat); **Colonel Hathi** 2 adults plus 3 children Jul-Aug €2400/week, May-Jun and Sep €1100/3 nights (Fri-Sun) or 4 nights (Mon-Thu), Apr, Oct-early Nov €900/3 nights (Fri-Sun) or 4 nights (Mon-Thu), mid Nov-Mar €500/2 nights (Fri-Sat); **Maisonette Akela** 4-5-person house Jul-Aug €1900/week, May-Jun and Sep €850/3 nights (Fri-Sun) or 4 nights (Mon-Thu).

Snooze beneath the stars in one of these cute wooden treehouses, each one with its own private terrace and

hammocks for lounging. Children will adore King Louie in particular, connected by a bridge through the treetops to the separate, kids-only Mowgli treehouse. At the centre of the property there's a swimming pool, surrounded by shady oak, cherry trees and palms.

Splashing out

Le Canberra

120 rue d'Antibes, 06400 Cannes, T04 97 06 95 00, hotel-cannes-canberra. com. Doubles €140-330, 4-person suite €220-500.

Set between boutique-lined rue d'Antibes and Cannes' main thoroughfare, La Croisette, Le Canberra is quiet, welcoming, and best of all it has a secluded swimming pool surrounded by sunloungers. Cots available at no extra charge; free Wi-Fi.

Le Havre Bleu

29 blvd Maréchal Joffre, 06310 Beaulieu-sur-Mer, T04 93 01 01 40, lehavrebleu.com. Doubles €63-85, triples €78-98, 4-person family room €93-115.

A blue-and-white clapboard façade hides an excellent budget hotel. The 20 rooms feature Wi-Fi and air conditioning, private parking and a terrace. Beaulieu's beaches and train station, plus Villa Keryos and Cap Ferrat, are a few minutes' walk away.

Hôtel Martinez

73 La Croisette, 06400 Cannes, T04 92 98 73 00, hotel-martinez.com. Doubles €610-760 (online bookings from €152/double, €200/2 adults plus 2 under 12s).

Cannes' most glamorous hotel boasts a swimming pool overlooking La Croisette and ZPlage, the town's coolest beach club. But best of all, it offers the most terrific kids' club in town (Jul-Aug daily 1400-1800, 4-12 years, free), available to children staying in the hotel only. Organized activities include face-painting, making your own comic strips and ceramics.

(€7.50) against the backdrop of stupendous sea views. A ten-minute bus ride from Monaco's port and town centre

Nice Garden Hotel

11 rue du Congrès, 06000 Nice, T04 93 87 35 62, nicegardenhotel.com. Doubles €65-110, triples €90-135, €15/night extra bed.

Within easy walking distance from the railway station, the Old Town and the beach, Nice Garden Hotel sits in a quiet, residential neighbourhood. Rooms are airy, some have frescos and hardwood floors and all beds are laid with traditional Provençal quilts. Winter visitors can pluck oranges and lemons from the trees in the garden. Particularly friendly, free Wi-Fi.

Hôtel Patricia

Av de l'Ange Gardien, T04 93 01 06 70, hotel-patricia.riviera.fr. Doubles €55-79, triples €71-79, quadruples €79-85.

A veritable – and shockingly cheap – Eden. Past the friendly welcome are a dozen or so unique bedrooms: some (recommended) with gorgeous sea views. There's a sun terrace with loungers, marble tables, citrus groves, mobiles and Moroccan lamps, as well as free parking, Wi-Fi, and new in 2010, a spa and a jacuzzi. The downside? The local train rattles past every hour.

Hôtel Miramar

126 av du 3 septembre, 06320 Cap d'Ail, T04 93 78 06 60, monte-carlo. mc/hotel-miramar-capdail. Closed Feb. Doubles €54-88, triples €65-95, quadruples €95-115.

Twenty-five simple rooms perched on the *basse corniche* and a 10-minute walk from Cap d'Ail's Mala Plage. Plump for one with a private sun terrace, where you can enjoy breakfast

Eating The Riviera

Local goodies

With mild winters and year-round sunshine, it's little surprise that the Riviera is home to a handful of France's finest food markets. For picnic heaven, hit Cannes' Marché Forville (rue Forville, 06400, Tue-Sun 0730-1230): producers pile their harvests high and there's a dedicated organic section. Menton's covered market, Les Halles (place du Docteur Théophile Fornari, 06500, daily 0800-1300), is packed by almost 40 stallholders come summer, and it's a great place to pick up a mix of French and Italian fruits, veggies and cheeses. Nibble morsels of hazelnut-spiked saucisson, or dip crunchy baguette rounds into varieties of locally produced olive tapenade at Antibes' Marché Provençal (cours Masséna, 06600, Tue-Sun 0730-1300, Jun-Aug daily). Head into Fréjus's Old Town (place Paul-Albert Février and place Formigé, 83600, Wed and Sat 0800-1300) to scoop up goodies farmed by local producers; alternatively, stock up at St-Raphaël's fruit and vegetable market (place République, 83700, Tue-Sun 0800-1300). Over the Italian border, Ventimiglia's weekly *mercato* (throughout town, 18039, May-Oct 0600-1800, Nov-Apr 0600-1700) takes over the city's seafront streets, and draws visitors by the thousand.

Look out for Sicilian tomatoes in summer, Clementine oranges at Christmas and Piedmontese wines, Ligurian olive oils and scores of other foodie souvenirs year-round.

Pâtisserie La Cigale

7 av Carnot, 06500 Menton, T04 93 35 74 66. Wed-Mon 0700-1930. Locals boast that Menton grows the world's best lemons. What better way to test their theory than a stop at this citron-centric pâtisserie and salon de thé? Indulge in crème brûlée au citron and tarte au citron.

Quick & simple

Boulangerie-Pâtisserie des Pins

5 blvd Pinède, 06160 Juan-les-Pins, T04 93 61 13 45. Tue-Sat 0800-1900. A mouth-watering array of sandwiches (aubergine and feta, roast chicken salad and tuna-filled *pan-bagnats*, all around €4 apiece), as well top croissants and éclairs – perfect picnic fodder for the nearby beaches.

Café de Paris

Casino Square, 98000 Monaco, T00 377 98 06 76 23, montecarloresort.com. Daily 0800-0200. Posh though it is, a cool drink on an outdoor table in the sun in this most ritzy of squares won't break the bank.

Celebrity-spot from the terrace: Monte Carlo's famous Hotel de Paris is opposite, with its exclusive Casino just over the road. Racing fans will love the café's history: in 1897 during the first Marseille-Monte Carlo rally, Edouard Michelin (of Michelin tyre fame) veered off the road at top speed, spectacularly smashing his car straight into the Café de Paris' dining room.

Café de la Place

Place Général de Gaulle, 06570 St-Paul-de-Vence, T04 93 32 80 03. Daily 0800-2000, closed Nov. Café-bar with simple sandwiches and plat du jour lunches (€12-16) like steak and frites, served up in front of St Paul's premier *pétanque* ground. Plenty of space makes it ideal for young kids.

Le Rustic

33 place Nationale, 06600 Antibes, T04 93 34 10 81. Daily 1200-1430 and 1800-2300. At first glance it may not stand out from the other restaurants on bustling place Nationale.

But Le Rustic is a notch above. Perfectly executed cuisine comes direct from the 1980s: bouquet of prawns, salad with lardons, grilled lamb and crème brûlée. Set menus start at €15, wood-fired pizzas around €10.

La Taverne du Safranier

Place Safranier, 06600 Antibes, T04 93 34 80 50. Daily 1200-1430 and 1900-2230, closed mid-Nov to early Feb. Sunny street restaurant liberally sprinkled over place Safranier, with plenty of space for little ones to run around. Colourful menus hung from the square's walls are chalked up with solid, unshowy dishes: grilled bream with garlic, prawns à la Provençale.

Posh nosh

African Queen

Port de Plaisance, 06310 Beaulieu-sur-Mer, T04 93 01 10 85, africanqueen.fr. Daily 1200-2400. On a row of great terraced restaurants in Beaulieu marina, the African Queen may be celeb-showy (Stallone and Jack Nicholson are regular diners) but its cuisine is down-home traditional. Tasty salade Niçoise is tossed together with over-the-top pizzazz at your table, while crisp pizzas, burgers and grilled fish arrive steaming from the oven. In high season reservations are a must.

Caveau 30

45 av Félix Faure, 06570 Cannes, T04 93 39 06 33. Tue-Sun 1800-2400. Seafood specialist brasserie where platters of fruits de mer and buckets of mussels are served up with aplomb. Service is extravagantly friendly, although kids will prefer the outdoor terrace rather than the more elegant interior. Two fixed price menus (€24 and €36) feature oysters, grilled fish and squid, plus pasta and lamb chops for non-fish fiends.

La Colombe d'Or

Place Général de Gaulle, 06570 St-Paul-de-Vence, T04 93 32 80 02, la-colombe-dor.com. Daily 1200-1400 and 1900-2200, closed Nov-mid Dec and 2 weeks Jan. St-Paul-de-Vence's must-eat restaurant and high-end hotel where the likes of Picasso and Matisse once paid for their keep in canvases (now adorning the walls of the dining room inside). The ambience could be stuffy but it most certainly isn't: there's a wonderful stone terrace where friendly, suited-up waiters serve the house speciality, roast chicken.

Le Cosmo

11 place Amélie Pollonais, 06230 Villefranche-sur-Mer, T04 93 01 84 05. Daily 0800-0300. In Villefranche's pedestrian main square, with a seaview terrace opposite the Jean Cocteau-frescoed Chapelle St-Pierre. Shady canopies and friendly staff make this place perfect for an unhurried lunch. Grown-ups will adore their famous anchoïade and crudités dipping-platter and exotic salads (try the avocado, crab and pink grapefruit); kids will revel in the great omelettes and giant plates of spaghetti.

La Potinière du Palais

13 square Mérimée, 06400 Cannes, T04 93 39 02 82, lapotiniere.fr. Mon-Sat 1200-1430 and 1900-2230, closed 1st 2 weeks Dec. Opposite Cannes' Palais des Festivals, La Potinière's streetside terrace is a sunny spot to stop for a light lunch. Plats du jour (giant salads with soft eggs for dipping, big creamy bowls of pumpkin soup) are around €15, two-course lunch menus €18. Staff are super-accommodating with little eaters.

La Salière

14 quai Jean-Charles-Rey, Fontvieille, 98000 Monaco, T00 377 92 05 25 82. lasaliere.mc. Daily 1200-1430 and 1930-2300. Mediterranean specialist popular with hip locals and celebs. Go for the *skizze*, a type of Tuscan pizza piled high with artichokes, mozzarella and mortadella ham, or robiola cheese and truffle oil (both €16).

For restaurants and markets in Nice, see page 47.

St-Tropez harbour.

Contents

St-Tropez to Hyères

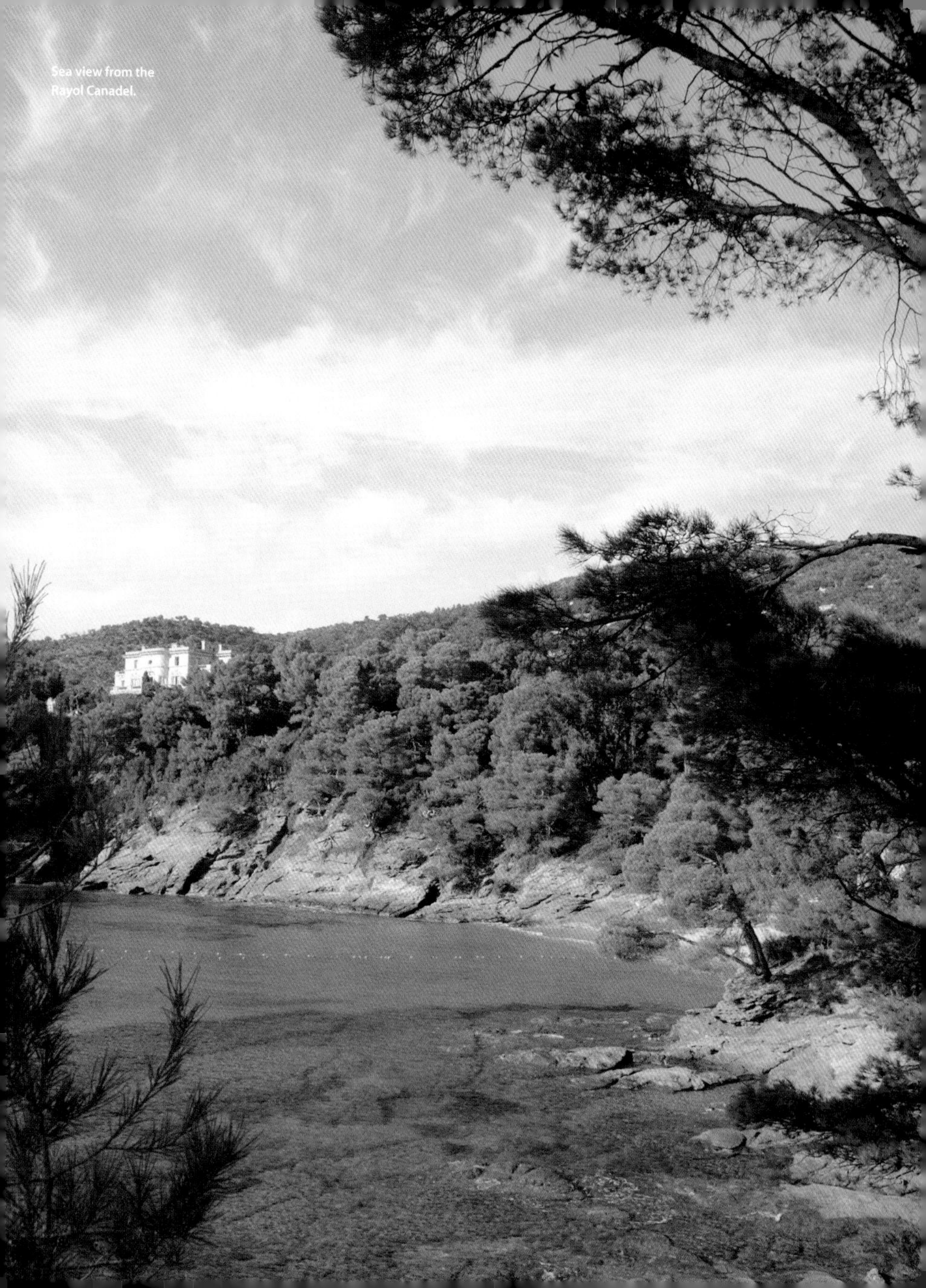

Sea view from the Rayol Canadel.

Le Lavandou.

Less crowded than the Riviera, tamer than Western Provence and a whole lot gentler than Haute-Provence, the coast and countryside between St-Tropez and Hyères is ideal for families who want a holiday with easy hiking, a splash of glamour and plenty of sandy beaches.

St-Tropez is this region's star. The name may evoke visions of snootiness, but little could be further from the truth. Sure, celebrities are a dime a dozen come summertime (keep those eyes peeled for the likes of Paris Hilton and Jennifer Lopez!), but this pretty seaside village has managed to retain its small-town heart. Behind the port's mega-yachts, there's a fleet of wooden boats, still hauling in piles of fish every day at dawn. Pedestrian place des Lices is packed with local *pétanque* players (see page 71 for where to borrow free *boules*), giving way twice a week to a teeming produce and antiques market. And frequent ferries zip from the town's new port across the bay to **Ste-Maxime** and **Port Grimaud**, the former great for cheap, beachside accommodation, the latter the South of France's very own little Venice.

St-Tropez sits in the northeast corner of the creatively named St-Tropez peninsula. This chunk of land is dusted with vineyards, edged by a *sentier du littoral*, or coastal walking path, and home to scores of blissfully beautiful beaches. The 5-km **Plage de Pampelonne** has stretches of sand to suit all tastes, from the splashiest tiny tot to the trendiest of all supersized-shade-clad teen. Near **La Croix-Valmer**, on the peninsula's southern coast, tranquil **Plage Gigaro** is perfect for a game of beach volleyball or a scamper along the shore.

The D559 weaves its way west along the coast. For the most part, beaches here are sandy, shallow, not too crowded and backed by the natural shade of umbrella pines. Most can be reached by the coastal bus; otherwise you can simply park up by the sand, usually for free. Days can fly by enjoying snorkelling, devouring endless ice-lollies and perfecting sand sculptures on the beaches that cluster around **Rayol-Canadel**, **Le Lavandou** and **Bormes-les-Mimosas**.

Too sedate? Pop into **Hyères'** vibrant Old Town or visit extreme water sports haven **Plage de l'Almanarre** to its south. Hankering after a remote idyll? Head instead to the **Îles d'Or**, three protected islands that include Port-Cros, France's smallest national park. The tiny islands are vehicle-free, studded with abandoned forts and ringed by crystalline shores.

You must

- Build a sand castle at one of the dozens of white-sand beaches.
- Get lost in the twisty turns of Cogolin's Labyrinthe des Sens maze.
- Hop aboard a ferry to car-free paradise: the tropical Îles d'Or.
- Snorkel along a *sentier sous-marin*, or underwater discovery trail.
- Snap a pic of the heady vistas from the Routes des Crêtes driving trail.
- Stargaze from a café in St-Tropez's celebrity-sprinkled port.
- Take the plunge: try your hand at scuba-diving, sailing or windsurfing.

Fun & free

Fly a kite
Running between windy Plage de l'Almanarre and the vast salt marshes to its east, Hyères' **Route du Sel** (salt road) connects the Giens Peninsula with the mainland. It's long, paved and closed to traffic, which means it's excellent for strolling. The strong, constant winds, teamed with the wide-open spaces, also make for top kite-flying and kitesurfing terrain. Look out for flamingos and herons hunting for food here, or orchids and sea lilies.

Play in the park
Visit the animals at **Le Parc Olbius Riquier** (av Ambroise Thomas, 83400 Hyères, T04 94 00 78 65, Apr-Sep 0730-2000, Mar and Oct 0730-1900, Feb 0730-1800, Jan and Nov 0730-1730, Dec 0730-1700), a small, free zoo set around the park's central lake. As well as a play area, there's also a mini train, pony rides and tennis courts (the latter all for a fee).

Take a walk on the wild side
A *sentier du littoral*, or coastal walking path, rings the whole of the St-Tropez peninsula. Some sections are rocky and uneven, others smooth and well trodden. For families with young children, racing along the 5-km shore of **Plage de Pampelonne** makes for a fantastic afternoon out. Leave the wheels at the Baie des Canoubiers and follow the *sentier* eastwards for sandy beaches and swimming. Free *navette* buses also run from St-Tropez's place des Lices to Plage des Salins, Cap du Pinet and other points on this easterly section of the coastal path – ask about seasonal schedules at St-Tropez's Tourist Office (see page 71).

Appropriate for older kids only is the beautiful yet challenging **southern coastal walk** between Plage de Gigaro and Plage du Brouis (allow one hour each way) – see who can spot Ilot du Crocodile first, the tiny nearby island shaped like a crocodile.

For additional walking around St-Tropez, stop by any local Tourist Office and pick up *Stepping Out*, a free map marked with 48 hiking,

biking and horse riding trails. Alternatively, visit golfe-saint-tropez-information.com.

Tour Little Venice

The zany space-age vision of architect François Spoerry, Port Grimaud rose from the sand dunes near St-Tropez in the 1960s. Spoerry envisaged a futuristic seaside village, with each property possessing its own boat mooring. But what could have turned out as a dull Docklands developed instead into a high-tech Venice, with the settlement expanding in stages until the 1990s. Leave your vehicle in the car park outside, then explore the town's canals on foot or on one of the little four-person electric boats (€20/hr from inside the city walls).

Routes des Crêtes

Movie-scene vistas combine with sweaty palms on the cliff-top Route des Crêtes (translated into English as the tamer sounding 'Ridgetop Road'). This guide covers three stunning South of France drives, all coined with this same moniker, all dusted with staggering panoramas and all edged by the very occasional scary sheer drop (most often behind a chunky guardrail). It's impossible to drive faster than around 40 kph on any of them and none are suitable for drivers or passengers prone to motion sickness. Picnic stops line each route, as do summer-only restaurants.

Route des Crêtes no 1: Bormes-les-Mimosas to Col du Canadel, 20 km Head north out of Bormes-les-Mimosas on the D41. After a couple of kilometres, keep an eye out for a small 'Piste des Crêtes' sign on the right. Seemingly only wide enough for one vehicle, this road is indeed the Route des Crêtes. It slowly ascends, eventually opening onto breathtaking views over the Iles d'Or. You'll likely cross paths with only a handful of cars (this road is primarily a favourite with cyclists). As the route begins its slow descent, it dips inland and the vistas flip: from this section you'll see the Gulf of St-Tropez, the Estérel Mountains and the runway of La Môle airport, where private jets fly in the super-rich all summer. The Route des Crêtes finishes at Col du Canadel, with more top views along the coast. It's another twisty 7 km from here down to the D559 at Rayol-Canadel-sur-Mer.

There's a café and one pizzeria on the Route des Crêtes. Both are open daily May to September. Alternatively, there are plenty of rural spots to stop for your own roadside picnic.

For **Routes des Crêtes nos 2 and 3,** see pages 95 and 105 respectively.

Out & about St-Tropez to Hyères

Best beaches

While topless sunbathing is the norm on all of the beaches in the South of France, many of the ones that surround the St-Tropez peninsula take achieving that all-over tan a step further. Nudism, while not exactly condoned (except on nudist beaches, of which there are plenty), is definitely optional, particularly in smaller coastal coves and out of season. For the most part, it's low-key and inoffensive, with elderly couples and families with young kids being the first to strip off.

The following beaches are grouped together geographically, beginning in Ste-Maxime and moving westwards to Hyères. Within each geographical area the beaches are listed in alphabetical order.

La Nartelle
Av Général Touzet du Vigier, 83120 Ste-Maxime.
This sandy beach is east of Ste-Maxime's town centre, and just off the coastal road. East facing, it's ideal for early risers, getting plenty of sun. Easy pushchair access.

La Pointe des Sardinaux
Av Général Touzet du Vigier, 83120 Ste-Maxime.
A beautiful park pokes into the sea, ringed by this sand and shingle beach. It's a fairly easy hike to reach, best for families with older kids. Its turquoise waters make it worth the effort.

La Mouette
83994 St-Tropez.
This wild, sandy beach sits between St-Tropez town centre and Les Salins (below), and is only accessible via the *sentier des douaniers*, or coastal footpath.

Les Salins
Chemin des Salins, 83994 St-Tropez.
Far from Pampelonne's bustle further south along the coast, this sandy beach has a great sand-in-the-toes restaurant and clear views across the St-Tropez bay to the Estérel Mountains. Easily accessible via one short set of stairs.

Le Cap Taillat
83350 Ramatuelle.
One of this region's most stunning beaches, and a paradise for trekkers dedicated enough to reach it. Just a narrow strip of sand connects Cap Taillat, a skinny peninsula jutting out into the sea, with the mainland. Difficult access (around half an hour from Plage de l'Escalet) is exclusively via the *sentier du littoral*.

Pampelonne
Various access points from route des Plages, 83350 Ramatuelle.
It was Brigitte Bardot who made this strip famous during Roger Vadim's 1956 movie *Et Dieu créa la femme* (And God Created Woman). Now a whopping 30,000 sun-worshippers flock to this 5-km stretch of beach every day during the summer, running the gamut from über-wealthy to utterly unpretentious. Pampelonne is home to 25 beach clubs (including some nudist ones) and public areas of sand: Club 55 is where the A-list flock, while merchant

Plage de Pampelonne.

bankers and the like run up bills of tens of thousands of euros at the Voile Rouge. Other *plages*, like Aqua Club, are way more relaxed; all have sunloungers to rent for around €20-30 per day. The beach clubs are backed by various car parks, making it a breeze to drag buckets, pre-inflated toys and buggies down to the water.

Les Brouis

83420 La Croix-Valmer.

For an afternoon on this lovely wild beach, scramble along the *sentier du littoral*, eastwards from Gigaro (below) towards Cap Lardier. The snorkelling is supreme. The relatively difficult access means Les Brouis is more suitable for families with older kids and is much quieter than nearby Gigaro. Allow about an hour to hike each way.

Gigaro

Boulevard de Gigaro, 83420 La Croix-Valmer.

This strip of sand is the antithesis to some of the peninsula's more posey beaches. A hop from a nearby cluster of restaurants, snack bars and shops, the beach is accessed via a smooth wooden walkway. Plus, it's great for young children, as the water deepens gradually.

Bonporteau

Off av des Alliés, 83240 Cavalaire-sur-Mer.

This large beach is tucked well off the main coastal road, with fine golden sands and natural protection from the wind.

Le Canadel

D559 to av de la Méditerranée, 83820 Rayol-Canadel-sur-Mer.

It may be much smaller than nearby Pramousquier (below), but Le Canadel possesses the same shimmery mix of black and white sand. As the beach is fairly protected, its water is very clear.

Gigaro.

Pramousquier

D559 to rue St-Pierre, 83820 Rayol-
Canadel-sur-Mer.

😎 🌊 🎵 ⚫ ➕ 🚽 Ⓟ

Just east of Cap Nègre (with
Carla Bruni's family home at its
tip), this long stretch of black
and white sand has plenty of
public space.

Cavalière

Off D559, 83980 Le Lavandou.

😎 🌊 🎵 ⚫ 🏖 ➕ 🚽 Ⓟ

A mecca for water sports
enthusiasts, including
waterskiing and wakeboarding.

St-Clair

D559 to bd de la Baleine, 83980 Le
Lavandou.

😎 🌊 🎵 ⚫ 🏖 ➕ 🚽 Ⓟ

Like many of the beaches in this
immediate area, St-Clair is an
attractive sweep of sand, yet in
close proximity to a clutch of
shops and cafés. It's edged with
palm trees and lapped by clear
waters. Easy pushchair access.

L'Argentière

Bd de la Plage de l'Argentière, 83230
Bormes-les-Mimosas.

😎 🌊 🎵 ⚫ ➕ 🚽 Ⓟ

This wide sandy beach is most
popular for its Jardin des Mattes
sentier sous-marin, or underwater
discovery trail. Seven numbered
buoys are dotted around the
headland to the beach's east,
with panels flagging up spots
to look out for urchins, starfish
and the protected Posidonia
seagrass (also called Neptune

grass). This type of seaweed
forms an important thick barrier
(or 'mat') over the seafloor.

Cabasson

Av Guy Tezenas, 83230 Bormes-les-
Mimosas.

🌊 🎵 ⚫ 🏖 ➕ 🚽 Ⓟ

Make like the French presidents
come summertime: this sandy
beach looks out onto Fort de
Brégançon, the presidential
retreat on a solitary island
opposite. The beach is easily
accessed with pushchairs and
there's a small children's play
area near the car park.

L'Estagnol

Off route de Léoube, 83230 Bormes-
les-Mimosas.

🌊 🎵 🚽 Ⓟ

This beautiful white-sand beach
arcs around a perfectly sheltered
lagoon, with views of the Iles
d'Or on the horizon. The canopy
of pine trees makes wonderful
natural shade, and there are
lovely vineyards just behind.
Highly recommended.

Le Pellegrin

Off route de Léoube, 83230 Bormes-
les-Mimosas.

🚽 Ⓟ

West of L'Estagnol, the longer
Le Pellegrin beach shares many
of its attributes: white sand,
shady pines, a wild feel yet easily
accessed by car. For adventure
seekers, there's a coastal path
that connects it to L'Argentière
to the west.

Les Brouis.

L'Almanarre

Route du Sel, 83400 Hyères.

😎 🌊 🎵 ➕ 🚽 Ⓟ

Facing the Gulf of Giens, this
4-km beach stretches along the
western *tombolo*, or the thin
strip of land linking the Giens
peninsula with the mainland.
The beach is a mix of sand and
shingle. It's extremely windy,
and popular for all levels of kite
and windsurfers; the IFCA World
Championships for windsurfing
take place here annually.

La Baume

Off route de Giens, 83400 Hyères.

🌊 🎵 🏖

On the east side of the Giens
peninsula, this small beach is
sheltered from the constant
wind buffeting the peninsula's
opposite side. There are plenty
of pines for shade. It's also
possible to hire canoes, small
sailboats and pedalos.

For beaches on the Iles d'Or, see
page 74.

Out & about St-Tropez to Hyères

Action stations

Adventure courses
Ecopark Adventures
Route de la Farlède, 83210 Solliès-Ville, T07 60 29 67 89, ecopark-adventures.com. Jul-Aug daily 1030-1930, mid-Mar to Jun and Sep to mid-Oct Wed, Sat and Sun 1300-1930. Minimum age 6, minimum height 1 m. €19 adult, €16 child 9-13 years, €11 child 6-8 years.

After a trial run at the *parcours d'initiation*, little (and big) monkeys can hit Ecopark's six courses. Each one is progressively harder, culminating in the *adrénaline's* zip line and daredevil Tarzan leap.

Boat hire
Octopussy Boat Rental
Le Port, 83990 St-Tropez, T04 94 56 53 10, octopussy.fr.
No-licence 6hp five-person speedboats (€160/day), plus bigger powerboats for hire.

Cycling
Cycles Evasion
61 av Georges Clemenceau, 83310 Cogolin, T04 94 54 71 13. Bike rental from €15/day adult, €10/day child (7-11).

For cycling around St-Tropez, its peninsula and inland, stop by any local Tourist Office and pick up the free hiking and biking map *Stepping Out*. Alternatively, visit golfe-saint-tropez-information.com.

L'Horizon
14 av de la Méditerranée, 83400 Hyères, T04 94 58 03 78. Daily 0800-1900. €5.90-6.30/2 hrs adult, €3.90/2 hrs child (bike height 40-50cm), helmets, baby seats and baby helmets provided free.

For cycling on the Ile de Porquerolles, see page 74.

Go-karting
Grimaud Karting Loisir (GKL)
RD61 Chemin des Blaquières, 83310 Grimaud, T04 94 56 00 12, gkl-karting.com. Daily Jul-Aug 1000-2100, Jun and Sep 1000-2000, Apr-May and Oct 1000-1900, Nov-Mar Wed, Sat-Sun and school holidays 1000-1800. Minimum age 7. 270CC go-kart €20/10 mins, 270CC Kart FunSport €84/2 hrs over 14s, 120CC go-kart €15/10 mins, 120CC Kart FunKid €69/2 hrs child (7-14).

Twist, turn and leave your competitors in the dust on this 800-m-long course.

Kids' Beach Clubs
Le Jardin des Mers
Plage de la Favière, 83236 Bormes-les-Mimosas, T04 94 41 77 20, portdebormes.com. Jul-Aug Mon-Sat 0930-1230, Fri also 1500-1800. Half day €10.

A club for three- to seven-year-olds that caters both to local children and to visiting tourists, Le Jardin des Mers plans a range of supervized daily activities, including introductory swimming, beach hunts, pirate play and crafts.

Sailing
Ecole de Voile
Plage du Débarquement, 83420 La Croix-Valmer, T06 48 23 51 04, voile-lacroixvalmer.com. Mar-Oct. Minimum age 7. Five 2-hr lessons: Hobie Cat 16 €150 adult, Hobie Cat 13 €130 child (11-15), Optimist €130 child (7-11).

A friendly sailing school popular with French families. Competent sailors can rent Hobie Cats by the hour (€30-37).

La Moune
Route de St-Tropez, 83580 Gassin, T04 94 97 71 05, lamoune.com. Apr-Sep. Minimum age 6. Five 1½-hr lessons: catamaran €160 adult, €140 child (10-15), mini-catamaran €125 child (6-10).

Learn how to sail a catamaran in the sheltered Gulf of St-Tropez. Windsurf (€18/hr) and kayak hire (€10) also available.

Scuba-diving
Both the coast off Le Lavandou and the sea surrounding the Iles d'Or are littered with aeroplane and shipwrecks, as well as spots of outstanding natural beauty.

European Diving School
Route des Plages, 83350 Ramatuelle, T04 94 79 90 37, europeandiving.com. Minimum age 8. CMAS Open Water course (includes 6 dives) €399 or €37/single dive adult, junior beginner's course (includes 3 dives) €199 child (8-13).

European Diving also has a school in Hyères. Highly recommended.

Porquerolles Plongée

Zone Artisanale 7, 83400 Porquerolles, T04 98 04 62 22, porquerolles-plongee.com. Mid Apr-mid Nov. Minimum age 8. €60 half-day 'baptism' dive, €45-60 per 2- to 3-hr dive.

Family-run dive school in Porquerolles's village port, with dives for all levels plus full day guided tours of Port-Cros's *sentier sous-marin* (€135 combo fee, including 'baptism' dive, lunch and supply of snorkels, masks and flippers for the underwater discovery trail).

Snorkelling
Balades Aquatiques

Office de Tourisme, Esplanade de la Gare, 83420 La Croix-Valmer, T04 94 55 12 12. Jul-Aug Mon-Fri. Minimum age 8. €18 adult, €12 child (8-16). Exploratory snorkelling trips to various coastal locations, including Gigaro. Masks, snorkels and flippers provided.

See also the *sentiers sous-marin* on the L'Argentière (Bormes-les-Mimosas, see page 65) and La Palud (Port-Cros, see page 75) beaches, as well as guided underwater tours at Domaine du Rayol (see page 68).

Water sports
Bormes Ski & Wake

Plage de la Favière, 83230 Bormes-les-Mimosas, T06 13 61 27 18. Jun to mid-Sep. Minimum age 6. €30/10 mins, €150/hr.

Waterskiing and wakeboarding lessons geared towards all levels; the same spot also offers tubing.

Funboard Center

Route de l'Almanarre, 83400 Hyères, T04 94 57 95 33, funboardcenter. com. Open year round. Minimum age 10. Funboard rental €25/hr, €60/3 hrs, 1½-hr lessons €30, five 1½-hr lessons €150.

Owned and run by Erik Thieme and Pascal Boulanger, world funboard champions (a variation on traditional windsurfing). Kayak hire also available.

Kaupo-Sport

Bd Patch, Plage Pampelonne, 83350 Ramatuelle, T06 09 21 19 80, kauposport.com. Various prices according to season and activity. Windsurf, kitesurf, canoe, pedalo and sailboat rental, plus waterskiing, wakeboarding and tubing.

Out & about St-Tropez to Hyères

Azur Park

Quartier La Foux 83580 Gassin, T04 94 56 48 39, azurpark.com. Jun-Sep 2000-0100, Apr 1600-2400, May 1900-2400. Free entrance. Rides €3-20, Baby Pass (13 rides) €10, Fun Pass (20 rides) €20, Xtreme Pass (4 really expensive rides) €25.

The region's biggest amusement park, with roller coasters, water rides and giant slides. There's also a crazy golf course, Tropical Golf (Jun-Sep 1200-0200, Apr-May 1200-2400, €12 adult, €7 under 12s).

Domaine du Rayol

Av des Belges, 83820 Le Rayol-Canadel, T04 98 04 44 00, domainedurayol.org. Daily Jul-Aug 0930-1930, Apr-Jun and Sep-Oct 0930-1830, Nov-Mar 0930-1730. €9 adult, €6 child (6-18), under 6s free. Landscapes of the world's Mediterranean-type climatic zones, from Mexico to Chile and Australia, are set over 50 seaside acres. Tropical plants wind themselves along narrow trails, around the organic café, up Inca-like staircases and into moisture-drenched palm plantations. Pick up a children's sheet (a short, trivia-based scavenger hunt around the Domaine) on the way in, or ask kids to hunt down the 65 different plants – including pistachio trees, the New Zealand Tea Tree and prickly pears – tagged with numbers around the gardens.

To check out life beneath the waves, don a mask and snorkel (provided) on the Domaine's private beach and follow the guided *sentier sous-marin* (mid Jun-mid Sep, minimum age 8, €17 adult, €14 child (8-18)) nature trail. Or opt for the longer 2-km trail every Sunday morning during July and August (minimum age 12, €40 adult, €34 child (12-18)).

Sentier sous-marin tickets include entry to the Domaine gardens. Highly recommended.

Kiddy Parc

Av de l'Aéroport, 83400 Hyères, T04 94 57 68 93, kiddyparc.com. Jul-Aug daily 1000-2030, Apr-Jun Wed, Sat-Sun and weekdays over Easter 1000-1900, Sep-early Oct Wed 1200-1800

Village des Tortues.

and Sat-Sun 1000-1800, Oct and Feb school holidays daily 1000-1730, Nov-Mar Wed and Sat-Sun 1200-1730. €4.70-7.90 adult, €13.90-17.50 child (over 2 years/over 90 cm), under 2s/under 90 cm free, free entry for 1 adult per paying child. A fun park geared towards two- to 12-year-olds, the sprawling Kiddy Parc offers children the chance to saddle up a pony, squeal their way down the toboggan chutes, race mini go-karts (over 6s) or bounce around on an inflated whale. During the summer, the park stages circus performances and magicians. There's a restaurant and crêperie on site, as well as picnic areas.

Labyrinthe des Sens

Quartier des Trois Ponts, 83310 Cogolin, T04 94 49 07 07, labyrinthedessens.com. Daily mid-Jun to mid-Sep 1000-2400, Apr to mid-Jun and mid-Sep to mid-Nov 1000-1900, mid-Nov to mid-Dec Sat-Sun 1000-1900. Day ticket €12 adult, €10 child (5-11), night ticket (from 2000) €14 adult, €12 child (5-11), under 5s free.
Billed as a maze that will send your senses 'into turmoil', this lush labyrinth is divided into four worlds: air, earth, fire and water. Using your senses, you'll investigate them all with the help of a scavenger-hunt booklet, learning more about the world's limited resources, sustainable development and different cultures. There's also a shop and a market on site.

Seascope.

Petit Train des Plages

Quai Gabriel Péri, 83980 Le Lavandou, T06 21 24 47 40. Jul-Aug 6/day, Apr-Jun and Sep 3/day. Adult return €8, single €4, one stop €1.50, child (3-12) return €4, single €3, one stop €1, under 3s free.
The best petit train in the South of France. The Petit Train des Plages chugs 16 km along the coast from Le Lavandou to Plage de Pramousquier, stopping at each of the nine beaches along the way. The circuit it traces – now a dedicated cycle and walking path – is along the old railway route between Toulon and St-Raphaël.

Seascope

Vedettes Iles d'Or, Port, 83980 Le Lavandou, T04 94 71 01 02, vedettesilesdor.fr. Jul-Aug 10/day, Apr-Jun and Sep 5/day, Oct-Mar Thu-Tue 1400. 35 mins. €12.50 adult, €9.50 child (4-12), under 4s free.
Climb aboard one of these spaceship-like vessels to discover the world beneath the Mediterranean's surface. Passengers sit below sea level, peering out into the water through bubble-like windows. Vedettes also runs 90-minute sea promenades, boat trips that circle the three Iles d'Or without stopping (daily Jul-Aug 1145 and 1830, Apr-Jun and Sep 1130 and 1430, Oct-Mar Sat-Tue 0930 and 1600, Thu 1600, Fri 0930 and 1630, €20.80 adult, €16.40 child (4-12), under 4s free).

Village des Tortues

Quartier les Plaines, 83590 Gonfaron, T04 94 78 26 41, villagetortues.com. Daily Apr-Sep 0900-1900, Oct-Mar 0900-1800. €4-10 adult, €2-6 child (3-16), under 3s free.
Home to more than 2500 turtles, tortoises and terrapins, including France's only indigenous land species, the endangered Hermann's tortoise. This recommended educational park teaches kids what turtles eat, what their insides look like and how to help an injured one.

Let's go to…

St-Tropez

Too often dismissed as a mythical celeb-land, pretentious or too pricey by those who've never set foot here, in fact St-Tropez is a far cry from some stilted designer resort. Instead, the town is unassuming and often downright welcoming, with plenty of fun family activities to boot.

Spot octopus at the daily fish market, or go for a swim on the town's beach. Play *pétanque* in place des Lices, scramble up to the 17th-century citadel or take a boat trip along the coast from the port. Or simply dig into the town's namesake dessert, the squidgy custard-filled *tarte tropézienne*. St-Tropez merits a visit, and a lingering one at that.

Getting here

Come summertime, traffic around St-Tropez is pretty much one giant jam. Although many may opt to drive, wise are the visitors who opt to float in by boat instead. **Les Bateaux Verts** (14 quai Léon Condroyer, 83120 Ste-Maxime, T04 94 49 29 39, bateauxverts.com) zip back and forth across the Gulf of St-Tropez from Ste-Maxime (every 15-40 mins, 20-min journey, €7 adult, €3.70 child (4-12), under 4s free) and Port Grimaud (hourly, 20-min journey, €6.50 adult, €3.50 child (4-12), under 4s free). **Trans Côte d'Azur** (trans-cote-azur. com) ferries passengers to here

from Cannes (T04 92 98 71 30, daily Jul'to mid-Sep, Jun and last 2 weeks Sep Tue, Thu and Sat-Sun, 1½-hr journey, day return €41 adult, €28 child (4-10), under 4s free) and Nice (T04 92 00 42 30, Jul to mid-Sep Tue-Sun, Jun and last 2 weeks Sep Tue, Thu and Sat-Sun, 2½-hr journey, day return €55 adult, €41 child (4-10), under 4s free).

Get your bearings

The town is compact and entirely walkable, so if you've arrived by car, park up at **Parking des Lices** (place des Lices) or **Parking du Port** (Nouveau Port), both clearly signposted as you're funnelled towards St-Tropez's centre. Head to the port, then along quai Suffren to the corner of quai Jean Jaurès, where the **Tourist Office** (T08 92 68 48 28, ot-saint-tropez.com, daily Jul-Aug 0930-1330 and 1500-2000, Apr-Jun and Sep-Oct 0930-1230 and 1400-1900, Nov-Mar 0930-1230 and 1400-1800) is located. Local maps can be purchased here (€2).

Fun & free

St-Tropez is still a fishing village – although definitely an overgrown one – at heart. Get a feel for the place with a **stroll** around the port. Duck into the Porte de la Poissonnerie, an old city gate that's now home to a miniscule **fish market** (summer daily 0800-1200, winter closed Mon). Fishermen slap down their dawn haul on marble slabs, the walls decked out with a mosaic of sea creatures behind them. Look out for bumpy red scorpion fish (*rascasse*), plump octopus (*poulpe*) and slithery moray eels (*murènes*). Exit into tiny **place aux Herbes**, where a handful of stalls sell local produce, flowers, seafood and cheese. Loop back down to quai Jean Jaurès, walking north until you hit the rotund **Tour de Portalet** at the far end. Formerly a 16th-century defensive tower, it's now lined with benches looking out to sea. Energetic toes can scamper left onto Môle Jean Réveillé, where there's a stocky **harbour wall** to run along. St-Tropez's historic fishing fleet is lined up here, while visiting mega-yachts are moored opposite.

Try your hand at *pétanque*, Provence's favourite sport: **Le Café** (place des Lices, T04 94 97 44 69, lecafe.fr, daily 0800-2400, closed 1430-1800 out of season) lends free *boules* to its patrons, and you can play anywhere on the dusty gravel of place des Lices. Rules vary, but to play a simple version of the game start by scraping a line on the ground. Divide up the *boules* between the players. Nominate one person to throw the jack, or *bouchon*. Each player takes turns standing behind the line and trying to gently toss or roll his or her *boules* as close to the jack as possible. It's entirely acceptable to hit the jack, or smash other players' *boules* out of the way with your own. At the end of the game, the *boule* closest to the jack wins.

Go for a **swim**. No need to leave the town centre: join the locals taking a dip on **Plage de la Ponche** (🚻 🔵 🔵 🅿), just outside Porte de Révélen, one of the city's old 16th-century gates. The beach is a mix of sand, shingle and tiny coloured pebbles, and flanked by rows of pastel fishing cottages.

Toting a **celebrity**-crazed teen? Pick up a copy of the local newspaper, *Var Matin*, to see who's in town this week, then star-spot with a Diet Coke from the café terraces at **Papagayo** (Le Port, T04 94 97 95 95, papagayo-st-tropez.com, Jun-Aug daily 1200-0500, Apr-May and Sep Fri-Sat 1200-0500) or **Sénéquier** (quai Jean Jaurès, T04 94 97 00 90, senequier.com, daily 0700-2400): Jade Jagger and Beyoncé frequent the former, Kate Moss hangs out at the latter.

Hit the town

Strange as it may seem for a town seething with tourists, even during summer's peak you'll often have much of St-Tropez's **Citadelle** (T04 94 97 59 43, daily Apr-Sep 1000-1830, Oct-Mar 1000-1230 and

Out & about St-Tropez to Hyères

I think it's very cool to take a Bateau Vert (see page 70) to Ste-Maxime. It takes just 20 minutes, but you get the best views. Especially on the trip back to St-Tropez. When you go early you have the whole boat for yourself. In Ste-Maxime you can go to Les Glaciers Italiens (84 av Charles de Gaulle), an ice cream parlour where they scoop your ice cream to look like a rose. But the very best ice cream you get at Barbarac (2 rue du Géneral Allard) in St-Tropez!! Soooo yummy!
Felix, 12

I love to go sailing! We do it with the school at the Ecole de Voile in the Baie des Canoubiers (ecole-de-voile.fr). I have lots of friends who come here on holiday and take sailing classes there. It's great fun to sail the little Optimists!
Anton, 10

Brothers Felix and Anton live in St-Tropez.

1330-1730, €2.50 adult, under 8s free) to yourself: perhaps it has something do with scaling the zillion stairs (or equally steep ramp) to reach it. But the lack of crowds makes poking around this naval fort a pleasure. The Citadelle is roughly the shape of an eight-pointed star, protected by high walls, a drawbridge,

fat ramparts and a line of cannons. A single-roomed museum shows how the fort has dominated the town since the 17th century, while below, the creepy dungeons are soon to be opened to the public. Photographers should head up to the Citadelle just before closing time, when the Côte

d'Azur's pink twilight makes the seascapes even more fabulous.

Although art museums may not top most kids' favourite-things-to-do-on-holiday lists, **Musée l'Annonciade** (place Grammont, Le Port, T04 94 17 84 10, saint-tropez.fr, Jun-Sep 1000-1300 and 1500-1900, Oct-May Wed-Mon 1000-1200 and 1400-1800, closed Nov, €5 adult, €3 under 18s, under 12s free) is one of the region's best, and a very compact (read two large rooms only) introduction to Provence's modern art scene. Impressionist painter Paul Signac 'discovered' this little fishing village in 1892, when he sheltered from a storm in the bay. Enamoured, he settled in and was soon joined by his artist pals Matisse, Derain and Dufy. Today, Musée l'Annonciade pays homage to these greats. Its permanent collection (upstairs) includes canvases by all of them, many depicting St-Tropez, some of the resorts listed in this book and the harbour just outside. Downstairs, the museum hosts huge-name temporary shows: 2010's schedule featured back-to-back Auguste Rodin and Amadeo Modigliani exhibitions.

Seaward bound
Get out of town with a *promenade en mer*, or one-hour boat ride around St-Tropez and nearby peninsula. **Brigantin II** (T04 94 54 40 61, lebrigantin. com, 6 daily departures in

season, €9 adult, €5 child (5-10), under 5s free) hugs the coast as it heads eastwards to the Baie des Canoubiers, pointing out celebrity villas and film locations en route. There are toilets and a small snack bar on board.

Grab a bite
Although a little pricier than others along the coast, place des Lices's **market** (Tue and Sat 0800-1300) is still a fab place to buy local cheeses, stuffed, focaccia-like *fougasses*, fresh fruit and other treats to pack up for an afternoon on the beach. Also on the square, **La Tarte Tropézienne** (place des Lices, T04 94 97 04 69, tarte-tropezienne.com, daily 0630-2000) is inventor of Brigitte Bardot's favourite squishy custard tart; it's also purveyor of the town's best sandwiches. Opposite, **La Renaissance** (place des Lices, T04 94 97 02 00) serves well-priced French *plats du jour*, including coq au vin, as well as standard salads and pizzas. Its terrace under plane trees affords plenty of space for kids to run around.

For a ham and cheese *croque-monsieur* (€7), unpretentious breakfasts (€7.50-14) or just a giant pile of *frites*, **Le Gorille** (1 quai Suffren, T04 94 97 03 93, legorille.com, Thu-Tue 0700-1900) has been a quayside institution for half a century. During July and August, it stays open around the clock.

Squeezed into a row of souvenir shops and cheap cafés, new hotspot **Petrus** (13 quai de l'Epi, T04 94 43 12 94, restaurant-petrus.com) is low-key at lunch, elegant come evening and very friendly all day long. Cuisine is Mediterranean with a playful Asian punch; the daily catch is always super fresh.

All wood panelling and tiny tables, **Pizzeria Bruno** (2 rue de l'Eglise, T04 94 97 05 18, Tue-Sat 1900-2200) has been home to the finest pizza in town for over sixty years. The killer salads are also great. Try the *pizza Provençale*, topped with tomatoes, cheese, parsley and garlic, or the *salade de Saint-Jacques*, a mix of scallops and green beans. Mains are €10-15, and wine is served by the jug.

Money no object? Gear up for a stratospheric meal at Michelin-starred chef Pierre Gagnaire's new **Colette** (route des Salins, T04 94 55 31 55, hotelsezz-sainttropez.com), located in St-Tropez's equally brand-new Hotel Sezz. Terrace tables are relaxed and poolside, which means you can release your little gourmets for a splash while you savour chef Jérôme Roy's sublime creations (lavender-infused oysters, or mango topped with Campari ice cubes and basil foam). The restaurant also offers simple sandwiches and salads at lunchtime. Unpretentious and recommended.

Shopping
Shopping is a sport in St-Tropez, albeit an expensive one. Show you're au courant with matching father and son trunks from **Vilebrequin** (24 rue Gambetta, T04 94 97 62 04, vilebrequin. com, Apr-Oct Mon-Sat 1000-1930), the hip local swimwear brand. The town is also home to **Le Temps des Cerises's** (11 rue Sibille, T04 94 97 32 58, letempsdescerisesjeans.com, Apr-Oct Mon-Sat 1000-1930) only dedicated kids' boutique, packed to its trendy rafters with the finest French jeans. For forgotten or replacement beach gear, **Kiwi** (10 rue des Commerçants, T04 94 97 41 67, kiwi.mc, Apr-Oct Mon-Sat 1000-1930, other branches around town) sells everyday bikinis, shorts, towels and bags.

If your little ones are in need of a soother, **Rêve d'Enfant** (6 rue Henri Seillon, T04 94 97 06 32, Wed-Sat 1000-1230 and 1530-1900) stocks yoyos, brightly coloured cars and other wooden toys. A block away, the interiors of sweet shop **La Pause Douceur** (11 rue du Général Allard, T04 94 97 27 58, Tue-Sat 1000-1230 and 1530-1800) take fluffy pinkness to a whole new level. Gorge on home-made chocolate, lollies and marshmallows, or Provençal veggies made of marzipan.

Iles d'Or

Once the children have stopped yearning for the props of civilization, they'll find the moor is a great place to listen to skylarks, watch sheep being silly, mess about over stones and go slightly feral.

Also referred to as the Iles d'Hyères, Porquerolles, Port-Cros and Levant are just this side of paradise. All three islands are strictly protected natural reserves. They are owned by the French state for the most part so development has been kept to a bare minimum. They are studded with Aleppo pines, eucalyptus and wild strawberry trees, plus a flurry of white-sand beaches and turquoise waters. Each island has its own appeal, and come summertime a day trip to any of the three, snorkelling, exploring ancient forts or building sand castles in the sun, is an idyllic way to escape the crowds along the coast.

As the islands are protected reserves, there are a few tips to keep in mind as you drift ashore. Smoking (except in the ports) and cars are strictly prohibited. Be sure to bring ample cash with you: Port-Cros has no ATM, Porquerolles has just one. Drinking water is only available in each island's port, so be sure to stock up before heading into the wilderness. From mid-October until Easter most activities on the islands close down. And unless indicated, the beaches have no facilities.

Ile de Porquerolles: The Tropical One
porquerolles.com

The largest of the three islands, Porquerolles is over 3 km wide and stretches for 7 km. Action centres around Porquerolles' small village and port. For maps and island tips, visit the kiosk in the port or the **Maison du Parc** (Apr-Oct daily 0930-1230 and 1400-1800) on the southern edge of the village. Be sure to investigate **Fort Ste Agathe** (T04 94 58 07 24, mid May-Sep 1000-1200 and 1400-1800), built to protect the island against pirate sieges.

The island's northern coast is dotted with **beaches** boasting waters so transparent you'd be forgiven for thinking you've been plonked down in the Caribbean. **Plages du Langoustier**, at the western tip of the island and 4 km from the village, are two beaches back-to-back: one white (300 m), one black (100 m). Both **Plage d'Argent**, west of the port, and the often windy, kilometre-long **Plage de la Courtade**, the first beach to the east of the port, are cloaked in powdery white sand lapped by shallow turquoise waters. Continue on eastwards from La Courtade and you'll hit oak and pine-backed **Plage Notre Dame**, another white sandy beach.

Porquerolles is laced with more than 50 km of **walking** trails. The most popular are Circuit de la Repentance (2½ hrs), Circuit du Phare (1½ hrs) and Circuit du Langoustier (4½ hrs). None of the walks are navigable with pushchairs. The island is also waymarked with four **cycle** paths, ranging from a 45-minute shortie to two longer than two hours each. There's an information board detailing these routes in place d'Armes. Bikes can be hired (€11-14/day adult, €6-11/day child) from one of the shops in the village. Tandems are also available. These hire spots usually provide a map of the paths too.

Ile de Port-Cros: The Wild One
portcrosparcnational.fr

Port-Cros is a Jurassic Park-like paradise. Four by two and a half kilometres, the mountainous island was declared France's smallest national park in 1963. As such, it's strictly protected: there's no camping, fish-feeding or flower-picking allowed. An untouched shoreline means Port-Cros is teeming with schools of fish and untouched **beaches**. Hit **Plage du Sud**, southwest of the port, for crystal clear waters and a sandy shore. It's more white sand at petite **Plage de la Palud**, northeast of the port. Serious snorkellers will love the *sous-marin*, or underwater trail, that follows the buoys posted with information about the island's sea life out to Rascas Island.

The island is criss-crossed by 35 km of hiking trails. Lengthy **Circuit de Port-Man** (4 hrs) passes the island's five ruined forts by way of 192-m, amusingly named Mont Vinaigre (Mount Vinegar) and the cliff-top route des Crêtes. You can only explore inside Fort de l'Estissac (open for temporary exhibitions) and Fort de l'Eminence (daily 1000-1700, summer only). The vertiginous **Circuit des Crêtes** (3 hrs) loops Plage du Sud, the interior valley and southern cliffs of the island, with parts of the path extremely steep and suitable for steady feet only. Tamest is the **Sentier des Plantes** (1 hr), a trail of Mediterranean flora that passes Plage de la Palud. None of the walks are navigable with pushchairs.

Ile du Levant: The Nudie One
iledulevant.com.fr

A skinny stick of an island (1 x 8 km), almost 95% of Levant is owned by the French military (although they plan to leave the island in the next few years). The small part of Levant that's currently public is mostly occupied by Héliopolis, a nudist colony – with a school, town hall and post office, as well as restaurants and hotels – established in 1931.

Although all of Levant's **beaches** are nudist, there are plenty of uninhibited families splashing around here. Southwest of the port, **Plage des Grottes** is the island's most popular, with a small strip of sand and large, low rocks for investigating.

Getting there

Vedettes Iles d'Or (Port, 83980 Le Lavandou, T04 94 71 01 02, vedettesilesdor.fr) offers year-round crossings from Le Lavandou (Jul-Aug 6/day, Apr-Jun and Sep 4/day, Oct-Mar Thu-Tue 2/day) to Port-Cros and Levant (€25 adult, €20.60 child (4-12), under 4s free), as well as to Porquerolles (€32.50 adult, €25.30 child (4-12), under 4s free). There are more expensive daily summer crossings from La Cavalaire port and La Croix-Valmer beach.

It's faster and cheaper to visit Porquerolles from Giens. **TLV** (T04 94 57 44 07, tlv-tvm.com) has year-round services from La Tour Fondue to Porquerolles (every 30 mins in summer, €17 adult, €15 child (4-10), under 4s free) and from Hyères' port to Port-Cros or Levant (€25 adult, €22 child (4-10), under 4s free). There are also two-island itineraries in July and August. All prices are return.

Sleeping St-Tropez to Hyères

Camping International

1737 route de la Madrague, Giens, 83400 Hyères, T04 94 58 90 16, international-giens.com. Mid-Mar to Oct. €20.50-23.50 2 adults, pitch and car, €5 extra adult, €4.50 child (4-12), €3 under 4s; 2-person apartment €460-860/week, 4-5-person apartment €480-1300, 4-person mobile home €370-720, 5-person mobile home €380-790.

⚓ 🛁 🚿 🔥 💧 🐕 🛒 🍴 ♿

A popular site at the southern tip of Plage de l'Almanarre. Although it's a 500-m walk to the sandy beach, the campsite has a paved 'solarium' with sunloungers and direct access to the sea, as well as its own summertime windsurfing school.

Camping les Palmiers

Rue du Ceinturon, L' Ayguade, 83400 Hyères, T04 94 66 39 66, camping-les-palmiers.fr. Mid-Mar to mid-Oct. 4-person mobile home €40-149/night, €483-994/week; 6-person mobile home €50-160/night, €553-1064/week; 8-person mobile home €60-179/night, €679-1204/week. Minimum stay 2 nights-1 week depending on season.

🔌 ⚡ 🛁 🍴 🐕 Wi-Fi

Looking for non-stop entertainment? Les Palmiers may be the campground for you. Not only does it boast a children's club (Jul-Aug mornings and afternoons, 4-12 years), daily water aerobics, a disco and regular tennis tournaments, it's also home to a swimming pool trimmed with massive slides, waterfalls and floating rafts. Note that Les Palmiers' accommodation is exclusively mobile homes. On the coast southeast of Hyères, 300 m from the beach.

Les Eucalytpus

Chemin des Moulins, 83350 Ramatuelle, T04 94 97 16 74, leseucalyptus.com. Camping Jun to mid-Sep, apartments Apr to mid-Oct. €17-27 2 adults, pitch and car, €5.50-9.50 extra adult, €2.50-4 child (2-6), under 2s free; 2-person studio €465-750/week, 2-3-person apartment €455-750.

⚓ 🛁 🚿 🐕 Wi-Fi

Set 100 vineyard-filled metres back from Plage de Pampelonne, Les Eucalyptus is a heavenly place to pitch a tent. Studios and apartments are blissfully cute, each with private terrace and free parking. There's also a garden space dotted with chairs, olive trees and a shared BBQ.

Le Mas des Oliviers

Quartier de la Croisette, 83120 Ste-Maxime T04 94 96 13 31, hotellemasdesoliviers.com. Feb-Nov. 2-4-person studio €320-830/week. Twelve studios centred around a pool, *pétanque* ground, tennis courts and gardens, 1 km from the St-Tropez ferry terminal. Décor is a charming mix of colourful Provençal features and modern fittings. There's also a 20-room hotel (€59-165/night) on site.

Plage de l'Almanarre.

Château de Valmer.

Le Refuge

Plage Gigaro, 83420 La Croix-Valmer, T04 94 79 67 38. Apr to mid-Oct. Doubles from €77, triples and studios from €84, breakfast included.

A line of basic but beautiful rooms and studios – ground floor with open terrace, first floor with giant balconies – within wave-crashing distance of Plage Gigaro. Classic French furniture inside, shared gravel garden full of succulents outside. Books up months in advance. Between the *chambres d'hôtes* and the sea is Le Refuge's separate terraced restaurant (mains around €20).

Residence Les Medes

Rue de la Doune, 83400 Ile de Porquerolles, T04 94 12 41 24, hotel-les-medes.fr. Closed mid-Nov to mid-Dec. 2-person studio €66-203/night, €462-1330/week; 2-4-person apartment €120-227/night, €841-1832/week; 2-6-person duplex €193-421/night, €1383-2784/week. Free baby cots.

Spacious, modern apartments – some with bunk beds or private terraces, all with kitchenettes – in Porquerolles' village centre. Breakfast and half board also available.

Villa du Plageron

Quartier Pramousquier, chemin du Plageron, 83820 Rayol-Canadel-sur-Mer, T04 94 05 61 15, plageron.com. Closed Nov-Mar. Mid-Jun to mid-Sep doubles €900-1300/week, suite €1100-1600, minimum stay 1 week; Jan to mid-Jun and mid-Sep to Oct doubles €125-135/night, 2-bedroom suite €165, extra bed €35, minimum stay 2 nights. Children 7 and over.

Out-of-this-world B&B tumbling into the azure sea by Plage de Pramousquier, owned by the wonderfully welcoming Bruno and Virginie. The villa hosts three individually designed rooms and one two-bedroom suite, each with its own outdoor space. Breakfast on fresh fruit, yogurt, chestnut compote, nutty bread and piles of pastries, then slip through the scented Mediterranean garden down to the sandy beach area and pebbly plage. Highly recommended.

Cool & quirky

Château de Valmer

Gigaro, 83420 La Croix-Valmer, T04 94 55 15 15, chateauvalmer.com. May-Sep. Les Cabanes Perchées €355-490/night 2-person, €480-690 4-person.

Two ultra-luxurious treehouses, set among Château de Valmer's private vineyards. Fabrics and furniture are all natural, and the treehouses are ringed with spacious wooden decking. There's a private beach (shared with hotel residents) with sunloungers and umbrellas just five minutes away, accessed via an idyllic palm-lined alley. The Château's equally sumptuous private villa, Le Cabanon (€530-850/night, sleeps 4) sits in a nearby lavender field.

Tiki Hutte

Plage de Pampelonne, 83350 Ramatuelle, T04 04 55 96 96, tiki-hutte.com. Apr-Oct. 4-person Tiki Huts €70-360/night, €560-2520/week; 6-person Tiki Huts €90-390/night, €680-2730/week; 4-person Garden Huts €55-260/night, €420-1610/week; 6-person Garden Huts €60-310/night, €490-1890/week. Luxury Thai-style beach bungalows lined up by St-

Tropez's longest, coolest beach. Each hut has a full kitchen plus its own sunloungers and covered terrace. There's a supermarket, swimming pool, games room, beach volleyball and diving school on site, plus two dedicated kids' clubs (infants to 6 years, 6-12 years). Restaurants run the gamut from pizza parlour to Thai. The big swing in rates is due to position, with premier huts spilling out directly onto the beach; architecturally, Garden Huts are similar to more traditional mobile homes.

Splashing out

Pastis

61 av du Général Leclerc, 83990 St-Tropez, T04 98 12 56 50, pastis-st-tropez.com. Jan-Nov. €175-600. Remodelled from a former *hôtel particulier*, or wealthy private home, Pastis still feels like one. Ten wow-factor rooms, each with their own outdoor space, are equal parts cool contemporary (colourful prints, 20th-century photography) and enveloping cosiness (clawfoot tubs, superb linens), making them a splurge-worthy

treat for families with older children. Striped bathing cabins, sunloungers and ancient palms frame the large tiled swimming pool. Amazing.

Hôtel Provençal

Place St-Pierre, Giens, 83400 Hyères, T04 98 04 54 54, provencalhotel. com. Mid-Apr to mid-Oct. Doubles €111-174, triples €158-216. Fashionable it is not, but the Provençal sums up laid-back Giens: pleasantly dated guestrooms, a tasty terraced restaurant and dozens of kilometres of sea views all round. There's also a magnificent seaside swimming pool, plus nearby tennis courts.

Villa Naïs

1568 route de Martegasse, 83230 Bormes-les-Mimosas, T04 94 71 28 57, villanais.com. Doubles €75-160, triples €101-170, quadruple/family suite €130-250, breakfast included. A 10-minute drive from the coast, Villa Naïs is a lovely getaway with gorgeous vistas. As well as the nearby beaches, there's plenty to keep the family busy on site, including a 3-ha garden, pool, tennis courts, ping-pong, a *boulodrome* (for *pétanque*), outdoor barbeque and free Wi-Fi.

Eating

L'Atelier de Cuisine Gourmande

4 place Gambetta, 83230 Bormes-les-Mimosas, T04 94 71 27 80. Hours vary.

Tiny *traiteur* owned by Mireille Gedda, specialising in high-end Provençal dishes (ratatouille, slow-cooked beef *daube*), wines, home-made jams and chutneys to take away.

Fruits et Legumes

Place de La Tour-Fondue, Presqu'île de Giens, 83400 Hyères.

Before hopping aboard the ferry to Porquerolles, stop here (opposite La Tour Fondue) to stock up on peaches, plums and picnic veggies.

Chez Gaetano

2 rue de Limans, 83400 Hyères, T04 94 03 75 32, Mon-Tue and Thu-Sat 1200-1500 and 1900-2200.

Family-run establishment in Hyères' Old Town, dishing up crispy, authentic Italian pizzas since 1964. The large-sized pizzas are perfect for sharing: try the *Norma*, topped with aubergine, ricotta, garlic and mint. Sister restaurant to the equally excellent Chez Gaetano in Toulon (158 av de la République, 83000 Toulon, T04 94 93 02 02, chez-gaetano.com).

Chez Richard

1631 plage de l'Estagnol, off route de Léoube, 83230 Bormes-les-Mimosas, T04 94 71 60 22, restaurant-chezrichard.com. Daily Jul-Aug 1200-1500 and 1900-2200, May-Jun and Sep 1200-1500.

Beachside restaurant in a stunning toes-in-the-sand setting. Dishes range from simple *salade l'Estagnol* (with shrimp, octopus and mussels, €9.50) to *bouillabaisse du pêcheur* (order at least a day in advance, €50 per person, minimum portion for two). Richard also serves up daily pizzas, sandwiches, lamb kebabs and steaks for those who are less keen on bounty from the sea. Much of the produce used is organic.

Le Krill

22 rue Patron Ravello, 83980 Le Lavandou, T04 94 89 62 20. Daily 1200-1430 and 1800-2100.

A cheerful, low-key spot for *moules frites*, superb steaks and *loup grillé*. Two-course menus for €16, good wine by the *pichet*. Overlooks the busy port Promenade area and rates as possibly the best euro-for-euro eatery in town.

Magic Markets

Whether you're tracking down foodie souvenirs, shopping for dinner or filling up the picnic hamper, all of these markets are great spots to stock up on the treats this region has to offer.

In **Ste-Maxime**, there's a daily produce market (rue Fernande Bessy, summer daily 0800-1300 and 1630-2000, winter Mon 1630-2000, Tue-Sun 0800-1300 and 1630-2000) in the Old Town. On Thursday mornings (0800-1300), the winding city streets are crowded with farmers plying their regional specialities, including salami, fresh goat's cheeses and home-made tapenade.

Tumbling downhill from place aux Palmiers, stalls at **La Croix-Valmer's** *marché Provençal* (Sun 0800-1300) sell pots of pâté and piles of fresh produce: in late August, look out for the first of the purple figs.

For sun-dried tomatoes, cheeses, hams and baskets of strawberries, hit **Le Lavandou's** weekly market (av Vincent Auriol, Thu 0700-1400).

Hyères' produce market (Tue-Sun 0800-1300) takes place in place de la République, while on Tuesdays, Thursdays and Saturdays there's an organic market (0800-1300) in place Vicomtesse de Noailles.

St-Tropez also hosts a bountiful market twice a week (place des Lices, Tue and Sat 0800-1300); see page 71 for more details.

Eating St-Tropez to Hyères

St-Tropez's
fish market.

Tamaris Plage

Plage de Pramousquier, 83980 Le Lavandou, T06 26 16 60 25. Easter-Oct daily 1200-1500 and 1900-2200. Easy-going beach bar and restaurant with shoreline dining, midway between Le Lavandou and Le Rayol-Canadel. Tuck into *fruits de mer* or the catch of the day (freshly grilled), while your little ones play on the sheltered shoreline or dip into the waters.

Posh nosh

Café de France

Place Neuve, 83310 Grimaud, T04 94 43 20 05. Daily 1200-1500 and 1800-2200.

Perched on one of Grimaud's ultra-cute cobbled squares, this family-run restaurant serves up quality cuisine minus any hint of stuffiness. Opt for the hearty *menu du jour* (€25) then settle into one of the wooden tables on the front terrace. Look out for the *tarte à la tomate*, stellar in its simplicity; bottles of great local reds from around €25.

La Ferme Ladouceur

Quartier La Rouillère, 83350 Ramatuelle, T04 94 79 24 95, fermeladouceur.com. Daily 1900-2230, closed Nov-mid Dec.

Midway between St-Tropez and Ramatuelle, this idyllic garden restaurant makes a great getaway from the summer coastal chaos. Exquisite creations are served up at simple wooden tables underneath fig and olive trees. A little on the swish side, it's best suited for families with older kids. Picky eaters beware, as there's only one set menu (€42) each day: call ahead to be sure everyone is tempted by the options on offer. Dishes can include thyme-infused lamb with spinach or raspberry spring rolls.

Le Poisson Rouge

Port du Niel, Giens, 83400 Hyères, T04 94 58 92 33, restaurantlepoissonrouge.fr. Jul-Aug daily 1930-2200, Apr-Jun and Sep Tue-Sun 1200-1400 and 1930-2200, mid- to end Mar Tue-Thu 1200-1400 and 1930-2200, Fri-Sun 1930-2200. Few foreign tourists make it to Port Niel, a picturesque port on the southern coast of the Giens peninsula. And how they miss out! At dawn, local fishermen drift in with their catch; later in the day, Le Poisson Rouge steals the show. Under a canopy of pines, exemplary fish and seafood are this delicious spot's *raison d'être*. Many items have a Middle Eastern or South American flair. Set menus €28-42, yummy children's menu €13.

Le Relais des Maures

Av Charles Koeklin, 83820 Le Rayol-Canadel, T04 94 05 61 27, lerelaisdesmaures.fr. Jun-Sep Mon-Sat 1200-1430 and 1900-2200, Sun 1200-1430, Mar-May and Oct Wed-Sat 1200-1430 and 1900-2200, Sun 1200-1430.

A family restaurant and pension for close to a century, positioned between the D559 coastal road and the fine sands of Plage du Canadel. Menus (€28-38, children's €17) are modern spins on tasty traditional dishes (*soupe de poissons*, John Dory with candied vegetable rissoles); ice cream is home-made and the six top-notch flavours change daily.

La Tonnelle

23 place Gambetta, 83230 Bormes-les-Mimosas, T04 94 71 34 84, la-tonnelle-bormes.com. Jul-Aug daily 1230-1430 and 1900-2130, May-Jun and Sep Fri-Tue 1230-1430, daily 1900-2130, Oct and Dec-Apr Fri-Tue 1230-1430 and 1900-2130.

Chef Gil Renard's modern French cuisine is super seasonal and so carefully constructed. There are four different set menus (€27-50), plus a market-fresh kids' menu (€13) and a lunchtime *plat du jour* (€11). Little ones will be entranced in the toy-scattered boutique, l'Antre Nous, at the entrance to the restaurant. There are weekly embroidery workshops here (Mon 1500), and the boutique also hosts afternoon tea on weekends (Sep-Jun Sat-Sun).

For places to eat in St-Tropez, see page 73.

Contents

Haute-Provence

The stunning Castellane countryside.

Gorges du Verdon.

Gorges du Verdon.

Skyscraping mountains? Tick. Translucent rivers? Tick. Rafting, trekking, canyoning? Tick, tick and tick. Combine its crisp, cool air with the dozens of adventure sports options that riddle the region, and Haute-Provence is a superb destination for the great outdoors. Millions of people may funnel onto the Riviera's coastal resorts every summer, but just a tiny portion of these visitors head to Haute-Provence.

The region is home to two stunning national parks. Nestled up against the Italian border, the wild **Parc National du Mercantour** is ringed by craggy snow-topped mountains and perennially popular ski resorts. Animal-lovers will adore the park's pristine natural habitat, home to chamois, wild boar and ibex, as well as owls, eagles and scores of other species. They're easy to spot, either in the wild or in designated breeding grounds.

To the west, the **Parc Naturel Régional du Verdon** cradles the region's most popular site: the jaw-dropping **Gorges du Verdon,** Europe's answer to the Grand Canyon. Get up close and personal with the shimmering Verdon River, which carved out the canyon over millions of years. Or peek at the Gorges' depths from the vertiginous heights of the **Route des Crêtes**, a driving route close to a kilometre above the canyon floor. Whatever your perspective, the Gorges du Verdon's staggering expanse can't fail to impress.

The Verdon River tumbles along, connecting four placid mountain lakes: **Lac d'Esparron de Verdon, Lac de Quinson**, **Lac de Ste-Croix** and **Lac de Castillon.** If you're travelling with toddlers, a cool splash around on one of the lake's beaches makes for an idyllic summer's afternoon. Daredevils in tow? There are plenty of experienced sports operators that can arrange for your family to join adventure-seeking groups, whether you're yearning to hike the Gorges du Verdon, paraglide over Lac de Castillon or ski in the Provençal Alps. All ages and abilities are catered for, and the whole family will likely make some fantastic new friends along the way.

You must

- Chug through the Provençal Alps aboard the historic Train des Pignes.

- Explore the Gorges du Verdon, Europe's largest canyon.

- Try rafting, canyoning or hiking along the Verdon River.

- Splash along the gentle shores of Lac de Ste-Croix, or explore the lake by pedalo.

- Spy on protected packs of wolves at Alpha Wolf Park.

- Swoosh down the slopes at one of Haute-Provence's four ski resorts.

- Spend a night snoozing among herds of bison and Mongolian horses at the Monts d'Azur Nature Reserve.

Fun & free

Take a walk on the wild side

If you're a family of walkers, Haute-Provence is an ideal place to plunge into the wilderness.

Hugging the Italian border north of the Riviera's coastline, the 685-sq km **Parc National du Mercantour** (mercantour. eu) was designated a National Park in 1979. Almost a million visitors flock here yearly to enjoy the scenery, which takes in several 3000-m-plus peaks and a vibrant flora, and is home to reclusive chamois, stags, eagles, ermine, marmots, ibex and the odd old deer. Fifty-six walking trails are available on an extension of the park's website (mercantouralpimarittime. com) as printable maps with descriptions in English; many are also written-up in the Randoxygène guides (randoxygene.org, see Family Favourites page 20). Routes range in difficulty from an easy hour's hike in the hills surrounding St-Martin-Vésubie to a three-day trek departing from Allos, with overnight stays in refuges along the way.

For a gentler excursion, head to the heart of Gorges du Verdon territory. Here **Castellane Tourist Office** (rue Nationale, 04120 Castellane, T04 92 83 61 14, castellane.org, Mon-Sat 1000-1800) distributes a free walking map that charts an easy trail (45 mins, suitable for all ages) up to the early 18th-century Chapelle Notre-Dame du Roc overlooking the town. You can download three free, hand-drawn hiking maps that explore the eastern shores of Lac de Ste-Croix from **Bauduen Tourist Office** (bauduen-sur-verdon.com, in French only). **Gourdon Tourist Office** (tourisme-gourdon.com) also offers 13 free walking trails in and around the town, again downloadable in French only.

Climb a mountain

An extreme version of the adventure courses found in other areas of the South of France (see pages 23 and 130), Via Ferrata is the (safety harnessed) sport of traversing Alpine areas using zip lines, aerial walkways and iron stairs built into rock. Experienced climbers can hike 45 minutes out of Digne-les-Bains' town centre to the 500-m **Via Ferrata du Rocher de Neuf Heures** (Office du Tourisme, place du Tampinet, 04000 Digne-les-Bains, T04 92 36 62 62, ot-dignelesbains.fr, mid Apr-mid Oct 0600-2000, mid Oct-mid Apr 0800-1700; rental of harness, helmet and ropes with shock absorbers €12/4 hrs adult, €10/4 hrs under 14s) trail; alternatively, the town's Tourist Office can help you reserve an excursion with a guide.

Although access to this course is free, if you don't have any Via Ferrata experience or your own gear, you'll need to hire both a guide and the necessary equipment for your first few forays. The Via Ferrata is not suitable for young children but older kids will love it.

Spend a day at the beach

The Verdon River connects four Alpine lakes: Lac d'Esparron de Verdon, Lac de Quinson, Lac de Ste-Croix and Lac de Castillon. Each one of these is fringed with lovely beaches. If you have tiny tots in tow, mild afternoons on the Bauduen shores of Lac de Ste-Croix or beachside in St-Julien-du-Verdon on the Lac de Castillon are a welcome respite from the Mediterranean coast's intense summer heat.

Lac de Ste-Croix.

Out & about Haute-Provence

Action stations

For SpaceBetween's **adventure holidays** in the Mercantour National Park, see Family favourites, page 20.

Canyoning, kayaking & rafting

In Haute-Provence there are scores of waterways to kayak, and literally loads of organized rafting trips down the rapids. Fearless families can try canyoning: this activity mixes swimming, sliding, jumping through waterfalls, rock climbing and abseiling. To participate in any canyoning, kayaking or rafting trips, note that all participants must know how to swim.

Aboard Rafting

8 place de l'Eglise, 04120 Castellane, T04 92 83 76 11, aboard-rafting.com. Apr-Sep. Minimum ages: rafting 8, canyoning 10.

Hit the Verdon River with this established outfit. Beginners can navigate the rapids on their Discovery Middle-Verdon trip (€33/2 hrs), while the brave can try the Discovery Jabron canyoning trip (€33/2½ hrs).

Base Sport & Nature

Camping du Brec, 04320 Entrevaux, T04 93 05 41 18, basesportnature.com.

These family rafting specialists offer kids-only Baby-Raft (€25/1 hr, 6-10 years), tubing (€33, 1 hr, minimum age 12) and a scaled-down version of canyoning, the easy La Chalvagne River-Hike (€33/2 hrs, minimum age 6). The company also has a base in Castellane (T04 92 83 11 42).

Horse riding
Verdon Equitation

Route du Lac, 83630 Les-Salles-sur-Verdon, T06 07 39 62 57, terre-equestre.com/verdon-equitation. Saddle up for a gallop along the shores of Lac de Ste-Croix (€40/ 2 hrs), or pick from a range of riding tours through the Parc du Verdon, adapted for all ages and levels, from absolute beginners to budding jockeys.

Paragliding
Aerogliss Parapente

Base de Loisirs des Iscles, 04170 St-André-les-Alpes, T04 92 89 11 30, my-paragliding-tandem.com. Minimum age 4. €65 Discovery Flight, €95 Thermal Flight. Paragliding experts François and Philippe offer tandem flights over the north end of Lac de Castillon and the Verdon River, where it's common to

spot wild boar or chamois from the air. All gliders are given a free CD with photos from their sky-high experience.

Watersports
Biké-Beach

Baie du Touron, 04170 St-Julien-du-Verdon, T06 76 48 79 71, bike-beach. com. Mid Jun-mid Sep.

Motorboats (4-6 person, €29-38/hr, no licence needed), pedalos (€13/hr), canoes (€10/ hr) and kayaks (€9/hr) for hire on Lac de Castillon.

Centre Nautique

Bauduen Quartier Aires, 83630 Bauduen, T04 94 70 09 22, centre-nautique-bauduen.com.

Spend a day splashing around the southern side of Lac de Ste-Croix: rent a canoe (€7-10/ hr), catamaran (€20-30/hr), windsurfer (€10/hr) or electric motorboat (€20-30/hr, no licence needed). There's also a sailing school on site; courses run from two to five days and are open to beginners aged seven and up.

Club Nautique des Salles-sur-Verdon

Base Nautique, 83630 Les-Salles-sur-Verdon, T04 94 70 21 49, cnsv.fr. Rent pedalos (€12/hr), windsurfers (€15/hr), dinghies (€15/hr) and canoes (€10-12/hr) on Lac de Ste-Croix's eastern shores.

Get active down the Verdon River.

King of the mountain

Blue skies, shimmering sunshine… and piles of powdery snow? Winter sports may not be the first activity you associate with the South of France, but surprisingly, the Southern Alps make up a great chunk of this region. Snow cloaks their peaks for much of the year, and ski resorts are generally open from early December through to March (although the resorts also offer a mixture of mountain hiking, biking, horse riding, fishing, tennis and archery over the spring to autumn off-season). Hugely popular with local families on winter weekends, all of these ski spots are at their quietest during the week.

If it's your first ski trip as a family, be sure to check out the other activities nearby should it turn out that the kids aren't keen on downhill runs. And remember that you may be just a hop from the Mediterranean seaside, but it's plenty chilly in the mountains: pack thermals and cosy clothes to ensure everyone stays warm.

L'Ecole du Ski Français (esf. net) offers downhill and cross-country ski lessons for both kids and adults at Auron (esf-auron. com), Isola 2000 (esf-isola2000. com) and Val d'Allos-La Foux (esf-valdallos.com). They also run Club Piou-Piou (3-6 years, age group can vary depending on the resort): the kids' club mixes ski time with snow games.

Auron Grange Cossa, 06660 Auron, T04 93 23 02 66, auron. com. Day ski pass €29.50 adult, €25 12-16 years, €22 child

(5-12), under 5s free. Forty-two runs over 135 km, plus a three-level snowboard park for boarders, a bouncy elastic band trampoline (€6, minimum weight 15 kg) for releasing non-snowy giddiness and Les Oursons crèche (3 months to 5 years). The cross-country ski and snowshoeing resort of St-Dalmas-le-Selvage (T04 93 02 46 40, saintdalmasleselvage.com) is 20 minutes away.

Isola 2000 Immeuble Le Pélevos, 06420 Isola, T04 93 23 15 15, isola2000.com. Day ski pass €29.50 adult, €25 12-16 years, €22 child (5-12), under 5s free. The closest resort to Nice (just over an hour by car from Nice airport), Isola 2000 has 42 runs over 120 km; it's also deservedly popular for its extensive snowboarding park. Handiski (a tandem ski for disabled children and adults), snowshoe trekking, snowmobiling and bowling also available. In 2010, the popular Aquavallée (1 chemin Longon, 06420 Isola, T04 93 02 16 49, Fri-Wed 1100-1930, €5 adult, €4 child (4-10), under 4s free) reopened, an indoor sports complex with a large pool and dedicated kids' area.

Val d'Allos-La Foux 04260 La Foux d'Allos, T04 92 83 80 70, valdallos.com. Day ski pass €30 adult, €25.70 13-24 years, €24.20 child (6-12), under 6s free. A super family resort, with 80 pistes over 180 km. Children will revel in the sledge runs, trampoline, playgrounds, ice-skating rink, crèche (15 months to 6 years) and kids' club.

Valberg Place Ginesy, 06470 Valberg, T04 93 23 24 25, valberg.com. Day ski pass €27.90 adult, €23.50 students, €20.70 child (5-12), under 5s free. Over 90 km of stunning pistes. Kids can start skiing here at age three, and there's sledging, horse riding, snowshoe treks, a 'solar system' hike (the 3-km pathway is built to scale, albeit a million times smaller), a swimming pool and a crèche (3 months to 6 years).

Getting there
Auron, Isola 2000 and Valberg are just a €1 bus ride (cg06.fr) from Nice's main train station, via the airport, where pick-up is also possible. There are express *navettes* (reserve on lignesdazur. com Dec-Mar, €4, under 4s free) that operate twice a day too.

To reach Val d'Allos-La Foux, Haut Verdon Voyages (haut-verdon-voyages.com) operates buses from Digne-les-Bains (2 hrs), Thorame (on the Train des Pignes line, 1 hr, see page 93), Nice airport (Sat only, 3 hrs, €23 adult, €18 child (5-12), under 5s free) and Aix-en-Provence TGV station (Sat only, 3 hrs, €35 return adult, €17 return child (2-15)).

Out & about Haute-Provence

Alpha Wolf Park

Le Parc des Loups du Mercantour,
Le Boréon, 06450 St-Martin-Vésubie,
T04 93 02 33 69, alpha-loup.com.
Jul-Aug daily 1000-1800, ticket desk
closes 1630, Apr-Jun daily, Sep-Oct
Wed-Sun and Jan-Feb Sat-Sun 1000-
1700, ticket desk closes 1545. €12
adult, €10 child (4-12), under 4s free.
During the 20th century, the
Alps' indigenous wolf population
came close to extinction. Today,
this 12-ha, contained nature
reserve teaches visitors all about
these wonderful wild animals,
and is home to three thriving
packs of wolves. There are five
observation huts, informative
films about the animals, a kids'
playground, snack bar, picnic
area and various hiking trails. If
you're lucky, you may even catch
the park's caretakers feeding
the wolves. Note that the park
sits at 1500 m and can be chilly:
even during summer, be sure to
bring an extra layer of clothing.
A full visit of the reserve will take
around 2½ hours.

Musée de Préhistoire des Gorges du Verdon

Route de Montmeyan, 04500
Quinson, T04 92 74 09 59,
museeprehistoire.com. Jul-Aug daily
1000-2000, May-Jun and Sep Wed-
Mon 1000-1900, Feb-Apr and Oct
mid-Dec to Wed-Mon 1000-1800,
ticket desk closes 1 hr earlier. €7
adult, €5 child (6-17), under 6s free.
Europe's largest museum

Try heading up to Lac des Merveilles in the Parc du
Mercantour, accessible via a great little hike not too far
from Nice. We trekked up to the lake from Casterino (near Tende), spent the
night in the Refuge des Merveilles (cafnice.org, reservations advised) up
there and hiked back the next day. We saw mountain goats and marmots
while on the trail, which Mia loved.

Jen, Mickael and Mia (16 months)
*For this hike and others around the Parc du Mercantour,
visit mercantouralpimarittime.com.*

dedicated to all things
prehistoric, many of them
discovered in the nearby Grotte
de la Baume Bonne, with a cool
collection of life-sized dioramas,
reconstructions and films
to really bring 400 millennia
of local history to life. The
museum's ultra-contemporary
architecture, designed by
Norman Foster and Partners,
provides a neat contrast to its
ancient exhibits. Cave dwellers
were purportedly eking out
an existence in the Gorges du
Verdon until a century ago.

Réserve des Monts d'Azur

Domaine du Haut-Thorenc, 06750
Thorenc, T04 93 60 00 78, haut-
thorenc.com. Closed early Jan-Feb.
Walking safaris €18 adult, €10 under
12s, horse-drawn carriage safaris
€39 adult, €21 under 12s, both last
around 90 mins.
This 700-ha animal park is home
to herds of bison, red deer,
eagles and wild boar. It's also
a great place to catch a peek
of the critically endangered
Mongolian wild horse (also
called Przewalski's Horse),
whose numbers dropped down
to just 31 lonely creatures in
1945. Today, their population
is on the up, with around 1500
worldwide. Animal-lovers can
stay the night on site in one of
the reserve's eco-lodges (see
page 97).

Train des Pignes

Digne-les-Bains train station: av Pierre Sémard, 04000 Digne-les-Bains, T04 92 31 01 58; Nice Chemins de Fer de Provence train station: 4 bis rue Alfred Binet, 06000 Nice, T04 97 03 80 80, trainprovence.com.

Train des Pignes.

Shuttling its way from the French Riviera to Haute-Provence via the Provençal Alps, the Train des Pignes is a single-gauge railway that originally used pinecones (*pignes*) to fire the engines. It chugs from Digne-les-Bains to Nice and back again four times a day, and is a fantastic way to see the rivers, mountains and lakes of Haute-Provence.

Departures from Digne begin with a trundle through Alpine pastures, crags and cliffs to Mézel. The route then picks up speed in the dense primary forest – a patchwork of beech, oak, gorse, pine and heather – before running through St-André-les-Alpes, a great base for exploring Lac de Castillon.

Half an hour past the scary-but-stunning viaduct crossing at Méaille is the mountain stronghold of Entrevaux. Entrance to this gem of a walled town is via a creaky drawbridge over the raging River Var. A menacing 17th-century castle (€3, open all hours) casts a shadow from above; it's worth a trip up the 156 m of stairs to the 360° observation panel at the top. Some 15 km further on, Puget-Théniers has a pretty old town and is ringed by walking routes. The perched village of Villars-sur-Var, an hour north of Nice, is a further 20 minutes down the tracks.

Passengers can hop on and off at any of the mountain stations using the same ticket (Digne-Nice return ticket or vice versa €17.65 adult, €8.85 child (5-12), under 5s free). For the best view along the way, sit by the big windows next to the driver's seat at the very front, or very rear, of the carriage.

Don't miss Gorges du Verdon

It may be the biggest canyon in Europe, but incredibly, the skinny Gorges du Verdon lay hidden from the outside world until Edouard-Alfred Martel almost fell into it in 1905. Along with surveyor Isidore Blanc and a team of scientists, Martel was charting the Verdon River for France's Southeast Electricity Company. Instead of a few geological measurements, the group came back with shocking news: the discovery of the giant Gorges du Verdon, more than 20 km long and more than 700 m deep, and second in size only to the USA's Grand Canyon.

The entire area was given National Park status in 1977 (Parc Naturel Régional du Verdon, parcduverdon.fr). Today, the Gorges and the protected landscape that surrounds them are packed with wonderful wildlife. At the canyon's heart, the uniquely turquoise Verdon River slowly carved out the Gorges du Verdon over millions of years. Orchids, sweet peas and other wild flowers carpet its banks. Sheer cliffs shimmy skywards, and it's often possible to spot eagles and vultures circling overhead.

The Gorges du Verdon are particularly popular for whitewater rafting and rock climbing; to the canyon's west, the Verdon River spills into the gentler jade-green Lac de Ste-Croix, great for sailing, kayaking, swimming, boating and fishing. If you'd like to ride the river's rapids, climb cliffs or simply tool around Lac de Ste-Croix on an electric boat, refer to this chapter's list of experienced local operators (Action stations, page 88). The region around the Gorges is also laced with long-distance Grande Randonnée (GR) walking routes. For maps, practical tips and kid-specific advice, step into one of the local Tourist Information Offices (opposite).

Route des Crêtes no 2:
D23 clockwise loop from La Palud-sur-Verdon, 23 km

Driving this Route des Crêtes, which tiptoes its way along the vertiginous northern flank of the Gorges du Verdon, is the best way to gawk at daredevil rock climbers, spot swooping eagles and generally shock your system with the canyon's sensational grandeur. Expect plenty of cars and a good sprinkling of tour buses during the summer; out of season, you may very well have the road to yourself. Be aware that this itinerary is not suitable for drivers or passengers with a fear of heights.

To drive the route, follow the D952 west out of La Palud-sur-Verdon, in the direction of Rougon and Castellane. Less than a kilometre from town, the turnoff for the Route des Crêtes (D23) will be indicated on your right. The road inclines at a slow and steady pace, squeezing between horse farms and picnicking holidaymakers, until it reaches La Carelle, the first of the route's 14 *belvédères*, or panoramic viewpoints.

Incredibly, each perched lookout on the Route des Crêtes manages to be more awesome than the previous one. Most have a small space to pull over and park, as well as guardrails, although young children should be kept securely in hand. By the time you reach Dent d'Aire, the route's third viewpoint, the Verdon River slips noiselessly along the canyon floor close to a kilometre beneath you. Look out for massive brown Bonelli's eagles nesting near here, as well as fearless rock climbers scaling the canyon's cliffs. Further along, there are stunning views over the D71, which skirts the Gorges du Verdon's *rive gauche* (left bank).

It's essential to note that the Route des Crêtes cannot be driven in the opposite (counterclockwise) direction, as the middle portion of its loop is strictly one-way. There are plenty of road signs to alert you to this rule too. Gusty winter weather means the Route des Crêtes is closed between mid-November and mid-March, although you'll still be able to access the viewpoints closest to La Palud.

For Routes des Crêtes nos 1 and 3, see pages 61 and 105 respectively.

Tourist Information offices

All of these tourist offices stock maps, hiking guides and piles of information about activities in both the Gorges du Verdon and the surrounding region.

Moustiers-Ste-Marie 04360, place de l'Eglise, T04 92 74 67 84, moustiers.fr. Jul-Aug Mon-Fri 0930-1900, Sat-Sun 0930-1230 and 1400-1900, Sep daily 1000-1230 and 1400-1830, Apr-Jun daily 1000-1230 and 1400-1800, Mar and Oct daily 1000-1230 and 1400-1730, Nov daily 1000-1200 and 1400-1730, Dec-Feb daily 1000-1200 and 1400-1700.

Castellane 04120, rue Nationale, T04 92 83 61 14, castellane.org. Mon-Sat 1000-1800.

La-Palud-sur-Verdon 04120, Le Château, T04 92 77 32 02, lapaludsurverdon.com. Wed-Mon mid-Jun to mid-Sep 1000-1300 and 1600-1900, mid-Mar to mid-Jun and mid-Sep to mid-Nov 1000-1200 and 1600-1800.

Ste-Croix-du-Verdon 04500, Mairie, T04 92 77 85 29, saintecroixduverdon.com. Jul-Aug daily 1000-1230 and 1430-1830, May-Jun and Sep Mon-Fri 1000-1200 and 1500-1800, Jan-Apr Tue and Fri 1000-1200 and 1400-1700.

Sleeping Haute-Provence

Pick of the pitches

Camping Les Matherons

Les Bronzets, 04700 Puimichel, T04 92 79 60 10, campinglesmatherons. com. Mid Apr-Sep. €8.80 pitch, €4.80 adult, €3.60 under 9s, 2-5-person mobile home €270-515/week.

Dutch-owned, this rural campsite is north of the Plateau de Valensole. Twenty-five spacious pitches (some isolated) and two mobile homes dot the car-free terrain: you leave your wheels at the campground's entrance, and assistance is provided to help you shift your things to your site. There are swings, a sandpit, swimming pool and ping-pong, and during summer regular activities are organized for kids. Wednesday and Saturday evenings there are communal meals (additional fee) on the terrace. Nature-lovers will love this campground; internet addicts will not.

Domaine du Verdon

04120 Castellane, T04 92 83 61 29, camp-du-verdon.com. Mid-May to mid-Sep. €20-33 2 adults, pitch and car, free-€13 extra adult, under 4s free, 4-6-person mobile home €48-113/night, 4-8-person mobile home €74-139, 4-5-person chalet €54-113.

On the outskirts of Castellane, this sprawling campground is packed with tons of activities to please all campers. There's direct access to the Verdon

River, a heated swimming pool, crazy golf, archery, games room and a kids' lake for fishing. During summertime, staff organize a nightly campfire for teens (riverside from 2300); they can also help you arrange canyoning, kayaking and canoeing trips locally.

Best of the rest

Family Favourite

Rent the four-bedroom Wide Open Space Villa in Montauroux, one of just three South of France self-catering spots to snooze from Baby-Friendly Boltholes. See page 14 for details.

Une Campagne en Provence

Domaine Le Peyourier, 83149 Bras, T04 98 05 10 20, provence4u.com. Closed Jan-Feb. Doubles €90-125, minimum stay 2 nights, 4-person apartment €600-910/week.

Almost equidistant from the Gorges du Verdon, Hyères and Marseille, these three apartments and five B&B rooms are a great base from which to explore both Haute-Provence and the coast. Accommodation is spread over the massive estate, and its 170-ha grounds include a swimming pool, cellar cinema and library. Welcoming owners Martina, Claude and their son Fabrice are ecologically attentive (much of the electricity comes from solar panels, fresh veggies from the garden), and there are cooking, art and

Provençal *boutis* (a type of quilting) workshops on site.

Cool & quirky

Réserve des Monts d'Azur Eco-Lodges

Domaine du Haut-Thorenc, 06750 Thorenc, T04 93 60 00 78, haut-thorenc.com. Mid May-Oct.
Sleep out among the Monts d'Azur Nature Reserve's wild horses and herds of bison, within one of these five African-style eco-lodges (€195 covers 2 adults in half board with one walking safari, €45 per child under 12). Breakfast and dinner are served alongside an open fire (the camp is at an altitude of 1200 m), and there are outdoor showers and separate outhouses. Alternatively, you can opt to stay in one of the 15 rooms in the Manoir, an 18th-century country house with round corner towers (doubles €76, €20 child under 12, €30 for 2 children under 12, rates include breakfast). The Domaine also offers various Eco-Lodge/Manoir combination stays.

Terre d'Arômes

Ancienne route Napoléon, 06750 Séranon, T06 23 32 78 07, terre-d-aromes.com. 2-person yurt €80/night, €450/week, €30 per additional adult, €20 per additional child, rates include breakfast, half board optional; family yurts sleep 4-5 people, group yurts sleep 6-8. Beautifully decorated, snug Mongolian yurts dotted over five hectares of mountain terrain. Owners Olivia and Pierre Mérindol collect local plants (lavender, sage etc) and refine their essential oils (for sale) in a distillery on the premises, and are happy to share their knowledge with guests. Stellar organic breakfasts are provided, with lunches, exquisite dinners and unusual home-made beverages on request.

Splashing out

Le Chalet d'Auron

La Voie du Berger, 06660 Auron, T04 93 23 00 21, chaletdauron.com. Doubles €90-340, suite €272-660, out of season there may be a 3-night minimum stay; €60 per extra bed, €20 per cot.
Cosy set-up of 17 Alpine-style rooms, with two pairs that are interconnecting. Guests have free access to the jacuzzi, Turkish bath and indoor pool. Hearty dishes in the restaurant; half board available. Outdoor bar; piano bar, log fire and library inside for snowy nights.

Local goodies

Weekly regional **markets** are one of the best places to stop off and stock up on snacks, fresh fruit, veggies and traditional Provençal products. In **Castellane**, farmers pack the village's central square (in front of the Town Hall) on Wednesday and Saturday mornings (0800-1300). Both **St-André-les-Alpes** (place Marcel Pastorelli) and **Digne-les-Bains** lure local producers on Wednesdays and Saturdays as well (0800-1300). On Friday mornings, **Entrevaux** (place Moreau, 0700-1300) is the spot to shop.

Le Pain d'Epicerie
Rue du Milieu, 04320 Entrevaux, T04 93 05 49 89. Thu-Tue 1000-1200 and 1400-1800.

Home-made chutneys, herb-laden pastis, fruit jams and plenty of local honey sold from a vat, plus delicious variations on *pain d'épices*, a spicy sweet honey cake.

Quick & simple

Café Le France
54 bd Gassendi, 04000 Digne-les-Bains, T04 92 31 03 70, Tue-Sat 1200-1430 and 1930-2130.

A favourite with Digne locals, serving top traditional dishes (*confit de canard*, pumpkin soup) as well as more experimental cuisine (grilled langoustine and passion fruit salad). Two-course lunch menus are €13.50, and there's a summertime terrace.

Les Lacs de St-Auban

Chemin Viviers 06850 St-Auban, T04 93 60 40 90, lacsdesaintauban.fr. Jul-Aug daily 1200-1500, May-Jun and Sep Tue-Sun 1200-1500, Apr and Oct Wed-Sun 1200-1500, Mar Thu-Sun 1200-1500.

Located on a pretty little lake where kids can fish for rainbow trout and grown-ups can try fly-fishing, this laid-back restaurant spills over a terrace waterside. The menu is simple, and includes freshly grilled fish and lamb, piles of chips and big salads.

Le Vieux Four

3 rue Jacques Barraja, 06450 St-Martin-Vésubie, T04 93 03 36 06. Tue-Sun 1900-2230.

Pizzas and grilled meats exit sizzling from a massive wood-fired oven at the end of a narrow, cavernous dining room. Salads are heaped with local cheeses; early diners (from 1800) can grab a slice of *socca* (savoury chickpea flour pancake), served steaming straight from the oven during summer.

Posh nosh

Auberge du Teillon

Route Napoléon, La Garde, 04120 Castellane, T04 92 83 60 88, auberge-teillon.com. Jul-Aug Wed-Mon 1200-1400 and daily 1900-2130, mid-Mar Jun and Sep to mid-Nov Tue-Sun 1200-1400 and Tue-Sat 1900-2130.

Despite its basic appearance, the Auberge du Teillon lifts hearty regional cooking to gastro levels. Chef Yves Lepine dishes up roast beef in a thick port sauce, mushroom and scallop risotto and caramelized melon, all utterly *sans* pretension. Set menus are €22-48, with a children's menu at €10. The Auberge also has eight rooms (doubles €55-60, €10 per extra bed) with half board available (€57 per person per night).

Bastide Moustiers

Chemin de Quinson, 04360 Moustiers-Ste-Marie, T04 92 70 47 47, bastide-moustiers.com. Apr-Oct daily 1230-1400 and 1930-2130, Mar, Nov-Dec Thu-Mon 1230-1400 and 1930-2130.

Alain Ducasse's place of foodie pilgrimage. New head chef Alain Souliac serves two Michelin-starred menus (€55/70) of southern French country cooking, including John Dory with asparagus, pigeon-topped polenta and roasted local lamb. Kids are welcome to check out the Bastide's veggie garden (divided into five themed areas, e.g. herbs, salad, roots), where ingredients like courgette flowers and basil for pesto are harvested each morning. During summertime, there's a shady outdoor terrace that's great for younger families.

Le Grill de la Piscine

Moulin de la Camandoule, Chemin Notre Dame, 83440 Fayence, T04 94 76 00 84, camandoule.com. Late May-Sep daily 1200-1500, pool open until 1800.

Polished former olive oil mill set in 4.5 hectares of orchards, parks and riverside lawns, 2 km downhill from Fayence. Although gastronomic restaurant L'Escourtin is also on the grounds, families will love the Moulin's poolside grill, Le Grill de la Piscine. Two to three-course menus are €15.80-25, and use of the pool for the afternoon is free (although an extra €5 per person will get you a poolside lounger and towel). The on-site hotel also boasts a dozen rustic-chic bedrooms (doubles €60-148, children's room €50-78, 4-person apartment €120-179).

Contents

Boats in Cassis.

Marseilles & the Calanques

Bestouan beach.

Taking it all in.

Home to the South of France's largest city and newest national park, this coastal region is ringed with sub-tropical islands, fjord-like *calanques* and some of the best driving country in France. The national park offers plenty of pay-to-visit attractions, but it's the simple stuff such as scrambling over granite tors or boulder-hopping across streams that makes the greatest impression on kids.

Marseilles is a sprawling metropolis. And like any big city, it's not the epitome of kid-friendliness. But to the surprise of many a visitor, Marseilles is packed with parks, amazing shopping, summer festivals and a shoreline of beach after rolling beach. The city is currently spending millions on tourism development and new museums as it gears up to become European Capital of Culture in 2013.

The coastline unfurling west and eastwards from Marseilles' downtown offers a striking visual contrast. Limestone cliffs are speckled with turquoise inlets and tiny pebble or white-sand beaches. Known as *calanques*, these inlets are pristine, protected, and, in 2011, were reclassified as France's eighth national park, **Parc National des Calanques**. Families can hop aboard a local boat tour, join a kayaking expedition or choose a gentle stroll around them.

This region has fantastic **walking trails** to suit all abilities. Even better, some of them circle the tiny islands scattered off the Mediterranean shore. There are short, paved loops (eg around Ile de Bendor, see page 110) that are perfect for pushchairs. There are more challenging rural treks (eg Cassis's Vin et Terroir vineyard walk, see page 104), plus serious hard-core hikes (eg into the Massif des Calanques, see page 116) for more adventurous teens.

The landscape around here is stunning, and for visitors with tots, it can be appreciated from the cosy environs of a car. Peer at seagulls from on high while driving the **Route des Crêtes**. The rippling hills behind Bandol and Cassis are blanketed in vines: pick up a Tourist Office map of the area and cruise on inland. If you're lucky enough to travel out of peak season (July and August), you'll have all the roads pretty much to yourself.

You must

- Dare to drive along the scary Route des Crêtes.
- Dive beneath the waves to see underwater life by scuba or snorkel.
- Explore the region's *calanques* by organised boat trip, *petit-train* or trekking along on your own two feet.
- Investigate the 16th-century former fortress Château d'If, on an island opposite Marseilles' Vieux Port.
- Pack up buckets, beach toys, blankets and a picnic, then hit a shimmering stretch of sand.
- Spend a day hiking, fishing or lazing around on one of the coast's island hideaways.

Out & about Marseilles & the Calanques

Provence-on-sea

Almost entirely ignored by foreign tourists, the town of Martigues, west of Marseilles, makes for a very pleasant off-the-beaten-track day out. Charming and down-to-earth, it's laced with canals and bridges *à la* Venice (albeit much smaller). The town also boasts the 100-year-old Musée Ziem (blvd du 14 Juillet, 13500, T04 42 41 39 60, Wed-Sun Jul-Aug 1000-1200 and 1430-1830, Sep-Jun 1430-1830, free), which celebrates turn-of-the-century artist Félix Ziem, plus other great Provence-loving painters, including Paul Signac and Auguste Rodin. If you visit the town by train, wait for the bus link that covers the couple of kilometres into Martigues: the road into town is dangerously pavement-free.

Ramble through vineyards

With energetic kids in tow, a tour around the South of France's bountiful vineyards may seem as likely as a 0900 lie-in. Cassis's two-hour **Vin et Terroir** vineyard walk may come as a pleasant surprise. The easy trail loops past all twelve of the town's vineyards, as well as olive groves and traditional stone bastides. Pick up a map, marked with the walk, from Cassis's Tourist Office (quai des Moulins, 13260, T08 92 25 98 92, ot-cassis.fr, Jul-Aug Mon-Fri 0900-1900, Sat-Sun 0930-1230

The port at Cassis.

and 1500-1800; Mar-Jun and Sep-Oct Mon-Fri 0900-1230 and 1400-1800, Sat 0930-1230 and 1400-1730, Sun 1000-1230; Nov-Feb Mon-Fri 0930-1230 and 1400-1730, Sat 1000-1230 and 1400-1700, Sun 1000-1230). If you're travelling with tiny tots, try **driving** through the gently rippling vineyards and hilltop villages (Le Castellet and La Cadière d'Azur are two favourites) around Cassis and Bandol instead. Bandol's Tourist Office (allée Vivien, 83150, T04 94 29 41 35, tourisme.bandol.fr, Jul-Aug daily 0930-1900, Apr-Jun and Sep Mon-Sat 0900-1200 and 1400-

1800, Oct-Mar Mon-Sat 0900-1200 and 1400-1700) distributes free maps of the region.

Take a walk in the park

Exotic **Parc du Mugel** (av du Mugel, 13600 La Ciotat, daily Apr-Sep 0800-2000, Oct-Mar 0900-1800) is spread over 12 hectares on the Cap de l'Aigle, south of La Ciotat. Marked pathways wind their way through chestnut trees, palms, bamboo forests and a fragrant herb garden, with views over the Mediterranean from the higher lookout points. There's a kids' play area and plenty of spots for picnicking too.

Route des Crêtes no 3: D141, La Ciotat to Cassis, 15 km

The teetering Route des Crêtes connects the seaside towns of Cassis and La Ciotat, tracing its way along Cap Canaille's ridges, bumping past Europe's highest seaside cliff (the amusingly-named *Grande Tête*, or Big Head, at 399 m). For the most enjoyable driving experience, pack up the car and set off early – not so much to avoid the traffic (although skipping the jams of tour buses is a bonus), but to scoot across this route ahead of the pummelling winds that pick up from mid-morning onwards. Again, this itinerary is suitable only for drivers and passengers with a head for heights.

From La Ciotat, follow the Route des Crêtes signs along avenue Marcel Camusso and out of town. The road ascends, and entrance to the cliff-top route is clearly indicated. Suburban houses drop off, the coastline retreats and the landscape quickly grows more otherworldly: huge, smooth rocks poke out of the lush hilltops. The route winds westwards, dotted with panoramic spots to park up and peek out over the stunning seascapes. Most lookout points have wooden guardrails or are skirted by a thick rim of protective rocks. Regardless, younger children should be kept firmly in hand.

The route's final twist is its most breathtaking. As the road turns inland, unobstructed vistas of sea, Marseilles' Frioul Island archipelago and endless coastline come into sight in both directions. A dip westwards again, and the Route des Crêtes corkscrews downhill into Cassis town centre.

Note that this Route des Crêtes can be driven in either direction. For seriously sporty families, there's also a 12-km **Sentier des Crêtes** hiking trail that weaves among the cliffs. You'll need to pack a picnic and plenty of drinking water; the strenuous trail is unsuitable for young children.

Due to dangerous dry conditions that could spark forest fires or exceptionally strong winds, this Route des Crêtes is sometimes closed during summer. Check with the Tourist Offices in Cassis (quai des Moulins, 13260, T08 92 25 98 92, ot-cassis.fr) or La Ciotat (blvd Anatole France, 13600, T04 42 08 61 32, tourisme-laciotat.com), or call the info line T08 11 20 13 13 before setting out.

For Routes des Crêtes nos 1 and 2, see pages 91 and 95 respectively.

Winding through the
Route des Crêtes.

La Grande Mer.

Best beaches

The following beaches are grouped geographically, beginning in Bandol and moving westwards beyond Marseilles. Within each area, the beaches are listed alphabetically.

Centrale

Quai Charles de Gaulle, 83150 Bandol.

😎 🚗 ☕ ♿ ➕ 🐕 🅿️

Just east of the port, Centrale is Bandol's pretty town beach, shallow and backed by palms. Ideal for a quick cooling dip rather than a day on its sands.

Recrénos

Av Maréchal Foch, 83150 Bandol.

🚗 ☕ ✖️ ➕ 🐕 🅿️

An almost perfectly round turquoise lagoon, west of Bandol's town centre. Stake out a spot early during summertime, as this sandy, shallow beach is popular with local families.

La Résidence & du Grand Vaillat

Corniche François Fabre, 83150 Bandol.

🚗 ☕ ✖️ ➕ 🐕 🅿️

Hugging the coastline between Bandol and Sanary-sur-Mer, this long, powdery beach is shallow and sheltered, making it perfect for young children.

Les Lecques

Blvd de la Plage, 83270 St-Cyr-sur-Mer.

😎 🚗 ☕ ♿ ✖️ ➕ 🐕 🅿️

Wide, sandy and a massive 2 km long, this popular beach is one of the region's roomiest. Gentle waves lap the shoreline, and there's plenty of room for building sandcastles. Easy pushchair access.

Calanques du Grand & Petit Mugel

Av du Mugel, 13600 La Ciotat.

🚗 ☕ 🐕 🅿️

On the southeast corner of Cap de l'Aigle, these two pebble beaches boast crystal clear waters. Arrive early to snag a spot in the shade.

Calanques Figuerolles

Av de Figuerolles, 13600 La Ciotat.

🚗 ☕ 🐕 🅿️

Around the western section of Cap de l'Aigle's headland, russet-tinged cliffs back particularly chilly turquoise waters fed by cool currents. Access via steps makes it unsuitable for pushchairs.

Grande, Lumiere & Cyrnos

Blvd Beaurivage, 13600 La Ciotat.

🚗 ☕ ✖️ ♿ ➕ 🐕 🅿️

These three sections of beach dot their way along the coast of Golfe d'Amour, east of La Ciotat's town centre. All are sandy, shallow and sheltered.

Bestouan

Av de l'Amiral Ganteaume, 13260 Cassis.

😎 🚗 🐕 🅿️

A pleasant pebble beach, west of Cassis's port and en route to the Calanque de Port-Miou. Accessible via a short set of stairs.

La Grande Mer

Promenade Astride Briand, 13260 Cassis.

😎 🚗 ☕ ✖️ ➕ 🐕 🅿️

Cassis's central beach – a mix of sand and fine shingle – sits below the remains of the town's medieval castle. It's steps from both the snack shops lining the lovely port and a children's play area. Water is cooled by the seepage of mineral water from the rocks.

See also the beaches listed in Let's go to… **Marseilles** (page 112) and Off the beaten track: **the Calanques** (page 116).

La Corniche

Av Général Leclerc, 13960 Sausset-les-Pins.

🚗 ☕ ➕ 🐕 🅿️

Large rocks edge a portion of this wide sandy beach, perfect for curious climbing kids. There's also a pier poking out into the waves, and easy pushchair access.

Anse du Verdon

🚗 ☕ ➕ 🐕 🅿️

Chemin du Verdon, La Couronne, 13500 Martigues.

This spacious, sandy beach is a favourite, with beach volleyball nets set up for public use during the summer. Note that although it has a Martigues postcode, this beach is in the seaside town of La Couronne on the Mediterranean coast.

Out & about Marseilles & the Calanques

Adventure courses
Le Parc Grimpozarbres

Quartier de St Jérôme, 20 blvd Rémusat, 13013 Marseilles, T04 91 12 29 46, grimpozarbres.com. Mid-Jul to Aug daily 1000-1900, last entry 1700, end-Mar to mid-Jul and Sep-end Oct Wed, Sat-Sun 1000-1900, last entry 1700, end Oct-end Mar Wed, Sat-Sun 1000-1700, last entry 1500. €18 14 years and over, €16 child 8-13 years, €12 child 5-7 years, €4 child 3-5 years. Parcours Ouistitis minimum age 3, Parcours Jaune minimum age 5, Parcours Bleu minimum age 8, Parcours Rouge and Parcours Noir minimum age 14.

An outdoor adventure park for young children, with the Ouistitis course suitable for age three and up. There's also easy pushchair routes around the site, a *Parcours Nature* (nature walk) though the park and three resident fuzzy llamas to coo over.

Pastré Aventure

155 av de Montredon, 13008 Marseilles, T06 27 41 06 21, pastreaventure.com. Jul-Aug Mon-Fri 1330-1800, Sat-Sun 1000-1800, May-Jun Wed 1330-1700, Sat-Sun 1000-1700, Apr and Sep-Oct Wed, Sat-Sun and holidays 1330-1700, Nov-Mar Wed, Sat-Sun and holidays 1330-1600. Parcours Kids €12, minimum age 5, Parcours Super Kids €13, minimum age 7, Parcours Decouverte €14, minimum age 8, Parcours Aventure €16, minimum age 12.

Four adventure courses of varying difficulty, including ropes to shimmy up, walls to climb and bridges to dash across. On Marseilles' southern outskirts.

Boat hire
JCF Boat Services

Port (office next door to the Capitainerie), 13260 Cassis, T06 75 74 25 81, jcf-boat-services.com. Explore the calanques in one of JCF's motorboats (from €135/half day, excluding petrol). If you don't have a licence, opt to rent a five-person *aligator* boat (€45/hr or €90/half day) instead. Reserve in advance in summer.

Kayaking
Calankayak

Port, 13260 Cassis, T06 16 90 25 71, calankayak.com. €60/day, €100/weekend. Two- to four-person kayaks for rent from Cassis's port.

New Evasion Provence Canoe

Strade Deferrari, Base mer, 83150 Bandol, T04 94 29 52 48, provence-canoe.fr. Minimum age 5; children aged 5-10 years must be accompanied by adults in a 3-4 person kayak; over 11s can paddle a 1- or 2-person kayak; all participants must know how to swim.

Sea kayak rental in Bandol's bay (from €11/1½ hr adult, €7/1½ hr child (11-17)), plus half-day outings around the Ile de Bendor (€16 adult, €12 child (11-17)) or full day trips to the *calanques* along the coast (€22 adult, €16 child (11-17)).

Provence Kayak Mer

3 rue Rompicul, 83870 Signes, T06 12 95 20 12, provencekayakmer.fr. May-Sep. Minimum age 12 if paddling with an adult, minimum age 16 if paddling alone or with another teen. Guided kayak expeditions set off from Calanque de Port Miou (half day €35/person, full day €55/person); there are also sunset tours departing from La Ciotat (1½-2 hrs, €30/person).

Scuba-diving
Bandol Plongée

Quai de la Consigne, place no. 6, allée Vivien, Port, 83150 Bandol, T06 07 45 27 81, bandol-plongee.com. Minimum age 8. From €42/dive, €45 adult's instruction and baptism dive, kids' courses from €190 (4 dives). Specialists known for their kids' diving courses, targeting ages 8-13. Group dives visit around 30 sites off Bandol, La Ciotat and along the coastline.

Centre Cassidain de Plongée

3 rue Michel Arnaud, BP1, 13714 Cassis, T04 42 01 89 16, centrecassidaindeplongee.com. Mid-Mar to mid-Nov. Minimum age 12. From €38.50/dive, €63 instruction and baptism dive.

Friendly outfit based out of Cassis's port. For experienced divers, dive sites along the *calanques'* coastline.

For more outdoor activities, visit the **Faire du Sport à Marseilles** website, fairedusportaMarseilles.com (French only).

Castaway to distant shores

OK, so they aren't really that distant. But during summer's busy season, a day out on any of these three Lilliputian islands – Ile Verte, Ile de Bendor and Ile des Embiez – is a heavenly way of escaping the mainland's crowds.

Ile de Bendor
Port, 83150 Bandol, bendor.com. Daily ferries Jul-Aug 0700-0210 (every 30 mins-1 hr), Apr-Jun and Sep to mid-Oct 0700-1900 (every 30 mins) and 1920-2400 (by advance reservation), mid-Oct to Mar 0745-1700 (hourly); 7-min crossing. Apr-Sep €10 adult, €8 child (2-12), Oct-Mar €8 adult, €6 child (2-12), under 2s free; all prices return. Purchased 60 years ago by Paul Ricard, founder of Ricard pastis, the 7-ha Ile de Bendor was originally an exclusive retreat. Ricard revelled in his island getaway, throwing wild parties and wooing Europe's most famous celebs, including Salvador Dali. Whether lonely, weary of fame or simply feeling generous, Ricard eventually opened Bendor to the curious public. Today, local artisans sell handcrafted jewellery and sculpture from their ateliers, and there are three hotels and six spots to dine on the island.

A paved, 20-minute footpath (easily navigated with a pushchair) rings the island, passing the quirky *Exposition Universelle des Vins et Spiritueux* (Universal Exhibition of Wines and Spirits, T04 94 05 15 61, euvs.org, Jul-Aug daily 1100-1400 and 1540-1940, Apr-Jun and Sep

Wed-Sun 1100-1400 and 1540-1940, free), one small sandy beach, and, especially on its southern side, loads of crimson rocky outcrops for swimming. Note that although you'll see scores of families blatantly breaking the rule, picnicking isn't officially allowed on the island.

Ile des Embiez
Port du Brusc, 83140 Six-Fours, les-embiez.com. Daily ferries Jul-Aug 0700-0100 (every 30 mins-1 hr), Apr-Jun and Sep to mid-Oct 0700-2015 (every 30 mins) and 2030-2400 (by advance reservation), mid-Oct to Mar 0700-1930 (hourly); 12-min crossing. Apr-Sep €12.50 adult, €9 child (2-12), Oct-Mar €10.50 adult, €7 child (2-12), under 2s free; all prices return. Almost a decade after he purchased Bendor, in 1958 Paul Ricard snapped up the much-larger Ile des Embiez down the coast. Today, the 95-ha island is home to three hotels, eight restaurants, secluded beaches and an oceanographic institute (institut-paul-ricard.org). A fantastic – and fairly easy – *sentier nature* (nature trail, 1½-2½ hrs, depending on route) loops much of the island's perimeter,

passing pistachio trees and 16th-century Fort St-Pierre, meandering through the Domaine des Embiez, the island's own 10-ha vineyard, and skirting the Lagune du Brusc.

During July and August, ferries to Ile de Bendor and Ile des Embiez also run to and from the coastal town of Sanary-sur-Mer.

Ile Verte
Vieux Port, 13600 La Ciotat, laciotat-ileverte.com. Ferries Jul-Aug daily 0900-1900 (hourly), Sat-Sun 0700 early-bird fishermen's run, Apr-Jun and Sep Mon-Fri 1000-1200 and 1400-1700 (hourly), Sat-Sun 1000-1800 (hourly), Oct by advance reservation; 10-min crossing. €10 adult, €6 under 10s; all prices return. Pack plenty of beach toys and a picnic spread, then head to 12-ha Ile Verte, famed as the only wooded island in the region. The island has just four tiny beaches, each one partially sheltered by shady Aleppo pines; frequent ferries drop off day visitors in front of the island's only restaurant, Chez Louisette, in Calanque St-Pierre. Utterly chilled out, with all the makings for a perfect day splashing around.

Aqualand

ZAC des Pradeaux, 83270 St-Cyr-sur-
Mer, T04 94 32 08 32, aqualand.fr.
Jul-Aug daily 1000-1900, last 2 weeks
Jun and 1st week Sep daily 1000-
1800. €25 adult, €18.50 child (3-12),
under 3s free.

A massive water park, set just
back from Les Lecques beach.
There are steep spiral slides,
rapids, a surf beach and a big
bubble bath. This is a sure-fire
child pleaser.

Hit or miss?

Cacti collectors Maurice and Odile Clement opened the **Jardin
Exotique Zoo** (83110 Sanary-sur-Mer, T04 94 29 40 38, zoosanary.
com, May-Oct daily 0930-1900, Nov and mid-Feb to Apr daily
0930-1730, Dec to mid-Feb Sat-Sun and holidays 0930-1730,
€8.50 adult, €6 child (3-10), under 3s free) in 1948. Today, the
petite but packed zoo houses a huge range of exotic animals,
including parrots, zebras, wallabies, desert foxes and many a
monkey. Animal-lovers will find cages to be on the small side,
although keepers are attentive and docile peacocks ramble free.

If you're near Marseilles, you have
to go to the Western theme park
OK Corral (D8n, 13780 Cuges-
les-Pins, okcorral.fr, Jul-Aug daily,
Mar-Jun and Sep-Oct Sat-Sun,
€18.50 adult, €16.30 children
under 1.4 m, kids under 1 m free)
– it's my favourite!"
Maya, 10 years old

Let's go to...

Marseilles

Marseilles is big. For many families touring the South of France, it has the reputation of being too crowded, too hot or simply too urban. But don't be so quick to dismiss this seaside metropolis. It's packed with parks and popular beaches. It also has loads of summertime music festivals (see marseille-tourisme.com), and in 2013 will be crowned European Capital of Culture (marseille-provence2013.fr). Intrepid explorers should be sure to hit the waterfront west of the Le Panier neighbourhood, where the urban-regenerating Euroméditerranée project (euromediterranee.fr) is rising up fast, including Zaha Hadid's 33-floor skyscraper and film director Luc Besson's multiplex cinema.

Get your bearings

Marseilles is the largest city in the South of France. However, its downtown area is fairly compact, and you'll be able to cover most of it on foot, with a few forays to outlying neighbourhoods by bus, metro or with your own wheels.

If you've arrived by car, leave your vehicle at one of Marseilles' dozens of car parks *(parcs de stationnement)*. **Parking Gare Marseille St Charles** (1 av Pierre Semard, Esplanade St Charles, 13001, resaplace.com) is under the city's main train station, **Gare St-Charles** (square Narvik, 13001, T36 35, sncf. com), and conveniently located on metro lines 1 and 2. The latter will take you to the **Vieux Port,** Marseilles' tourist-friendly city centre harbour. To download a transport map or learn more about fares (€1.50 adult, under 6s free) and travel passes, see **Régie des Transports de Marseille** (rtm.fr).

The Vieux Port is Marseilles' bustling centre. From here, the shopping streets **La Canebière** and **rue de la République** shoot off to the east and north respectively, with **Le Panier**, the city's Old Town, sitting to the northwest. Ferries to Château d'If and the Frioul Islands depart from here, as do boat trips to the nearby *calanques*. The crowded **Tourist Office** (4 la Canebière, 13001, T08 26 50 05 00, marseille-tourisme.com, Mon-Sat 0900-1900, Sun 1000-1700) is just east of the port. There's a free ferry that runs across the Vieux Port from place aux Huiles to Hôtel de Ville.

Fun & free

Poke around Marseilles' **fish market**, held every morning on the Vieux Port's quai des Belges (0800-1300). Lovers of all things creepy and crawly will delight in buckets of conger eels (*congre*), scary-looking scorpion fish (*rascasse*) and giant diamond skate (*raie*). Foodie grown-ups are in for a culinary lesson too, as all of these fish are used in *bouillabaisse*, Marseilles' famous soup, which features on the menu at the restaurants.

Go for a swim

Join the locals on the sandy city beach, shallow **Plage des Catalans** (rue des Catalans, 13007, 30-min walk or bus no 83 from Vieux Port). During the summer months, there are beach volleyball nets; next door, Pizzeria des Catalans (3 rue des Catalans, 13007, T04 91 52 37 82) serves up pastas, pizzas and grilled meats on their seaside terrace.

Alternatively, head along the coast to the massive **Plages du Prado** (also called Parc Balnéaire, av Pierre Mendès-France, 13008, bus no 83 from Vieux Port) seaside park. Its shingle beach is divided into two large sections (north and south) and it's lined with loads of open green spaces, restaurants and water sports operators. Note that in some places the sea's depth drops off rapidly, so Prado is best for children who are comfortable swimmers. Keep an eye out for the bizarre yet weirdly fascinating replica of Michelangelo's *David*, towering above the seaside roundabout at the end of avenue du Prado.

Well south of Parc Borély (see below) and en route to the *calanques* (see page 116), **Pointe Rouge** (av de la Pointe Rouge, 13008, bus no 19 from place Castellane) is peaceful off season

City Pass

First time in Marseilles? Plump for a City Pass (one day €22, two days €29), which covers free entrance to 14 museums and monuments, return ferry rides to Château d'If and the Frioul Islands, plus all public transport. Holders also get a free ride on one of Marseilles' two *petit-train* routes, discounts on boat trips to the *calanques* and tons of freebies (including a taste of famously yummy *navette* biscuits) around town. City Passes can be purchased at Marseilles' Tourist Office.

The old port.

Visiting Château d'If & the Frioul Islands

Frioul If Express Ferry Service
1 quai Belges, 13001, T04 96 11 03 50, frioul.cityway.fr.
Return travel to Château d'If OR the Frioul Islands:
€10 adult, family ticket €7.50/person, minimum 4
people, minimum 1 child 4-12 years; under 4s free.
Return travel to Château d'If AND the Frioul Islands:
€15 adult, family ticket €11.25/person, minimum 4
people, minimum 1 child 4-12 years; under 4s free.

but teeming with local families during summer.
The beach is sandy and sheltered, and there's
windsurfing, kitesurfing and pedalos for hire.

Play in the park
Marseilles is home to three fantastic parks. Perched
alongside Napoleon III's Palais du Pharo, **Jardin du
Pharo** (blvd Charles Livon, 13007, daily 0800-2100)
has swings, slides and a wide green lawn perfect
for picnics, plus stunning views over the Vieux Port
and mountains beyond. To the east of the port,
Parc Longchamp's (blvd du Jardin Zoologique,
13004, daily May-Aug 0800-2000, Mar-Apr and
Sep-Oct 0800-1900, Nov-Feb 0800-1730) former
botanical gardens have been transformed into a
children's play area. The park's winding pathways
weave among waterfalls and the swirly, now-
empty cages of the park's 19th-century zoo, which
closed down two decades ago. South of the city
centre, manicured **Parc Borély** (av du Prado,
13008, daily 0600-2100) has four-person buggies
to rent (€15/hr) and a cute rowing lake (6-person
boat €11/30 mins). Wide, smooth and seemingly
never-ending **corniche JF Kennedy** is also great
for burning off extra steam; its northern section
has seascape vistas over the Château d'If and the
Frioul Islands.

Hit the town
For older kids only, the colourful **Musée Cantini**
(19 rue Grignan, 13006, T04 91 54 77 75, marseille.
fr, Tue-Sun Jun-Sep 1100-1800, Oct-May 1000-
1700, €2 adult, €1 child (10-18), under 10s free)
– including 20th-century artworks by Kandinsky,
Picasso and Bacon – is well worth a whirl. For a
spot of culture with tots in tow, head to the **Jardin
des Vestiges** (square Belsunce, Centre Bourse,
13001, T04 91 90 42 22, Mon-Sat 1200-1900, €2
adult, €1 child (10-18), under 10s free), where
little ones can dash between the ancient ruins
of Marseilles' Roman port and Greek city walls.
Access is via the ground level of the Centre Bourse
shopping mall.

Seaward bound
For **boat trips** to the nearby *calanques*, see page 116.

Château d'If (T04 91 59 02 30, if.monuments-
nationaux.fr, mid-May to mid-Sep 0930-1815, mid-
Sep to mid-May 0900-1730, closed Mon mid-Sep
to Mar, €5 adult, under 18s and EU citizens under
26 free) is the ultimate great escape for families,
although this was not the case for its two most
famous residents: a shipwrecked rhinoceros who
was washed ashore in 1515, and the fictional
Alexandre Dumas' character, the Count of
Monte-Cristo. Tantalizingly visible from Marseilles'
shoreline, this 16th-century former fortress and
prison crowns the smallest island in the Frioul
Archipelago. For a few hours scampering around
the Château, hop aboard the frequent Frioul If
Express (20-min journey, see box opposite).

For island fun without the history lesson, a
frequent ferry service from Marseilles' Vieux Port
to Château d'If also runs on to the **Frioul Islands**
(30-min journey, see box opposite). The two
largest, Pomègues and Ratonneau, are long, skinny
and connected by a man-made bridge, and boast
walking trails, turquoise inlets and beachy coves.
There are restaurants in the port area, but note
that there are no ATMs on the islands.

Vieux port entrance.

Grab a bite

To try Marseilles' famous orange-blossom *navettes* (a kind of cakey biscuit, from €8/dozen), a stop at the city's oldest bakery, **Four des Navettes** (136 rue Ste-Anne, T04 91 33 32 12, fourdesnavettes. com, Sep-Jul Mon-Sat 0700-2000, Sun and Aug 0900-1300 and 1500-1930) is a must. For juices (€3-5), smoothies, soups and salads, **Orange Basilic** (11a cours d'Estienne d'Orves, T06 03 80 06 94, Mon-Sat 0900-1830) is just off the Vieux Port.

Eating

Pique-nique en Villes (40 rue Montgrand, 13006, T04 91 33 76 88, ilove-eating.fr, Mon-Fri 0800-1600) tasty range of wraps and unusual sandwiches (like sweet curried chicken €4.50, meal combos €6.70-7.80) are indeed perfect for picnicking in the city's parks. For tiny eaters, there is also a selection of mini-sandwiches (ham and cheese, goat's cheese and tomato, €2 each). Nearby, **United Food** (40 rue Montgrand, 13006, T04 91 91 91 90, Mon-Sat 0900-1900) has a trendy canteen feel: grab a bowl of soup, a plate of pasta or a sushi spread (all around €5) and head upstairs to the terrace overlooking pretty place Félix Baret.

Hidden away in Le Panier's back streets, **Pizzeria Etiennes** (43 rue de Lorette, no reservations; Mon-Sat 1800-2300) ambience is old-school but its short menu shines: pizza, *côte de bœuf* and a smattering of starters.

OK, so most kids aren't keen on seafood. But if yours are the exception – or you're a bivalve-lover yourself – pick up a spread of prepared oysters, urchins, mussels and more from the kiosk outside **Toinou** (3 cours St-Louis, 13001, T04 91 33 14 94, toinou.com, daily 1100-2300). If you'd like to try authentic *bouillabaisse*, the Vieux Port's **Miramar** (12 quai du Port, 13002, T04 91 91 10 40, bouillabaisse.com, Tue-Sat 1200-1400 and 1900-2200) is a founding member of La Charte de la Bouillabaisse Marseillaise, a group of just 11 restaurants that serve up truly traditional versions of Marseilles' fish soup. Remember to allow ample time to dine, as *bouillabaisse* (€58/person) needs about 20 minutes of preparation time, then is served in two courses: first the soup, then the fish. You can find the dish for around a third of the price at other, less classy, restaurants.

Shopping

For visitors with a passion for fashion, rue Paradis and rue St-Ferréol thread through Marseilles' boutique-lined neighbourhood. Tread softly as you pass **Repetto** (24 rue Francis Davso, 13001, T04 91 91 53 09, repetto.fr, Mon-Sat 1000-1900): teenage girls are bound to fall hard for their exorbitantly expensive ballet shoes. Hit **La Sardine à Paillettes** (3 rue de la Tour, 13001, T06 18 31 46 04, lasardineapaillettes.com, Mon 1400-1900, Tue-Sat 1030-1330 and 1430-1900) for fabulous baby booties, colourful mobiles and unique lunchboxes. Pick up new reading material at brand-new **La Boîte à Histoires** (31 cours Julien, 13006, T04 91 48 61 60, laboiteahistoires.fr, Tue-Sat 1000-1900), Marseilles' only exclusively kids' bookshop. And for soapy souvenirs, **La Compagnie de Provence Marseille** (18 rue Francis Davso, T04 91 33 04 17, compagniedeprovence.com, Mon-Sat 1000-1900) is superb. At the back of the shop, there's a sink and a range of scented samples where kids can lather up while you browse.

The Calanques

Translated loosely as 'creeks', calanques – coastal limestone cliffs slashed by deep inlets – surround Marseilles for kilometres in both directions, providing an idyllic natural contrast to the city streets.

Southeast of Marseilles and en route to the seaside village of Cassis, the Massif des Calanques covers 20 km of rocky cliffs, deep inlets and translucent waters. The 4000-ha protected area is home to hiking trails, secluded beaches, jaw-dropping landscapes and plenty of get-out-and-shout outdoor appeal. In 2011 this glorious strip of land was classified as France's eighth national park, Parc National des Calanques (gipcalanques.fr).

To the northwest of Marseilles, the Côte Bleue calanques are less isolated but equally appealing: turquoise coves are tucked among pines and rugged shoreline, including the Calanques du Jonquier and de l'Everine, west of Niolon, Calanque de Méjean and Calanque de la Redonne.

By foot

Hiking into the Massif des Calanques from Marseilles is for families with plenty of trekking experience only. The adventurous have two options: hop aboard bus no 21 from La Canebière to Luminy, then hike into the Calanques, or take bus no 23 from rond-point du Prado. The latter's two final destinations allow access to the Calanques Sormiou and Morgiou respectively. Hikes between the bus stops and the seaside are around an hour each; be sure to pack plenty of snacks and drinking water. Marseilles' Tourist Office also runs organized hikes into the Massif between September and June (T04 91 13 89 00, Fri 1400, €15 per person, minimum age 8).

Accessing these limestone cliffs, turquoise waters and isolated beaches from Cassis is a whole lot gentler. Pick up a town map from Cassis's Tourist Office (quai des Moulins, 13260, T08 92 25 98 92, ot-cassis.fr, see page 104 for hours). Head west

During the dry summer months, the Massif des Calanques is frequently off-limits due to high risk of forest fires or strong winds. If your family is planning to explore the area solo, check for closures with the Tourist Office in Cassis or Marseilles, or call T08 11 20 13 13 before setting off.

Off the beaten track The Calanques

through Cassis's residential neighbourhoods to the Calanque de Port-Miou (45 mins), or drive over and leave your wheels at the Presqu'île car park. The panoramic **Découverte entre Terre et Mer** (Land and Sea Discovery, 1 hr) trail departs from here; younger kids will enjoy **Le Sentier du Petit Prince** (1-1½ hrs) around Cap Cable. Alternatively, Cassis's *petit-train* (May-Sep daily 1115, 1415, 1515, 1615, 1715 and 1815, Apr and Oct to mid-Nov daily 1115, 1415, 1515, 1615 and 1715, 40-min tour, €6 adult, €3 child (6-12), under 6s free) runs between the town's Tourist Office and the Calanque de Port-Miou.

By boat

During the summertime, setting out to see the *calanques* from the water is loads of fun: as these organized tours bob along past white sands and turquoise inlets, you'll be shocked you're so close to Marseilles' urban centre. Note that unless specified, these boat trips are return loops, with no stops to hop off and explore the *calanques* up close.

From Cassis

GIE des Bateliers Cassidains 13260 Cassis Port, cassis-calanques.com. Tours: three *calanques* Feb-Oct daily 0930-1700 every half hour, Jan-Feb from 1030 by reservation only, 45-min boat ride. €13 adult, €7 child (2-10). Five *calanques* Feb-Oct daily 1130, 1200, 1500, 1530, 1630, 1700, 65-min boat ride. €16, €10 child (2-10). Eight *calanques* Feb-Oct daily 1030, 1100, 1330, 1400, 1430, 1600, 90-min boat ride. €19, €13 child (2-10). Under 2s free. Tickets go on sale at the port's yellow kiosk 30 mins before tour departures. Fourteen local boats tour the *calanques* surrounding Cassis, taking on 12 to 96 passengers apiece. For hard-core hiker families (with sure-footed older kids only), occasional summer morning tours allow you to descend on the white sands of En Vau, where you can swim, snorkel and then hike back to Cassis. Inquire at the yellow boat kiosk in Cassis's port.

From La Ciotat

Les Amis de Calanques Quai Ganteaume, Port Vieux, 13600 La Ciotat, visite-calanques.fr. Circuit En Vau daily Aug 1400 and 1700, Jul 1400, 1½-hr boat ride. €20 adult. Circuit Morgiou daily Aug 1700, Jul 1730, 2-hr boat ride. €23 adult. Circuit Sormiou daily Jul-Aug 1000, 1030, 1430, 1545, Apr-Jun and Sep-Oct 1030 and 1500, Mar 1500, Nov 1430, 2½-hr boat ride. €26 adult. €3 discount for under 10s on all circuits, under 3s free. As well as dipping in and out of the *calanques* between La Ciotat and Marseilles, these boat trips also pass the tiny island of Ile Verte (see page 110) and the sheer cliffs plummeting from nearby Route des Crêtes (see page 105) into the sea. Some of the boats have vision *sous-marine*, or transparent panels for underwater viewing: ask at the boats' departure kiosk in La Ciotat's port.

From Bandol

Atlantide 1 Port de Bandol, 83150 Bandol, atlantide1.com. Apr-Nov, schedule varies, see website for details. Six *calanques*: 2½-hr boat ride, €21 adult, €12 child (4-12). Ten *calanques*: 3-hr boat ride, €25 adult, €14 child (4-12). Twelve *calanques*: 4-hr boat ride, €27 adult, €15 child (4-12). 14 *calanques*: 4-hr boat ride, €29 adult, €16 child (4-12). Under 4s free. For big boat lovers (or kids who have a hard time sitting still), *L'Atlantide* carries almost 200 people along the coast, taking in the *calanques* along the whole of the Massif des Calanques. Atlantide 1 also organises swimming and snorkelling day trips to Morgiou and Sormiou (1-hr journey each way, maximum 12 passengers, €36 adult, €25 child (4-12)), as well as dolphin-spotting. Dolphin Discovery excursions (€55 adult, maximum 12 passengers, €30 child (4-12)).

From Marseilles
Croisières Marseilles Calanques

Quai de la Fraternité, Vieux Port, 13002, croisieres-Marseilles-calanques.com. Apr-Nov, schedule varies, see website for details. L'Intégrale des Calanques (12 *calanques*): 3-hr boat trip. €25 adult, €18 child (4-15), €75 family ticket (2 adults plus 2 children 4-15 years). L'Essentiel des Calanques (6 *calanques*): 2½-hr-boat trip. €19 adult, €14 child (4-15), €57 family ticket (2 adults plus 2 children 4-15 years). Under 4s free.

Icard Maritime Vieux Port, 13001 Marseilles, visite-des-calanques.com. Côte Bleue Calanques: daily Jul-Aug 1130 and 1800, Apr-Jun and Sep-Nov 1130, 1¾-hr boat trip. €15 adult, €10 child (4-15), €40 family ticket (2 adults plus 2 children 4-15 years). Massif des Calanques (Marseilles to Cassis): Long circuit: daily Jul-Aug 0930, 1330, 1500 and 1700, Apr-Jun and Sep-Nov 0930, 1330 and 1500, Dec-Mar Wed, Fri-Sun and holidays 1330, 3-hr boat trip. €25 adult, €18 child (4-15), €75 family ticket (2 adults plus 2 children 4-15 years). Short circuit: daily May-Oct 1030, 1400 and 1600, Apr and Nov 1030 and 1400, 2¼ -hr boat ride. €19 adult, €14 child (4-15), €56 family ticket (2 adults plus 2 children 4-15 years). Under 4s free.

Kiosks for Croisières Marseilles Calanques and Icard Maritime sit side by side in Marseilles' Vieux Port. The companies operate similar excursions to the Massif des Calanques; only Icard Maritime run loops to the Côte Bleue north of Marseilles.

By train

The Côte Bleue Calanques are all accessible via local train between Marseilles and Miramas. If you're planning on stopping off at a few, opt for a **Carte Bermuda** (Jul-Sep, €5 per person), a pass valid for one day of unlimited travel along this stretch.

Sleeping Marseilles & the Calanques

Camping les Cigales

Av Marne, 13260 Cassis, T04 42 01 07
34, campingcassis.com. Mid-Mar to
mid-Nov. €6.25 adult, €2.60 under 7s,
€5 per pitch.
Ⓐ ⊕ ⓞ ⊛ ⊜ ⓕ ⓕ Wi-Fi
This modest but pleasant
campground is 1.5 km
(15-min walk) from Cassis's
town centre and the nearby
beaches. Caravans and camper
vans are welcome; reservations
not accepted.

Camping Marius

Plage de la Saulce, La Couronne,
13500 Martigues, T04 42 80 70
29, camping-marius.com. Apr to
mid-Nov. €16-22.50 2 adults, pitch
and car, €4-6.50 extra adult, €2-3.50
child (2-7), under 2s free; 5-person
Bengali canvas bungalow €189-518/
week, 6-person Funflower canvas
bungalow €294-623, 2-person
chalet €245-545, 3-person chalet
€343-728, 4-person chalet €294-728,
5-person chalet €343-728, 6-person
chalet €480-910, 8-person chalet
€525-1253.
Ⓐ ⊕ ⓞ ⊛ ⓖ ⊜ ⊕ ⓕ ⓖ ⓕ
Two hundred metres (albeit
a somewhat rough walk)
from a sandy beach on the
Med, Camping Marius has
shady pitches (70-90 sq m
each) for tents and a range
of rented accommodation,
including some chalets with
air conditioning. All rental
properties are fully equipped
(sheets, towels etc) and have

their own gas barbeques
outside. Off season, chalets can
also be rented by the night.

Clos Ste Thérèse

Route de Bandol, 83270 St-Cyr-sur-
Mer, T04 94 32 12 21, clos-therese.
com. Apr-Sep. €16.30-24.40 2 adults,
pitch and car, €3.70-5.90 extra adult,
€2.40-3.70 child (4-9), free-€1.70
under 4s; 2-person bungalow €300-
495/week, 4-person bungalow €215-
487, 5-person bungalow €266-524,
4-person chalet €280-699, 5-person
chalet €378-768, 4-person mobile
home €286-714, 5-person mobile
home €350-805, 6-person villa €518-
979, 8-person villa €658-1298.
Ⓐ ⊕ ⓞ ⊛ ⊜ ⊜ ⊕ ⓔ Wi-Fi
Set between Bandol and the
brilliant expanse of Les Lecques
beach, this well-equipped
campsite has ping-pong, a
swimming pool, a games room
and *pétanque* grounds. The
coast is about 4 km from the
campground, but lucky campers
can snag a pitch or rented
accommodation with sea views.

Hotel Les Lavandes

38 blvd de la République, 13600 La
Ciotat, T04 42 08 42 81, hotel-les-
lavandes.com. Doubles €50-62,
triples €60-72, quadruples €75-84,
6-person suite €105-125.
Run by mother and son team
Michelle and Bastien, this
bright backstreet spot is ideal
for budget-conscious families.
Seasonal home cooking comes

courtesy of Michelle both in the
evening (€15) and at breakfast
(€6.50). Rooms at the rear look
out over a vast garden, and
there's free Wi-Fi.

Old Creek Camp

Ranch Chaps Western, Chemin de la
Roque, 13780 Cuges-les-Pins, T06 17
70 36 11, campwestern.over-blog.
com. €60 adult, €30 under 12s.
Can't make it to the American
Wild West this year? Not to
worry – it's all recreated here.
Cowboys and girls meet up at
Ranch Chaps Western at 1830,
then hop into horse-drawn carts
to Old Creek Camp (15-min
journey). Evening activities range
from campfires and lassos to
rounding up horses and sleeping
in tepees. Prices include dinner
(drinks additional) and breakfast,
and you'll be returned to the
ranch around 1100 the following
day. Ranch Chaps Western can
also organize tailored days out
on horseback.

Hôtel Péron

119 corniche J F Kennedy, 13007
Marseilles, T04 91 31 01 41, hotel-
peron.com. Doubles €80, 4-person
family room €106.
A vision of pink and turquoise,
this family-run, seafront spot is
painted tip-to-toe in funky birds,
bucolic Roman ruins and other
unusual early-1960s murals. Best

The Big Wheel on Escale Borély.

are the corner rooms, which look out over Château d'If and the Frioul islands. Five minutes to Plage des Catalans, 20-minute walk to the Vieux Port. Free Wi-Fi.

Sofitel

36 blvd Charles Livon, 13007 Marseilles, T04 91 15 59 00, sofitel. com. Doubles €330-550 (significant discounts available online); Magnifique Family rate €295-390 for 2 double rooms (2 adults, 2 children 8-16 years plus 1 under 12), includes free breakfast for children. Between the city centre and Plage des Catalans (both around a 10-min walk), Marseilles'

Sofitel is luxury all the way, with a heated outdoor pool, interconnecting family rooms and underground parking. For parents (read no kids allowed), the hotel has a fabulous spa with jacuzzi pool, Turkish bath and sauna (free use included in room rate). And even if you're not spending the night, their killer buffet brunch (€25 adult, €12.50 child (4-12), under 4s free), served in the panoramic top-floor restaurant, is well worth slotting into your schedule.

Hôtel Splendid

83 av Maréchal Foch, 83150 Bandol, T04 94 29 41 61, splendidhotel.com. Apr-Sep. Doubles €63-282, triples €99-133, quadruples €126-179. Hôtel Splendid boasts 26 charming rooms and friendly local owners. But it's the hotel's position, perched on the edge of Bandol's stunning Renecros Bay, that steals the show. Decor is basic and there's no internet access, but with the beach literally steps from your bed, who's counting?

Eating Marseilles & the Calanques

Local goodies

If you're self-catering, or simply keen on storing up snacks to munch on the go, the South of France's **fruit and vegetable markets** are as practical as they are picturesque. Marseilles' weekly **organic market** (cours Julien, 13006, Wed 0800-1300) is one of the best in the region: look out for rounds of goat's cheese, nutty baguettes, wildflower honey and biodynamic wine. The same space hosts a more general food market every Monday, Tuesday and Thursday to Saturday (0800-1300).

Down the coast, the **weekly markets** in Cassis (place Baragnon and around, 13260, Wed and Fri 0800-1300), La Ciotat (place Evariste Gras, 13600, Wed 0800-1330 and Vieux Port, 13600, Sun 0800-1400) and Sanary-sur-Mer (blvd Estienne d'Orves and around, 83110, Wed 0800-1300) draw hundreds of producers from the region. They all offer the choicest seasonal produce, from baskets of Mara strawberries to piles of crisp apples.

For fresh scallops, squid and sea bream, you can't beat Marseilles' Vieux Port **fish market** (quai des Belges, 13001, daily 0800-1300). In Cassis, kiosks line the portside quays (Oct-Apr), selling sea urchins plucked fresh from the sea.

Quick & simple

Le Grand Café de la Liberté
2 place Portalis, 83270 St-Cyr-sur-Mer, T04 94 26 45 24. Tue-Sat 1200-1500 and 1900-2200.
Pick of the restaurants on pedestrian place Portalis and home to a golden 3 m-high scale replica of the Statue of Liberty, Le Grand Café serves *aïoli* (cod, veggies and garlic mayonnaise, €11) most Fridays, plus tasty home-cooked *plats du jour* (around €8 each) daily.

Pizzeria le Pinocchio
5 rue Docteur Louis Marçon, 83150 Bandol, T04 94 29 41 16. Daily 1200-1400 and 1900-2215.
Le Pinocchio's pizzas draw

Liberty at place Portalis.

crowds year round: they're a little pricey at around €14 apiece, but each one is cooked to a top-secret family recipe. Other lip-smacking dishes are seared in the roaring wood-fired oven too, including lasagne and Texan pork ribs. During the busy summer season, diners pack the restaurant's three dining rooms and pour out onto the small street-front terrace.

Sur les Quais
46 quai François Mitterrand, 13600 La Ciotat, T04 42 98 80 80, surlesquaislaciotat.com. Daily 0800-2400.
Uber-trendy it may be, but the open-air terrace of this bar-cum-restaurant-cum-club is a great spot to stop late afternoon or early evening for a cool drink and a few tiny plates of tapas (€3-6 each), including crispy squid and cod fritters. At the far end of the port and tucked behind berths of private yachts,

it's perfectly positioned for kids to run along the wide quay.

Posh nosh

Le Clos des Arômes
10 rue Abbé Paul Mouton, 13260 Cassis, T04 42 01 71 84, le-clos-des-aromes.com. Fri-Sun 1200-1430, Thu-Tue 1930-2300, closed Jan-Feb.
Dine under the giant fig tree in the flowery courtyard garden of this delicious Provençal restaurant, tucked into Cassis's back streets. Set menus (€26 or €38) include *daube* ravioli and veggie lasagne; there's also a hotel with 14 basic rooms on-site.

L'Escalet
21 quai François Mitterrand, 13600 La Ciotat, T04 42 08 29 52. Tue-Sat 1200-1500 and 1900-2200.
Cuisine centres around this restaurant's blazing wood-fired oven. Excellent set menus (€20) feature grilled lamb or swordfish,

and there's a great range of crispy pizzas for pickier eaters. On warmer evenings, the open terrace out front faces the town's picturesque port.

Auberge La Ferme
La Font de Mai, Chemin Ruissatel, 13400 Aubagne, T04 42 03 29 67, aubergelaferme.com. Tue-Fri and Sun 1230-1400, Fri-Sat 1930-2130, closed Aug and 2 weeks in Feb.
This spot of foodie pilgrimage serves up dish after dish of traditional Marseillaise treats, including gross-your-kids-out *pieds et paquets* (tripe stuffed with pork, served with lamb's feet). Dine on the leafy open-air terrace in summer, or by the snug fireplace during colder winter months. Decor is country-style Provençal; the abundant three-course set menu (€50) is good value.

For places to eat in Marseilles, see page 115.

La Bonbonnerie at Apt.

Contents

Aix-en-Provence & the Luberon

Gordes.

Grazy days in the Luberon.

Aix-en-Provence and the Luberon – the lavender-covered region to the north – is 100% real Provence. The rolling scenery is rollicking. The meaty cuisine is memorable. Best of all, that laid-back local lifestyle is there for the taking. If it's authentic country culture you're after, you've come to the right place.

The Luberon gives its name to the regional park, **Parc Naturel Régional du Luberon**, which ripples gently from Aix towards Haute-Provence. Hills are criss-crossed with hiking and biking trails, each one corkscrewing past the countryside's scarlet-stained ochre terrain. Keen to climb a mountain? Scale a stretch of **Mont Ventoux**, home to one of the trickiest stages on the Tour de France. Is your family a pack of pedallers? Hundreds of kilometres of cycle routes shimmy around *villages perchés* (hilltop villages) and through almost iridescent lavender fields. The **Luberon** takes the cake not just for the range of outdoor activities so widely available, but also for the heartstoppingly-perfect backdrops that unfurl anywhere – and everywhere – you look. It's little wonder that **Aix's** most famous son, artist Paul Cézanne, rarely strayed far from here.

The region's rich bounty will appeal to gourmets little and large. Peek round to backyard kitchen gardens and you'll find them thick with fig trees, tomato plants bent double with each one's plump summertime load. At the foot of every village, vintners tend to silvery tangles of grapevines, their edges stacked with beehives. In autumn, residents scoop up a basket and head into the woods, collecting mushrooms or hunting for truffles. The treasures they unearth are swiftly swapped around and soon piled high at Aix's morning market or served up on your plate.

Unsurprisingly, the region attracts a torrent of tourists each summer, particularly between mid-June and late July, when the lavender flowers are at their purpley peak. If you do visit Aix and the Luberon during this period, do your best to get off the main roads and explore independently. As well as the recommendations in this guide, ask locals for their favourite sunflower-dipped drive, home-made ice cream shop or fresh fruit market.

You must

- Dash around Roussillon's dusty ochre quarries, the Sentier des Ocres.
- Discover how to make chocolate, candy or soap.
- Explore the cobbled streets of the Luberon's hilltop villages.
- Follow the footsteps of famous artist Paul Cézanne through Aix-en-Provence.
- Hike, ski or ride a pony on Mont Ventoux.
- Pedal your way along the Parc Naturel Régional du Luberon's cycling tracks.
- Stop to sniff the fields of lavender.

Fun & free

Abbaye Senaque.

Drive the road less travelled

This region boasts some of the South of France's best hill, mountain and river landscapes. Even if your goal is to travel from A to B, it's often just as fast to take the scenic route. Use a good map to plan your route: Michelin regional maps – available at most local newsagents in France – highlight particularly scenic roads with a green marker. Cruise stretches of the D7n (between Sénas and St-Cannat), along the D543 (between Aix and Rognes) or from Lourmarin to Apt on the D943. Just off the D108, wind your way past 2000-year-old **Pont Julien**, which crosses the Calavon River. The dry-stone bridge is part of the old Via Domitia, the principal Roman trade route that linked Italy and the Iberian Peninsula. Whatever your itinerary, be sure to pack a few snacks for the trip, as you may find a roadside picnic irresistible.

Scamper the cobbled streets

Tumbling down hillsides, sitting in sleepy valleys or poking out on the horizon, picturesque Provençal villages crop up here at every turn. Most of them are trimmed with pale stone buildings, pedestrianized central squares, pavement cafés, a bubbling fountain or two and a fantastic weekly market: perfect for a coffee while the kids run around. **Gordes** is the region's most famous town, and throughout July and August, a steady stream of tourists bear witness to its enduring popularity. Both **Bonnieux**, with its panoramic vistas, and laid-back **Lourmarin** make more leisurely stops, either for lunch or simply a wander. Largely owned by fashion designer Pierre Cardin,

Lacoste is home to the infamous Marquis de Sade's former castle: a music festival (festivaldelacoste. com) is held in the castle every summer. **Apt**, although its population still a petite 12,000, is the regional capital. Explore its shaded and, for the most part, un-touristy Old Town on a sunny summer's day.

Stop to smell the lavender

The Luberon is *lavande* (lavender) land. Visit the region between early June and late July and the countryside will be awash in a perfumed purple haze. Cycle or drive along the D6, which threads its way from Manosque to Riez through the **Plateau de Valensole**'s dazzling lavender plantations. Local farmers set up roadside kiosks selling fragrant sachets of dried flowers and giant jars of lavender honey, while the landscape cries out for your own oh-so-French family photo shoot.

Four kilometres from Gordes, the 12th-century **Abbaye Notre-Dame de Sénanque** (RD 177, route de Venasque, T04 90 72 05 72, senanque.fr (abbey), abbayedesenanque.com (boutique); grounds always open, access to interior by guided visit only (in French, 1 hr); boutique Feb to mid-Nov Mon-Sat 1000-1800, Sun 1400-1800, mid-Nov to Jan 1400-1800) nestles in its own lavender-filled valley. It's free to park up and wander around the grounds; be sure to circle around the back for a peek at the resident monks' vegetable gardens. The on-site boutique sells soaps, perfumes, the abbey's own honey and vials of lavender essential oil. Note that it's best to give the abbey's guided tour a miss: only the most monastic of kids would survive the hour-long circuit through its ascetic interiors.

Lavender, the miracle flower

Lavender has traditionally been used as an insect repellent, an antiseptic, to aid sleep, relieve sunburn, get rid of nausea and as a generally soothing calmative. In the car with cranky kids? An irritated driver? Try putting a few drops of lavender essential oil on a handkerchief and setting it on the dashboard in the sun. Results will range from a blissed-out family to simply a sweet-smelling car.

Abbey days: soak up the lavender and sunshine.

Action stations

At the heart of what many consider to be the 'real' Provence, the Parc Naturel Régional du Luberon (parcduluberon.fr) blankets much of the area covered in this chapter. It sits at the crossroads of four southern *départements*: Vaucluse, Bouches-du-Rhône, Haute-Provence and the Var. In addition to the great outdoor activities listed below, pop along to the Maison du Parc in Apt (60 place Jean-Jaurès, 84404 Apt, T04 90 04 42 00, parcduluberon. fr, Mon-Fri 0830-1200 and 1330-1800), where you can pick up loads more ideas, local maps and weeks' worth of inspiration.

Adventure courses
Colorado Adventures

84400 Rustrel, T06 78 26 68 91, colorado-aventures.fr. Jul-Aug daily 0930-1930, last departure 1700, Mar-Jun and Sep-Nov Sat-Sun and holidays 1000-1900, last departure 1630. €18 adult (minimum height 1.7 m with arms raised), €13 child (minimum height 1.5 m with arms raised).

Four different adventure courses, including the scary Indiana, composed entirely of zip lines.

Cycling
Luberon Biking

90 chemin du Stade, 84740 Velleron, T04 90 90 14 62, luberon-biking.fr. Adults' bikes €18-40/day, kids' bikes from €10/day.

Hundreds of mountain bikes, hybrids, tandems and kids' bikes that can be picked up or conveniently delivered to

Mont Ventoux

The Tour de France's Holy Grail, 1912 m-high Mont Ventoux offers a whole lot more than just seriously gruelling hill climbs. Contact the **Bedoin Tourist Office** (Espace Marie Louis Gravier, 84410 Bedoin, T04 90 65 63 95, bedoin.org, mid-Jun to Aug Mon-Fri 0900-1230 and 1400-1800, Sat 0930-1230 and 1400-1800, Sun 0930-1230, Sep to mid-Jun Mon-Fri 0900-1230 and 1400-1800, Sat 0930-1230) to get your hands on a detailed map of the mountain plotted with 11 different hikes, ranging from six to 20 km. Or learn all about insects by following the marked **Sentier de Découverte Jean-Henri Fabre** (Station du Mont Serein, 84340 Beaumont-du-Ventoux, T04 90 63 42 02, stationdumontserein. com), a discovery trail named after famed entomologist Fabre. Throughout July and August (daily 1400-1800), Beaumont-du-Ventoux is also home to **pony rides** (€8/30 mins), an **adventure course** (4-12 years, €10) and a **giant bouncy park** (€8/hr).

Come wintertime, both Bedoin and Beaumont-du-Ventoux are transformed into snowy wonderlands, with downhill and cross-country *pistes* and luge runs. Station du Mont Serein boasts nine lifts and more than 12 km of ski slopes (day pass €15 adult, €10 under 12s). Hit the station's Information Office to pick up the free booklet, **Circuits de Randonnées en Raquettes**, which covers five fun trails to hike along in snowshoes. In Bedoin, the smaller Station de Ski du Chalet Reynard (84410 Bedoin, T04 90 61 84 55, chalet-reynard.fr) is home to six blue and red ski runs (day pass €12 adult, €8 under 12s).

Oh, and if you're carting a little Lance Armstrong-in-training (or you think you're a little like Lance yourself), **Luberon Biking** (see below left) runs guided **cycling** tours up the mountain's steep slopes.

locations around the region. Kids' bikes include tiny models too, starting at age two, and child seats are offered free.

Provence à Vélo

provence-cycling.co.uk (English), provence-a-velo.fr (French).
An easy-to-use, detailed resource for bike rental agencies and downloadable cycle routes through the Luberon and Mont Ventoux, as well as around Avignon (see page 156) and further west. Routes are broken down into categories ('family', 'discovery' and 'competitive'), and range from easy 2-km to village-to-village routes.

Vélo Loisir en Luberon

203 rue Oscar Roulet, 84440 Robion, T04 90 76 48 05, veloloisirluberon.com.
The Luberon's pioneering cycling organisation, waymarking more than 450 km of cycle paths throughout the region over the past decade. Their four lengthy routes (51 to 236 km) vary in intensity. Families can download itineraries from the website and select the sections best suited for members' ages and abilities. The site also lists bike rental agencies, plus places to stay and eat en route. Note that portions of the cycle paths are on paved pedestrian/bike trails through the Luberon's hills and vineyards, while other (shorter) sections roll along the same roads used by cars and buses.

Out & about Aix-en-Provence & the Luberon

For kids who are crazy about creatures big and small – including elephant-adoring Pierre-Elliott (2 years old) – head to one of the South of France's fantastic animal parks, like the Zoo de la Barben (see below).

Big days out

La Ferme du Brégalon

Mas du Brégalon, chemin du Gour, 13840 Rognes, T04 42 50 14 32. Feb-Nov Mon-Sat 1500-1900. €1.50/person.
At this small goat farm just north of Aix, owners Hugues and Christine Girard teach visitors how they make traditional raw milk *chèvre*, or goat's cheese. Kids are welcome to watch the goats' afternoon milking sessions; there are plenty of free cheese nibbles too.

Zoo de la Barben

Route du Château, 13330 La Barben, T04 90 55 19 12, zoolabarben.com. Daily Jul-Aug 0930-1900, Feb-Jun and Sep-Nov 1000-1800, Dec-Jan 1000-1730. €14 adult, €8 child (3-12), under 3s free.
The largest zoo in the South of France, housing more than 100 species over its 33 hectares. There are picnic areas, a playground and 9 km of trails snaking through the zoo, while a tiny train (€1) loops around about a third of it, passing elephants, brown bears and giraffes along the way. If you're up for a little French immersion, the zookeepers give informative lectures on different animals in the zoo every Wednesday, Saturday and Sunday, covering what they eat and how they survive in the wild.

Hit or miss?
Village des Bories

Les Savournins, 84220 Gordes, T04 90 72 03 48, gordes-village. com. Daily 0900-dusk. €6 adult, €4 child (12-17), under 12s free.
Tiny dry-stone dwellings created between the 7th and 19th centuries, these *bories* were abandoned around the turn of the 20th century. The conical spaces were used as agricultural warehouses, shelter for sheep, open-air bread ovens and even miniature silkworm farms. Although there's not actually much to see, most young kids are enchanted by the houses, dashing in and out of the little doors. L'Enclos de Bories (Quartier Le Rinardas, 84480 Bonnieux, T06 08 46 61 44, Apr-Nov daily 1000-1900, last entry 1800, €5 adult, under 12s free) is a smaller cluster of *bories* just west of Bonnieux.

How's it made? Fabulous factories

Whether it's rivers of chocolate, squeezy tubes of cream or vats of candied fruit purée, these **factory tours** are fact-filled, friendly and loads of fun. Note that you must reserve in advance for all of these tours.

Insider access to a chocolate factory? A Willy Wonka-flavoured dream is on the cards at **Chocolaterie de Puyricard** (La Plantation, av Georges de Fabry, 13540 Puyricard, T04 42 96 11 21, puyricard.fr; 2-hr tours, €8/person, minimum age 10). Follow your nose to this sprawling laboratory, where you can learn how to become a *maître-chocolatier* (chocolate master), pop nuts inside pralines and dip Puyricard's Palet d'Or chocolate disks into genuine 22-carat gold.

The countryside northeast of Puyricard is littered with **vineyards**: grown-ups can cut a deal on a treat of their own by combining a quick *château* visit – try **Domaine de Barbebelle** (RD543, 13840 Rognes, T04 42 50 10 20, barbebelle.com, daily 0900-1200 and 1400-1800) or **L'Oppidum des Cauvins** (RD543, 13840 Rognes, T04 42 50 29 40, oppidumdescauvins.com, Mon-Sat 0900-1200 and 1400-1900) – with a stop at the Puyricard chocolate factory.

In Manosque, world-famous **L'Occitane en Provence** (Z.I. St-Maurice, 04100 Manosque, T04 92 70 19 00, loccitane.com; bilingual tours Mon-Fri, closed 3rd week Aug and 3rd week Dec, free) has been producing organic soaps, bubble bath and perfumes since 1976. Contact the town's Tourist Office (T04 92 72 16 00, accueil@manosque-tourisme.com) to tour

the factory (75 mins). Visits peek into allegedly top-secret rooms where different products are developed as well as the dedicated candle-making lab. There's also a 'sensorial workshop', where you'll learn about ingredients, what they're used for and where they come from. The on-site boutique offers a 10% discount on all items.

Calissons are Aix-en-Provence's famous local sweets, made of almond paste and candied fruits. To learn their secret recipe, visit **Calissons du Roy René's** (Pôle commercial de la Pioline, 330 rue Guillaume du Vair, 13545 Aix-en-Provence, T04 42 39 29 89, calisson.com; tours Tue and Thu 1000, €1/person) factory. The 30-minute tours culminate with a *dégustation* (tasting) of *calissons*. Or drop into their Aix Old Town **shop** (13 rue Gaston de Saporta, 13100 Aix-en-Provence, T04 42 26 67 86, Mon-Sat 0930-1300 and 1430-1830, Sun 1600-1900), where there's a

dedicated *calissons* museum (free) in the basement. Little artists will enjoy a visit to former factory **Ancienne Usine Mathieu** (page 134), which details the transformation of ochre into paints and dyes in days gone by.

Don't miss The Ochre Quarries

The terrain that surrounds Roussillon and Rustrel is slashed with stripes of deep orange, crimson and gold. The earth here is thick with ochre, a natural iron-based pigment mixed with sand that is used to tint paints, dye textiles and colour cosmetics. Mining for ochre was this region's main source of income at the start of the 20th century, and there were once more than 100 quarries and 25 ochre factories here. By the 1940s, the deep quarries threatened to burrow underneath the towns. Foundations of homes and public buildings were in serious danger of collapsing, and mining quickly ground to a halt.

Today, you can explore the former quarries along the **Sentier des Ocres de Roussillon** (Ochre Footpath, entrance signposted a 5-min walk from the town centre, 84220 Roussillon; daily Jul-Aug 0900-1930, Jun 0900-1830, May and Sep 0930-1830, Apr 0930-1730, Mar 0930-1700, Oct 0930-1630, 1st 2 weeks Nov 1000-1630, mid Nov-Dec and last 2 weeks Feb 1100-1530, €2.50 adult, under 10s free, short walk 35 mins, long walk 50 mins). The track loops through oak forest, dusty ochre valleys and coloured cliffs. If your family would rather explore the surrounding terrain by bike instead, visit **Vélo Loisir en Luberon** (veloloisirluberon.com, page 131) to download a free map of the challenging **Les Ocres en Vélo** cycle route.

Just outside Roussillon's village centre, the **Ancienne Usine Mathieu** (RD104, 84220 Roussillon, T04 90 05 66 69, okhra.com, Jul-Aug daily 0900-1900, mid-Feb to Jun and Sep to mid-Nov 0900-1300 and 1400-1800, Nov to mid-Feb Wed-Sun 0900-1300 and 1400-1800, €6 adult, €6.80 adult joint ticket Usine Mathieu and Sentier des Ocres, under 10s free) is a former ochre factory that's been transformed into a cooperative learning centre. See how this region's ochre pigments were washed, processed and transformed from earthen clay into paints and dyes. There's also a neat **Jardin des Teinturiers** (Dyers' Garden), where plants traditionally used for dyeing, such as camomile and goldenrod, are cultivated. Guided tours last around 50 minutes.

Near the town of Rustrel, the 30-ha **Colorado Provençal** region was given its Wild West nickname during the 1950s, for its similar appearance to the US state's crimson cliffs. Signposted **hiking trails**, including one along the naturally ethereal Cheminées de Fées (Fairy Chimneys), depart from the public car park south east of the town of Rustrel. For more walking routes through the Colorado Provençal, pick up a detailed booklet (€4.60) from the Mairie de Rustrel (Town Hall, Le Château, 84400 Rustrel, T04 90 04 91 09) or at any Tourist Office in the region.

To take in an aerial view of the brilliant red topography, **Montgolfière Vol-Terre** (Hameau des Goubauds, 84490 St-Saturnin-les-Apt, T06 03 54 10 92, montgolfiere-provence-luberon.com) organizes dawn balloon rides over Roussillon and the surrounding countryside. Flight time is an hour to an hour and a half. **Montgolfière en Luberon** (Joucas, 84220 Gordes, T04 90 05 76 77, montgolfiere-provence-ballooning.com, mid-Mar to mid-Oct, minimum height 1.25 m) offers two types of flights (Vol touristique 40 mins, €175/person, Grand vol 80 mins, €245/person) taking in a similar area. If your family plans to visit a few of these ochre hotspots, you may want to look into acquiring a **Couleur Pass Luberon** (€5, valid for 1-4 persons, available from Tourist Offices throughout the Luberon). This pass gives discounts of up to 50% on 16 activities throughout the region, including the Ancienne Usine Mathieu and Montgolfière Vol-Terre (details for both above).

GR Trails

Grande Randonnée (GR) walking routes connect most of France's historic towns, including Rustrel and Roussillon. These ancient paths have criss-crossed the country for centuries and are now well-marked long distance hiking paths. They often meander over ancient bridges, mule tracks and mountain passes. The GR97 rolls through Roussillon and Rustrel on its loop around the Luberon, while the GR6 heads through Rustrel en route from the Atlantic coast to the Alps, by way of the Pont du Gard. Look out for the hiking signs and the red and white waymarks as you pass through Provence.

Let's go to…

Aix-en-Provence

Aix-en-Provence is a vibrant city. Its pretty Old Town is packed with shops and restaurants; you'll encounter its favourite son, painter Paul Cézanne, at every turn. While a great place to base your family for a few nights, note that Aix lacks activities targeted at tots.

Get your bearings

Although Aix is fairly large, a rough ring of a road neatly encapsulates its small downtown area. Inside of this loop, it's best to explore on foot, as streets are narrow and parking difficult. Park up at one of Aix's nine central **car parks** (parcs de stationnement, semepa.fr/category/parkings), all an easy walk from the city's central sights.

Aix has two train stations. The **TGV station** (RD 9, plateau de l'Arbois, T08 36 35 35 35, tgv.com) is 20 minutes outside the city centre. A navette (navetteaixtgvaeroport.com, departures every 15 mins, €3.60 adult, under 6s free) bus connects it with Aix's gare routière (av Europe, T08 91 02 40 25, infotelo.com), or main bus station. The latter is a five-minute walk from the **city centre train station** (rue Gustave Desplaces, T36 35, voyages-sncf.com), where local trains stop. Head to place du Général

de Gaulle, referred to locally as La Rotonde, or 'the roundabout', to visit the very helpful **Tourist Office** (2 place du Général de Gaulle, T04 42 16 11 61, aixenprovencetourism.com, Mon-Sat 0830-1900, Sun 1000-1300 and 1400-1800, Jul-Aug extended hrs). From here, **cours Mirabeau** unfolds eastwards, slicing Aix's city centre neatly into two: to the north lie the twisty **Old Town** alleys, which is where the action lies; to the south is the **Mazarin** neighbourhood.

Amble like an Aixois

Its pavements shaded by plane trees, **cours Mirabeau** is the city's main drag. You can eat here (step into Les Deux Garçons, page 139). You can shop here (every summer evening an evening **market** lines the street, selling Provençal tablecloths, homemade hats and the odd ceramic chicken). But best of all, cours Mirabeau is a great place to get acquainted with what has made the city so popular over dozens of centuries: water and art. The street is spacious, as horse-drawn carriages used to trot along it, which makes it perfect for an unencumbered **stroll**.

Two thousand years ago, the Romans chose to build a town on this site because they loved a good long soak in the hot thermal springs that ran underground. Cours Mirabeau is home to four of the town's famous **fountains**. Farmers used to bring their herds of livestock to drink at Fontaine des Neuf Canons. The mossy cube Fontaine Moussue bubbles up hot water. Fontaine du Roi René is topped with a giant sculpture of 'Good René', the beloved last king of Provence. But most impressive is La Rotonde, the city's biggest fountain, which sits in the middle of the roundabout by the Tourist Office at cours Mirabeau's western tip.

The pride of La Rotonde.

One of the world's most famous artists was born in Aix. Hunt down **55 cours Mirabeau**: throughout his childhood, Paul Cézanne lived here with his family, upstairs from his father's successful *chapellerie* (hat shop).

Aix's university was established in 1409 and draws thousands of French and international students every year, who in turn cultivate the city's offbeat, experimental art. Pop into **Galerie d'Art du Conseil Général** (Hôtel de Castillon, 21 cours Mirabeau, T04 42 93 03 67, Tue afternoon-Sun, summer 1030-1300 and 1400-1800, winter 0930-1300 and 1400-1800, free) to see some of the city's finest: four colourfully contemporary art shows are held here each year.

Walk in the park

Cézanne adored Mont Ste-Victoire, the giant purple shadow of a mountain towering to Aix's east: so much so that over the course of his lifetime he painted it a whopping 77 times. To really see Mont Ste-Victoire through Cézanne's eyes, continue 650 m northwards from Cézanne's Atelier (see page 138), along avenue Paul Cézanne to the crest of Les Lauves hill. The entrance to a terraced park, **Terrain des Peintres**, is on your left: Cézanne set up his easel to paint 28 different versions of his favourite mountain from here. Climb up to the top of the park for views of the stunning landmark. The highest tier of the park is crowned with nine reproductions of canvases.

Let's go to Aix-en-Provence

Atelier Cézanne

9 av Paul Cézanne, T04 42 21 06 53, atelier-cezanne.com. Jul-Aug 1000-1800, tour (English) 1700, Apr-Jun and Sep 1000-1200 and 1400-1800, tour (English) 1700, Oct-Mar 1000-1200 and 1400-1700, tour (English) 1600. €5.50 adult, €2 13-25 years, under 12s free.

Visiting Cézanne's atelier is like stepping into a century-old time capsule. The artist designed and built the studio in 1901. He worked here every day, following a very strict painting schedule (0600-1030, lunch in Aix, straight back to the studio until 1700) until he passed away in 1906.

After Cézanne's death the studio was immediately sealed shut. Fifteen years later, a man named Marcel Provence purchased the building and its land. He was such a fan of Cézanne that he kept the studio just as he found it. Nothing was thrown away, and today the bright, 50-sq m studio is just as it was when Cézanne put the finishing touches on *Grandes Baigneuses* and other famous masterpieces inside it.

When you visit the studio, take a look at the folder that contains reproductions of Cézanne's artworks. See if your family can spot the following items, in the pictures and in the atelier: chairs, a pitcher, a fruit stand, a skull, an armless statue, a coat and Cézanne's hat.

The atelier is just north of the Old Town. Walking there is doable, but about a 10-minute trek uphill. Or, hop aboard bus no 1 from La Rotonde.

Les carrières de Bibémus

3090 chemin de Bibémus, T04 42 16 11 61. 1-hr visits by guided tour only, Jun-Sep 0945, Apr-May and Oct Mon, Wed, Fri and Sun 1030 and 1530, Nov-Dec Wed and Sat 1500. €6.60 adult, €3.10 13-25 years, €1.10 under 12s, entrance includes return ticket for the shuttle bus (obligatory transport to site from Trois Bons Dieux car park, necessary even for visitors who arrive by bus).

Perfect for little legs aching to run free, a visit to the abandoned (and now lightly landscaped) Bibémus Quarries is an appealing ramble for art-loving adults too. These stripy red rock quarries were mined from Aix's Roman heyday until the mid-19th century, but it was only after Cézanne rented a tiny hut here in the 1890s that interest in the quarries peaked again. The orange, blocky paintings Cézanne created during his time here are generally considered the revolutionary foundations for the Cubist movement of the early 20th century.

The Bibémus Quarries are outside the city centre. You'll either need your own wheels to reach them (there's a free car park on site), or you can take bus no 4 from La Rotonde.

If you can't get enough of Aix's favourite former resident, visit **Cézanne en Provence** (cezanne-en-provence.com). The website details every spot around town associated with the artist, including his family home, Jas de Bouffan, where he attended school and the church where his children were baptized.

Grab a bite

Aix town centre is home to three morning (0800-1300) **markets**: place Richelme (daily), place de la Madeleine and place des Prêcheurs (both Tue, Thu and Sat). All are perfect places to load up on picnic goodies, stock the kitchens in self-catering accommodation or simply snack your way through the seasonal produce. Look out for stalls selling their own artisanal *calissons* (see page 133): tasty local flavours include fig and Cavaillon melon.

Just off La Rotonde, **Simply Food** (67 rue Espariat, T04 42 59 52 85, simply-food.fr, Mon-Sat 0900-1900) has a great range of healthy, speedy meals for families on the go. There's a daily soup (€3.50), creative sandwiches (try turkey salad with goat's cheese on sesame bread, €4.20) or salads, like the popular pasta with cherry tomatoes and Parmesan cheese (€4.70).

A visit to the city would hardly be complete without a stop at Aix's most famous pavement café, **Les Deux Garçons** (53 cours Mirabeau,

T04 42 26 00 51, daily 1200-2300), old stomping ground of Cézanne and novelist pal Emile Zola. Order up a plate of mini *pâtisseries* or a simple sandwich on their outdoor terrace on cours Mirabeau.

At the eastern end of cours Mirabeau, **rue d'Italie** is lined with great delis, *boulangeries* and snack spots. Head south along the street to **Italy Street Coffee Shop** (67 rue d'Italie, T04 42 51 30 43, coffee-shop-aixenprovence.com, Mon-Tue and Thu-Fri 0800-1800, Sat-Sun 0800-1500) for bagel sandwiches, muffins or cookies. On weekends, various brunch specials include fresh pancakes, and the cosy café has free Wi-Fi too.

Toting extreme eaters? For veggie, vegan and gluten-free visitors, **Toute une histoire's** (place des Tanneurs, T06 63 30 13 75, Mon-Sat 1130-1500) all-you-can-eat lunch buffet (€12) is a bountiful mix of salads, grains and roasted vegetables. Down the road, former pork butcher Christophe Formeau mans the grill at **Le Zinc d'Hugo** (22 rue Lieutaud, T04 42 27 69 69, zinc-hugo.com, Tue-Sat 1200-1430 and 1900-2230), a paradise for carnivores, with home-made terrines, pâté and piles of wood-fired meats.

When you've got the Gruffalo coming out of your ears, drop into little **Book in bar** (4 rue Joseph Cabassol, T04 42 26 60 07, bookinbar.com, Mon-Sat 0900-1900) for a new stash of kids' books in English.

Atelier Cézanne.

Sleeping Aix-en-Provence & the Luberon

Pick of the pitches

Camping Le Colorado

Quartier Notre Dame des Anges, 84400 Rustrel, T04 90 04 90 37, camping-le-colorado.com. Apr-mid Oct. €9.90-13.20 2 adults, pitch and car, €4-5.40 extra adult, €1.90-3.50 child (1-7), under 1s free; 3-person caravan €150-275/week, 4-person mobile home €290-625, 6-person mobile home €345-625.

🅐 🐍 🅞 😊 🅑 🅞 🅠 🚲 🅕 Wi-Fi

Set in the heart of the ochre-tinged landscape, Camping Le Colorado provides easy access to the crimson Colorado walking trails. On site, there's a swimming pool, ping-pong, a small equestrian centre and a library. Guests can also rent bikes to cycle around the striking countryside.

Domaine des Chênes Blancs

Route de Gargas, 84490 St-Saturnin-les-Apt, T04 90 74 09 20, pausado. com. Apr-Oct. €17-30 2 adults, pitch and car, €4.50-6 extra adult, €3.50-4.50 under 7s; 4-5-person mobile home €380-750/week, 4-5-person canvas bungalow €250-520.

🅐 🐍 🅞 😊 🅞 🅠 🚲 🅕

Taking its name from the white oak canopy above it, this cool campground has spacious pitches, modern mobile homes and bright bungalows. Two newly built children's pools complement the large one for adults; a kids' club, karaoke and various competitions make the long summer days fly by. There's also an ice cream parlour and a pizzeria on site.

Best of the rest

Au Ralenti du Lierre

Village des Beaumettes, 84220 Gordes, T04 90 72 39 22, auralentidulierre.com. Doubles €79-96, 4-person suite €146, breakfast included.

Within a restored 16th-century building, this lovely B&B is managed by the gregarious Thierry. The carefully selected decor is Provençal, breakfast breads and pastries are home-made, and there's a fabulous walled garden and pool out back. Its village setting is ideal for a stroll home after dinner.

Le Mas d'Entremont
Célony, 315 route d'Avignon, 13090 Aix-en-Provence, T04 42 17 42 42, masdentremont.com. 3- or 4-person apartments €235-350/night.
Located in the countryside north of Aix's city centre, Le Mas d'Entremont ticks all the right boxes: swimming pool, tennis courts, spacious fountain-dotted gardens and a fantastic terrace restaurant (closed Sun dinner and Mon lunch). There are also double rooms (€170-200) and two- to three-person suites (€235-285) on site.

Les Olivettes
Av Henri Bosco, 84160 Lourmarin, T04 90 68 03 52, olivettes.com. 3-person apartment €690-1320/week, 4-person apartment €720-1860.
This large Provençal farmhouse has been transformed into six self-catering apartments, each with private outdoor space and Wi-Fi. La Zidane boasts a huge covered terrace and its own barbeque; La Clairette has two bathrooms, three terraces and views over the communal swimming pool. Friendly owners Elizabeth, Joe and their children have lived in the area for 15 years, and are happy to share their local knowledge.

Family Favourite
Rent the luxurious Mas du Luberon in Bonnieux, one of three South of France self-catering spots to snooze from Baby-Friendly Boltholes. See page 14 for details.

Cool & quirky

Le Domaine des Grands Prés
26220 Dieulefit, T04 75 49 94 36, lesgrandspres-dromeprovencale. com. 4-person gypsy caravans and 4-person chalets €445-725/week, 4-person yurt €295-450.
For visitors who don't mind the drive, Le Domaine is north of the Luberon's beaten track, but its unique accommodation – brightly decorated gypsy caravans, yurts and chalets – makes it well worth seeking out. There's also a simple campsite (€11-15 for 2 adults, pitch and car, €4-5 extra adult, €2-3 child (2-10), under 2s free), swimming pool and Wi-Fi.

Splashing out

Auberge de l'Aiguebrun
Domaine de la Tour, RD943, 84480 Bonnieux, T04 90 04 47 00, aubergedelaiguebrun.fr. Closed mid Nov-Feb. Doubles €140-190, triples €170-240, 4-person family suite €200-290, 2-person chalet €100-170.
In the hills 4 km outside Bonnieux's town centre, Auberge de l'Aiguebrun is blissfully removed from Provence's tourist throngs. Kids will love splashing around the pool, exploring the property's woodland stream or scouting out birds, insects and wildlife. There's an on-site spa as well as an excellent restaurant (closed Mon-Wed, dinner service for Auberge guests only).

Hôtel Cézanne
40 av Victor Hugo, T04 42 91 11 11, cezanne.hotelaix.com. Doubles €179, suite €249-310.
Perfect for hip teens, Hôtel Cézanne is Aix's trendiest spot to snooze. Bright colours and animal prints grace the ground-floor common areas, while bedrooms are more neutral, but just as funky. There's a free guest car park around the corner and a big bowl of free caramel Carambars at reception.

La Grange
Le Clos Saint Saourde, route de St Véran, 84190 Beaumes-de-Venise, T04 90 37 35 20, leclossaintsaourde. com. €2650-3950/week.
A holiday cottage that sleeps eight to ten guests, La Grange sits at the foot of Mont Ventoux. The property's main, 18th-century *mas* is now a welcoming guesthouse, while the old barn (*la grange*) has been transformed into this lovely luxury accommodation, complete with its own pool, outdoor barbeque and open fireplace. Well worth the splurge for a large group.

Eating Aix-en-Provence & the Luberon

Local goodies

As well as a sumptuous way to stock up on snacks, **markets** are a great place to learn what's grown on local farms and when it's harvested. Every week, hundreds of stalls cram the streets of **Apt** (place de la Bouquerie and around, Sat 0800-1300); between November and March, truffles are sold here. Local producers pile up peaches, slices of chunky country-style pâté and fresh walnuts in **Lourmarin** (place Henri Barthélémy, Fri 0800-1300). No matter where you're shopping, look out for locally grown olives, honey, clusters of grapes and sweet Cavaillon melons (in season each summer).

Lacking in nutrients but plenty local, **La Bonbonnière** (57 rue de la Sous-Préfecture, 84400 Apt, T04 90 74 12 92, labonbonniere84.com) is the finest spot in town to sample Apt's speciality, candied fruit. Not your taste? Nibble this confectioner's nougat, *macarons* or one of the cartoon-shaped sugar figurines instead.

Quick & simple

Aux Fines Herbes
Rue de la République, 84220 Goult, T04 32 50 23 54. Thu-Tue 1200-2100.
Off the D900 between Gordes and Roussillion, owners Johan and Martine run this laid-back little spot. Top-notch *foie gras* and tiramisu; between the lunch and dinner services there's afternoon tea and nibbles. The restaurant also showcases local artists' works.

L'Encas
Place du Château, 84220 Gordes, T04 90 72 29 82. Daily 1200-1430 and 1900-2200, closed Nov.
Just off the town's main square,

this low-key locale dishes up simple regional specialties. Two-course menus (€14) include pork *mignons* with hand-cut chips, followed by home-made apple pie topped with a scoop of ice cream. In the small dining room, head for the two tables at the back, which have great views.

Les Gourmands Disent...

17 place du Septier, 84400 Apt, T04 90 74 27 97. Mon-Sat 0830-1900.
Tables cluster around the pretty *place's* fountain, making this tea room and terrace a perfect pit stop for lunch. Mixed tasting plates (€10 each) offer a selection of themed bites, including *Provençal* (with stuffed tomatoes), *Gourmand* (with duck tart) and *Végétarien* (roasted pumpkin with lavender honey). Home-made *pâtisseries* (€4) and ice creams (€2/scoop) also on offer.

Le Pont Julien

Route Pont Julien, 84480 Bonnieux, T04 90 74 48 44, lepontjulien.com.
Daily 1200-1345, Sat-Sun 1945-2045.
Taking its name from the adjacent Roman bridge, Le Pont Julien has a limited daily menu, but all their offerings are home-made and seasonal. Isabelle and Michel d'Isoard de Chénerilles smoke their own salmon and a dedicated dessert table is piled high with sweet daily delights. There's an outdoor terrace and a kids' play area; set menus €13-27, children's menu €8.

Posh nosh

Le Fournil

5 place Carnot, 84480 Bonnieux, T04 90 75 83 62, lefournil-bonnieux.com.
Wed-Sun 1230-1400 and 1930-2130, closed late Nov to mid-Dec and mid-Jan to mid-Feb.
Chef Guy Malbec has been creating inspired Mediterranean cuisine here since 1992, mixing gourmet *plats*, like mackerel 'marmalade' served alongside lemony goat's cheese and roasted pine nuts, with home-made pasta and other more traditional dishes. The unique locale is worth a visit in its own right: the shady terrace is cool in the summer, while the interior tables are arranged inside a cosy cave that once housed the village bakery.

La Récréation

15 av Philippe de Girard, 84160 Lourmarin, T04 90 68 23 73. Thu-Tue 1200-1400 and 1930-2200.
Be sure to show up early if you plan to stake out a table in the sun: this small restaurant draws crowds with both its attractive terrace and its all-organic menu.

Cuisine is traditional Provençal; the three set menus (from €25-34) include easy-to-please items (roast chicken, melt-in-your-mouth lamb *confit*) and there's a solid wine list.

Le Table du Pré Saint Michel

Le Pré Saint Michel, route de Dauphin, Montée de la Mort d'Imbert, 04100 Manosque, T04 92 72 12 79, la-table-du-pre-saint-michel.com. Mon and Sat 1900-2200, Tue-Fri 1200-1400 and 1900-2200, Sun 1200-1400.
A gastro-address for sure, but the welcoming staff and warm ambience make this the perfect spot for foodie families. Try the sublime goat's cheese and tomato tiramisu or the comforting *œuf cocotte* topped with porcini mushrooms. Both the three-course (€25) and the children's (€11) set menus are excellent value.

For places to eat in Aix-en-Provence, see page 139.

Contents

Western Provence

Place du Palais des Papes, Avignon.

Arles.

Looking out from Avignon.

Untamed, underpopulated and just a little rough around the edges, Western Provence is a Wild West *à la française*. From the lush Sorgue River to the famous flamingos of the Parc Naturel Régional de Camargue, this natural countryside is the place for your family to cast aside urban inhibitions and plunge in.

The Rhône River is the region's backbone, and is studded with its central cities. In **Avignon**, investigate the city's massive Gothic palace, the Palais des Papes – seat of the breakaway Popes during the 14th century – Pont St-Bénézet and Ile de la Barthelasse, its green river island. It's an easy hop from here to **L'Isle-sur-la-Sorgue**, criss-crossed by canals, or **Fontaine-de-Vaucluse**, dotted with water wheels. These towns are a haven for kids keen to kayak or cycle, with cool summertime campsites surrounding both.

Vincent Van Gogh was enchanted by **Arles** (before moving on to **St-Rémy-de-Provence**), creating hundreds of canvases here at the end of the 19th century. Today, this golden city exerts a similar pull, attracting crowds of dreamy art-lovers with its huge annual international photography festival, *Les Rencontres d'Arles*. Nearby, careering around hilltop **Les Baux-de-Provence**'s sprawling abandoned castle is bags of fun.

Just north of Arles, the **Rhône** River splits into two (the Grand and Petit Rhônes), tumbling on southwards into the Mediterranean Sea. Its resulting watery delta is the **Camargue** national park, home to clouds of pink flamingos and indigenous pale-grey coloured horses. Kids will love exploring these flatlands by boat, bicycle or on foot. Make sure to look out for the French cowboys, or *gardians*, who herd up the region's wild black bulls. At the tamer end of the activity scale, the Camargue's dune-dotted beaches will appeal to tots, as they're great for building sandcastles and splashing around the shallow shores.

On the region's western frontier, elegant **Nîmes** is an oft-missed pleasure, with a towering first-century amphitheatre complete with traces of gladiator battles, sun-dappled canals and wide green gardens. **Montpellier** is home to a fantastic zoo, as well as a large university and a buzzing young population; unsurprisingly, action centres mainly on the über-cool pavement cafés of the city's Old Town.

You must

- Visit Montpellier's free Parc Zoologique Henri de Lunaret, an open-air zoo that's home to lions, giraffes and rhinos.

- Kayak under willows along the serene River Sorgue.

- Clamber around giant catapults and medieval battling rams at the abandoned Château des Baux.

- Explore the Pont du Gard near Nîmes, the tallest Roman aqueduct ever built.

- Hunt for secret chambers at Avignon's Palais des Papes.

- Cheer on Roman Olympics, gladiator battles or a Camargue bull race at Arles' Amphitheatre.

- Peer at the herons, egrets and flamingos in the Etang du Fangassier.

- Saddle up like a cowboy and gallop through the Camargue countryside.

Fun & free

Follow Van Gogh's footsteps

Track down the 21 Van Gogh artworks that waymark the *Promenade dans l'Univers de Van Gogh* countryside trail. It winds from the 8000-year-old archaeological ruins of **Glanum** (glanum.monuments-nationaux.fr) past the artist's former residence **Monastère St-Paul de Mausole** (cloitresaintpaul-valetudo.com) and into St-Rémy-de-Provence's medieval town centre. (Alternatively, pop into St-Rémy-de-Provence's Tourist Office and pick up a 'Visiting St-Rémy-de-Provence' booklet, where the walking route is neatly mapped out.) Each image has been placed in the spot where Van Gogh was standing when he painted it.

For Ted (10 months), a whirl around on a carousel always goes down a treat! Many of the South of France's cities and larger towns – including Avignon, Aigues-Mortes, Nice, Antibes and Marseilles – boast elaborate old-fashioned ones.
Ted, 10 months

The market at L'Isle-sur-la-Sorgue.

Hike to the Source

Gushing forth from the base of a 230-m cliff, the River Sorgue first sees the light of day just east of Fontaine-de-Vaucluse's centre. To find it, grab a map from the town's Tourist Office or follow these instructions: starting your walk in place de la Colonne, head uphill, keeping an eye out for the mossy water wheel outside Vallis Clausa, a functioning mill that still creates and sells traditional handmade paper. Don't miss the internal walkway, which provides great views into the pulp-filled vats. Continue along chemin de la Fontaine for another 15 minutes to reach the Sorgue's signposted source. Note that the 90 sq m/second tumble of water is only visible in spring, as the snow on nearby Mont Ventoux melts and feeds the Sorgue. During the rest of the year, this amble along the gentle river's banks still makes a pleasant afternoon out.

Hunt for tattered treasure

The **market** (every Sun, 0900-1900, more than 300 market stalls cram the streets and canals of L'Isle-sur-la-Sorgue) is best known for its high-end antique dealers, concentrated around the train station, but cheese-makers, bakers and *charcuterie* stands, plus towers of lavender pillows and olive oil soaps, cluster around the town's 13th-century Baroque church, Notre Dame des Anges. Older kids with a flair for funky fashion or unusual décor will enjoy the piles of used clothes and brocante along the pavements of avenue des Quatre Oranges.

Skate the streets of Montpellier

Rando Roller (place du Nombre d'Or, 34000 Montpellier, rim.fr.cc, first Fri of the month, at 2045). Pack your rollerblades, helmet and protective pads and join this two-hour, 20-km rollerblading tour through the streets of Montpellier. Under 16s must be accompanied by an adult, and all participants must know how to skate, turn, brake and stop.

Talk to the animals

Parc Zoologique Henri de Lunaret (50 av Agropolis, 34090 Montpellier, T04 67 54 45 23, zoo.montpellier.fr. Mid Apr-Oct, Tue-Sun, Jul-Aug also open Mon 1000-1900, Nov to mid-Apr 1000-1700. Tram no 1 to St-Eloi, then shuttle bus no 22 to Zoo). North of Montpellier's historic old town, this 80-ha, open-air zoo houses over 90 species of animals, including lions, zebras, giraffes and rhinos, with more than 11 km of trails that wind beneath the fenced-off enclosures. Itching to see more exotic beasties? Pay the entrance fee and enter France's largest greenhouse, the excellent *Serre Amazonienne* (Amazonian Greenhouse, €6 adult, €3.50 12-18 years, €2.50 child (6-12), under 6s free), home to scary crocodiles and the blue poison dart frog. The Restaurant AmaZOOne (restaurant-amazoone.fr) is on site; alternatively, pack a hamper and lunch in one of the park's many picnic areas.

Take a walk in the park

Jardins de la Fontaine (30000 Nîmes. Apr to mid-Sep 0730-2200, mid-Sep to Mar 0730-1830). To reach these beautifully sculpted French gardens, follow sun-dappled quai de la Fontaine westwards from square Antonin. A ring of canals converges at the park's entrance, and elderly *pétanque* players cluster in place Picasso. Spot the swans nesting below the gardens' bridges, or scramble around the mysterious Temple de Diane, a 2000-year-old shrine built on the site of an ancient spring. Up the sweeping staircase sits the perched **Tour Magne** (daily Jul-Aug 0900-2000, Jun 0900-1900, Apr-May 0930-1830, Sep 0930-1300 and 1400-1830, Mar and Oct 0930-1300 and 1400-1800, Nov-Feb 0930-1300 and 1400-1630, €2.70 adult, €2.30 child (7-17), under 7s free), the city's 32-m Roman tower.

A sensible distance from the crocodiles at Montpellier zoo.

Action stations

Cycling
Commavélo

28 rue Emile Jamais, 30900 Nîmes,
T04 66 29 19 68, commavelo.com.
Bicycle rental half day from €7 adult,
€5 child's bike (135-155 cm), baby
seats €2/day, helmets provided.
Commavélo also organizes half-
day to week-long tours of Nîmes,
Pont du Gard and the Camargue.

Provence à Vélo

provence-cycling.co.uk (English),
provence-a-velo.fr (French).
An excellent resource for bike
rental agencies and cycle routes
around Avignon, Châteauneuf-
du-Pape and the River Sorgue,
as well as the Luberon and
Mont Ventoux (see page 131).
Itineraries range from an easy
2 km to lengthy climbs.

Vélo Provence

velo-provence.com.
Bicycle rental agencies and
directions for circuits around
Fontaine-de-Vaucluse and L'Isle-
sur-la-Sorgue, including routes
that take in the Galas Aqueduct.
Some of the website is in French,
but the downloadable routes
are bilingual. For cycling in the
Camargue, see page 164.

Hot-air ballooning
Les Montgolfières du Sud

64 rue Sigalon, 30700 Uzès, T04 66
37 28 02, sudmontgolfiere.com. €230
adult, €130 under 12s, minimum
height 1.20 m.

Year-round, hour-long hot-air balloon rides over Western Provence, with dawn departures. Allow three to four hours launch, flight time and landing. Flights over Pont du Gard and Gorges du Verdon (Oct-Mar by reservation, minimum age 12, minimum height 1.30 m, €375) also available.

Kayaking
Alpha Bateaux
Route des Gorges de l'Ardèche, 07150 Vallon-Pont-d'Arc, T04 75 88 08 29, canoeardeche.com. Easter-Sep. Minimum age 7, life vests provided but ability to swim essential. Half-day mini-descent (8 km) €18 adult, €9 child (7-12), 1-day descent (24-32 km) €29 adult, €14.50 child (7-12); 2- to 3-day trips also available.
Northwest of Avignon, the Ardèche River spent millennia wearing a deep groove into the limestone cliffs that flank its banks, eventually forming the 30-km-long canyon, the Gorges de l'Ardèche. Setting off from the Pont d'Arc, a 65-m natural stone archway, Alpha Bateaux operates a range of kayaking trips through this nature reserve. Keep an eye out for rare birds, including eagles and falcons; note that river rapids are at their roughest in early spring.
The Vallon Pont d'Arc & des Gorges de l'Ardèche Tourist Office (vallon-pont-darc.com) provides plenty of great links to guided walks, rock climbing and various water sports along the Gorges de l'Ardèche.

Treetop adventure courses

Itching to swing on wooden bridges, scramble through ropy spider webs and slip down chutes? Or ready to simply release your Tarzan and Jane to burn off buckets of pent-up energy? Look out for treetop adventure courses, popular throughout Western Provence. After a brief initiation and donning of protective gear, the forest canopy's the limit.

Two favourites include:

Passerelles des Cimes
Les Basses Capianes, 84800 Lagnes, T04 90 38 56 87, parcours-aerien. fr. Jul-Aug daily, Mar-Jun and Sep-Oct Sat-Sun and holidays, advance reservation required. Grands Parcours €18 per person, Petits Parcours €12 per person.
Five different woodland courses, plus a dedicated area for little ones. To tackle the Grands Parcours (allow 2½ hours) kids must be over 1.40 m and 9 years or older; Petits Parcours (allow 1½ hours), from 1.10 m and 6 years. Helmets and gloves are provided.

Les Rochers de Maguelone
Chemin de la Diligence, 34750 Villeneuve-lès-Maguelone, T04 27 04 44 44, les-rochers-de-maguelone.com. Jul-Aug daily 1000-1900, 2100-2400 by reservation, Apr-Jun and Sep to mid-Oct Wed and Sat 1300-1900, Sun 1000-1900, mid-Feb to mid-Mar and mid-Oct to mid-Nov Wed, Sat & Sun 1330-1800. €22.50 adult, €17.50 height 1.26 m to 14 years, €15 child (3 years to height 1.25 m).
Eighteen different adventure courses, ranging from gentle forest hikes and toboggan chutes to treetop suspension bridges and a 200-m zip line.

For other adventure courses in the South of France, see page 22.

Kayak Vert
Quartier la Baume, 84800 Fontaine-de-Vaucluse, T04 90 20 35 44, canoe-france.com. Late Apr-end Oct. Minimum age 6, life vests provided but ability to swim essential. Large canoe (2 adults and 2 under 8s) €45, standard canoe (2 adults and 1 under 8) €34, 1-person adult kayak €17, child's kayak (8 years and older) €14.
This two-hour, 8-km trip along the River Sorgue begins in Fontaine-de-Vaucluse and finishes in L'Isle-sur-la-Sorgue. Group leaders are on hand to tote the kayaks across two dams, and rates include the bus ride back to your Fontaine-de-Vaucluse starting point. See page 22 for further details. For kayaking in the Camargue, see page 164; for the Pont du Gard, see page 154.

Out & about Western Provence

Arènes de Nîmes

30000 Nîmes, T04 66 21 82 56,
arenes-nimes.com. Daily Jul-Aug
0900-2000, Jun 0900-1900, Apr-May
and Sep 0900-1830, Mar and Oct
0900-1800, Nov-Feb 0930-1700.
€7.80 adult, €5.90 child (7-17). Nîmes
Romaine Ticket (Arènes, Maison
Carrée and Tour Magne) €9.90 adult,
€7.60 child (7-17), Nîmes Romaine
Ticket and Château des Baux €14.80
adult, €10.70 child (7-17), second
child 7-17 and under 7s free, free
audioguide.

Nîmes' Roman amphitheatre
was constructed between
AD 90 and 120, serving as
a massive stage for *venatio*:
brawls between man and beast,
including lions, rhinos and bears,
and battles between gladiators.
During your visit, tasty trivia is
provided via the exceptionally
detailed audioguide (eg the
arena's sand floor was used
to soak up blood, and the
sand had to be raked several
times during performances
so the stench wouldn't make
spectators feel sick). Don't miss
the *Quartier des Gladiateurs*, a
gladiator changing room turned
mini-museum, stocked with
shields, helmets and gladiator
film excerpts. Nearby, there's
a room dedicated to *corridas*,
or bullfights, a popular use for
the amphitheatre throughout
the 20th century. To learn
more, Nîmes' *Maison Carrée*, a
first-century AD square building

Arènes de Nîmes.

in the Old Town, shows a 3D
film covering local history from
ancient times to the present

Note some steps in the
Arènes are steep and uneven,
and may be a little difficult for
young children.

Château des Baux

13520 Les Baux-de-Provence, T04 90
54 55 56, chateau-baux-provence.
com. Summer 0900-2030, autumn
0930-1800, winter 0930-1700, spring
0900-1830. €7.80 adult, €5.70 child
(7-17), Château plus Nîmes' Arènes,
Maison Carrée and Tour Magne
€14.80 adult, €10.70 child (7-17),
second child 7-17 and under 7s free,
free audioguide.

Built during the 10th century
by the Lords of Les Baux, the
crumbling ruins of Château
des Baux are perched atop an

Alpilles mountain peak. From
the moment the Château's first
foundation stone was laid, this
perfect military vantage point
– with its clear views over the
surrounding countryside and
the Mediterranean Sea – has
been a source of contention,
battled over by French kings
and coveted by Monaco's rich
Grimaldi family. It was eventually
destroyed on the orders of King
Louis XIII in 1633, and remained
abandoned and forgotten until
the early 20th century.

Today, visitors to the former
fortress will need to park
outside Les Baux's walled
village, then head uphill to the
ruins through the town's narrow,
pale stone streets. Inside the
Château grounds, giant replica
catapults, battering rams and

The Haribo Museum.

medieval siege weapons are displayed among the dungeon, Saracen and Paravelle towers, Chapelle St-Blaise and a squat windmill. Seven- to 12-year-olds are encouraged to discover more about the Château's history using a free treasure hunt and puzzle booklet.

Note that during winter, the mistral winds can be extremely gusty here and children should stay well away from the steep drops that surround the Château.

Les Grottes de Thouzon

2083 route d'Orange, 84250 Le Thor, T04 90 33 93 65, grottes-thouzon. com. Daily Jul-Aug 1000-1830, Apr-Jun and Sep-Oct 1000-1200 and 1400-1800, Mar Sun 1400-1800. 45-min guided tours, last tour

departs 30 mins before closing time. €8.20 adults and over 12s, €5.60 child (5-11), under 5s free. Advertised as an unbeatable "six million years of history in 5 minutes", these limestone caves were discovered in 1902 during local quarrying. Today, guided visits explore the shimmery stalactite-lined caverns; tours are in French, with informative handouts in English. Be sure to pack a jumper, as the cave is a brisk 13°C year-round.

Musée du Bonbon Haribo

Pont des Charrettes, 30700 Uzès, T04 66 22 74 39, haribo.com. Daily Jul 1000-1900, Aug 1000-2000, Sep-Jun Tue-Sun 1000-1300 and 1400-1800, closed 3 weeks in Jan. Last entry 1 hr before closing. €6 adult, €4 child (5-15), under 5s free.

A dreamy museum dedicated entirely to sweets. Just south of the medieval town of Uzès, this interactive spot tracks the history and production methods of Swiss candy maker Haribo. A token included in the entrance fee allows kids to magically activate one of the Willy Wonka-esque machines, filling four small bags (yes, four!) with a veritable *dégustation* of liquorice torpedoes. Looking for a more extreme sugar high? Fear not, the on-site boutique is stocked with heavily discounted cola bottles, faux fried eggs and gummi bears.

Don't miss Pont du Gard

30210 Vers-Pont-du-Gard, T04 66 37 50 99, pontdugard.fr.
Entrance to site free year-round. Mar-Oct €15 parking for
1 car, plus entrance to Museum, Ludo and Cinema for up
to five visitors; Nov-Feb €10 parking for 1 car.

The Pont du Gard is the king of all aqueducts.
Both a bridge straddling the Gardon River and
a supremely sophisticated water-channelling
structure, at a skyscraping 49 m it's also the
tallest Roman aqueduct ever built. The site is free,
although it's necessary to pay for parking and
entrance to the on-site cultural activities.

Rive Droite & Rive Gauche
The Pont du Gard is composed of three levels
of limestone arches of varying sizes. Visitors can
walk over the lower level to explore both banks
of the river. Access to the bridge is wide, and easy
to navigate with pushchairs. The more energetic
can scale the Rive Droite side right up to the
top level (signposted) for a bird's-eye peek at
the monument.

On the Rive Gauche, a **Museum** charts the
Pont du Gard's history. The **Ludo** children's centre
targets five- to 12-year-olds with archaeological,
Roman and environmental interactive games and
role-play. Between the two, the **Cinema** screens
the 25-minute fictionalized history film, Le Vaisseau
du Gardon (Vessel on the Gardon). The Museum,
Ludo and Cinema are open daily May-September
0930-1900, March-April and October 0930-1730;
entrance to each is part of the package fee (ie free
with parking) above.

Both riverbanks boast restaurants. The Rive
Droite's **Les Terrasses** (T04 66 37 50 88) serves
various plats du jour (€15) and a children's menu
(€9.50). On the Rive Gauche, there's a small
crêperie opposite the Museum's entrance. But the
prettiest dining spot is definitely **Le Vieux Moulin**
(T04 66 37 14 35, vieuxmoulinpontdugard.com,
opening days vary according to season 1200-1430
and 1900-2100; see also page 169), a former mill
house, now a hotel-restaurant with gorgeous
views over the Gardon River.

The Gardon River
Visitors are encouraged to explore the Gardon
River too. For half-day kayak trips, contact **Kayak
Vert** (Berges du Gardon, 30210 Collias, T04 66 22
80 76 canoe-france.com, Mar-Oct, minimum age
6, life vests provided but ability to swim essential;
€20 adult, €10 child (6-12)). The simple 8-km
paddle begins in nearby Collias, finishing with a
float beneath the Pont du Gard itself. Rates include
the bus ride back to the Collias starting point.

Alternatively, pack a picnic and swimming
costumes, then stake out one of the small, pebbly
beaches that flank the Gardon. Lifeguards are
present on the large Rive Droite beach area during
July and August. Along the riverbanks, look out
for herons, kingfishers and egrets. Keep your eyes
peeled and you may even spot a beaver, or a
Bonelli's eagle soaring overhead.

The countryside
Mémoires de Garrigue (Garrigue Memories) is a 15-
ha open-air exhibition in the countryside behind
the Rive Gauche. Taking its name from garrigue,
mixed scrubby vegetation that includes bushy
oak, wild thyme and lavender, the landscaped area
demonstrates the dependence of local agriculture
on the nearby aqueduct. A guidebook to this area
(€4) can be purchased from the Pont du Gard
reception desk.

Getting there
There are two car parks on the site: the Rive Droite
and the Rive Gauche. The latter is just off the D981,
handy if you're planning to continue on to Uzès.

If you don't have your own transport, public
buses to Pont du Gard depart from the gare
routière (bus station) in Nîmes. Buses are very
infrequent outside of summer. Alternatively, join
one of **Provence Reservation**'s tours (provence-
reservation.com, €55 half day, €100 full day). Tours
depart from Arles mid-April to mid-September and
from Avignon year round.

Fun facts

What? The Pont du Gard was a portion of the 50 km-long Nîmes aqueduct, which sourced water from springs at Eure, near Uzès, and channelled it to the Roman city of Nîmes.

How? Through a tiny inclination in the aqueduct's angle – a decrease of just 12 m over its full 50-km length – the incredible aqueduct was able to shift water through gravity alone.

How much? At its peak, the aqueduct transported 30 million litres of water a day!

Why? The water was used for irrigation of farmers' fields en route, then thermal baths, under-floor heating and a complex sewage system in Nîmes.

When? The aqueduct was constructed between AD 40 and 60, and was essential to local livelihood until the sixth century, when it was abandoned. The Pont du Gard portion of the aqueduct was restored during the late 19th and early 20th centuries, although water no longer flows over it, and it's now a UNESCO World Heritage Site.

A perfect place for contemplation at the majestic Pont du Gard.

Avignon

Built under Pope Benedict XII and Pope Clement VI during the city's 70-year stint as the Catholic papal headquarters, the Gothic **Palais des Papes** is Avignon's main attraction. For any child – or indeed grown-up – with fairy-tale fantasies, the enormous palace, with secret chambers, is a delight to explore.

But impressive as the palace is, Avignon can offer its more energetic visitors so much more. Check out the nearby **Pont St-Bénézet** from below, kayaking your way along the Rhône River. Spend an afternoon in **Rocher des Doms**, Avignon's hilltop park with dazzling views. Or hop aboard the free shuttle boat that ferries families (and bikes) across the river to the quiet island of Île de la Barthelasse.

Get your bearings

Although Avignon's centre is walled and easy to navigate on foot, note that the enclosed town is relatively large. Ditch the car at **Parking de l'Ile Piot** (over the bridge Pont Edouard Daladier) then hop aboard the free shuttle bus to the city centre (every 10-20 mins). Avignon has two train stations: the **Gare Avignon TGV** is a 10-minute bus ride (tcra. fr, €1.20 adult, under 6s free, 10-min journey, departures every 20 mins) from downtown, while the **Gare Avignon Centre** is just outside Porte de la République. Dip through this gate into the city and along cours Jean Jaurès to visit the central **Tourist Office** (41 cours Jean Jaurès, T04 32 74 32 74, ot-avignon.fr, Jul daily 0900-1900, Apr-Jun and Aug-Oct Mon-Sat 0900-1800, Sun 0945-1700, Nov-Mar Mon-Fri 0900-1800, Sat 0900-1700, Sun 1000-1200). Continue northwards to **place de l'Horloge** (home to an antique carousel, daily mid-Jun to Aug 1100-2330, Sep to mid-Jun 1330-1900) and the **Palais des Papes**.

For an effortless overview of the city, Avignon's **Petit Train** (with multilingual commentary including English, petittrainavignon.fr, Jul-Aug daily 1000-2000, mid-Mar to Jun and Sep-Oct daily 1000-1900, Nov to mid-Mar Wed and Sat 1400-1800, €7 adult, €4 child (4-9), under 4s free) makes a 40-minute loop around much of the Old Town, departing from place du Palais des Papes every half hour.

Fun & free

Teetering between place du Palais des Papes and the **Rhône, Jardin du Rocher des Doms** (daily Jun-Aug 0730-2100, Apr-May and Sep 0730-2000, Mar 0730-1900, Oct 0730-1830, Nov and Feb 0730-1800, Dec-Jan 0730-1730) is a lovely spot to while away an hour or two. Trim gardens surround a pond packed with koi carp, ducks and geese. Amble past the park's vineyard to take in the views over Pont St-Bénézet, Ile de la Barthelasse and Villeneuve-lez-Avignon, then explore a portion of the city ramparts (access on to Pont-St-Bénézet open daily Aug 0900-2000, Jul and Sep 0900-1900, Mar-May and Oct 0900-1800, Nov-Feb 0900-1700).

Looking to prolong the peace? Little ones can pedal the miniature tricycles drawn by toy horses (daily during summer, year-round Wed and Sat-Sun, ages 1-8, €2.50/10 mins, €6/30 mins), while older kids will love the chunky four-wheelers (ages 6-12, same times and prices). Parents can park themselves at the pond-side café, **Buvette** (open daylight hours), for a glass of local wine (€2).

Float over to Ile de la Barthelasse for a peek at Avignon's medieval outline from afar. A free **shuttle boat** (daily Jul-Aug 1100-2100, Apr-Jun and Sep 1000-1230 and 1400-1830, Oct-Dec and mid-Feb to Mar Wed 1400-1730, Sat-Sun and holidays 1000-1200 and 1400-1730) runs every 10 minutes or so between Avignon's quai de la Ligne and the island. The latter's riverfront promenade makes a great place for a picnic, while skateboarders and bladers can roll over to the free **skate park** just near the Parking de L'Ile Piot.

Action stations

Explore Avignon from the seat of a **Vélopop** (velopop.fr) bicycle. A bike-sharing scheme suitable for teens or adults (one size only with adjustable seat), Vélopop passes can be purchased by the day (€1) or week (€3). Use of any of the city's 200 bikes is free for up to 30 minutes at a time, then €1 per additional half hour. Tool around town, or pick up a cycling map for **Ile de la Barthelasse** from the Tourist Office.

Too hot to pedal? Spend the day swimming, splashing and lounging in the hammocks at **Piscine Palmeraie** (135 allée Antoine Pinay, Ile de la

Let's go to... Avignon

Barthelasse, T04 90 82 54 25, clublapalmeraie.com, mid-Jun to mid-Sep daily 1000-2000, €10 adult, €6 child 5-17 years, €4 child 2-4 years, under 2s free, free Wi-Fi). The on-site restaurant serves snacks all day and meals at midday and in the evening.

Otherwise, get paddling. Rent a kayak from **Balade Kayak** (on the west side of Pont Edouard Daladier, T04 26 03 17 25, kayak-avignon.fr, Jul-Aug daily 1400-1830, life vests provided but ability to swim essential; 1-person kayak €6/30 mins, €9/hr, 2-person kayak €10/30 mins, €15/hr; under 9s free in parents' kayak) and explore Pont St-Bénézet, or simply drift along the Rhône.

Hit the town

Allow at least a couple of hours to explore the vast **Palais des Papes** (place du Palais des Papes, T04 90 27 50 00, palais-des-papes.com, daily Jul and first 2 weeks Sep 0900-2000, Aug

0900-2100, mid-Mar to Jun and mid-Sep to Oct 0900-1900, Nov-Feb 0930-1745, ticket desks close 1 hr earlier; Mar to mid-Nov €10.50 adult, €8.50 child (8-17), Palais and Pont €13 adult, €10 child (8-17); mid-Nov to Feb €8.50 adult, €7 child (8-17), Palais and Pont €11 adult, €8.50 child (8-17); 3rd child and under 8s free, free audioguide). The audioguide commentary ranges from informative to obscure, as you're guided through the *Palais Vieux* (Old Palace), Treasury – with recessed floors for the aforementioned treasure – and on to the vine-frescoed Pope's Chamber. Passing into the *Palais Neuf* (New Palace), the opulent *Chambre du Cerf* (Stag's Room) is decked out in floor-to-ceiling frescos, all 500-year-old hunting and fishing scenes. Any excess energy can be safely burnt scaling the steep stairs up to the palace's panoramic viewing platform. Last is a dash through

the Great Audience Hall, before you're funnelled into La Bouteillerie wine shop and then through the palace gift shop, the latter well stocked with dart-shooting crossbows, music boxes and medieval-themed colouring books.

Head down to the banks of the Rhône to explore Avignon's other star attraction, the **Pont St-Bénézet** (rue Ferruce, entrance to left of Porte du Rhône, T04 90 27 51 16, palais-des-papes.com, daily Jul and first 2 weeks Sep 0900-2000, Aug 0900-2100, mid-Mar to Jun and mid-Sep to Oct 0900-1900, Nov-Feb 0930-1745 (ticket desks close 1 hr earlier); Mar to mid-Nov €4.50 adult, €3.50 child (8-17), Palais and Pont €13 adult, €10 child (8-17); mid-Nov to Feb €4 adult, €3 child (8-17), Palais and Pont €11 adult, €8.50 child (8-17); 3rd child and under 8s free, free audioguide). Half a bridge poking out over the river, Pont St-Bénézet is named after Bénézet, a 12th-century shepherd instructed by God to spearhead its building. Today the bridge is best known as the inspiration for the 18th-century hit, composer Pierre Certon's song *Sur le Pont d'Avignon*.

For aspiring chefs, **Hôtel de La Mirande's** much sought after cooking school, **Le Marmiton** (4 place de la Mirande, 84000, T04 90 14 20 20, lamirande-avignon.com), runs fun children's workshops (usually one per month, Wed 1530-1830, €46,

minimum age 6). Bilingual classes take place in the 19th-century kitchen; kid-friendly menus cover burgers and chocolate lollies. Reserve well in advance, as classes are limited to 12 students.

Take a cruise

Get out of town with a cruise along the Rhône. **Les Croisières Mireio** (Allées de l'Oulle, 84000, T04 90 85 62 25, mireio.net) offer four different day-long cruises (4-6 daytime cruises most weeks, see website for calendar; €48-65 adult, €25-29 under 12s, under 2s free, 1 under 12 free with every paying adult on Wed). Best for families are Croisière du Royaume, which includes a two-hour stop in the nearby town of Villeneuve-lez-Avignon, and Croisière en Arles, which gives passengers a similar amount of time to explore Arles. Cruises include lunch on board.

Between April and September, Les Croisières Mireio also organize 45-minute **bateaux promenades**, sightseeing trips that loop around the southern tip of Ile de la Barthelasse (Jul-Aug daily 1400, 1500, 1600, 1700 and 1800, Apr-Jun and Sep 1500 and 1615, €8 adult, under 8s free).

Grab a bite

Pick up picnic goodies at **Les Halles** (place Pie, Tue-Fri 0600-1330, Sat-Sun 0600-1400; free cooking demonstrations by local chefs Sat 1100), Avignon's covered market. The exterior of the building is covered with a neat 30-m vertical garden, the first of its kind in France.

Tartines, or open-faced sandwiches (approx €4-7), are the specialty at **Ginette et Marcel** (place des Corps Saints, T04 90 85 58 70, daily 1100-2330), with toppings that range from avocado, anchovy and hard-boiled egg to goat's cheese and thyme. A chalkboard lists eight types of home-made cakes daily, and there's a selection of child-friendly afternoon snacks (eg bowl of cornflakes, €1.70).

For interactive dining, it's hard to beat Japanese barbeque specialist **Tanoshii** (8 rue Galante, 84000, T04 90 85 59 43, Tue-Sat 1200-1400 and 1900-2300): each

table is furnished with its own grill, where you're able to sear your fish or meat (approx €20 per mixed plate) to your liking.

Seek out **L'Epicerie** (10 place St-Pierre, 84000, T04 90 82 74 22, Mon-Sat 1200-1430 and 1930-2230), a hard-to-find terraced restaurant in a square outside Eglise St-Pierre. The menu is pan-Mediterranean, and large mixed plates are good for sampling.

Swish **La Vache à Carreaux** (14 rue de la Peyrolerie, T04 90 80 09 05, vache-carreaux.com, Sun-Fri 1230-1430, daily 1930-2330) is a haven for all things cheesy, including duck topped with Manchego and Camembert.

Fashionable plates-in-training will enjoy the atmosphere at **La Cour d'Honneur** (58 rue Joseph Vernet, T04 90 86 64 53, cour-honneur.com, Wed-Mon 1200-1430 and 1900-2230), located inside a walled garden on rue Joseph Vernet.

Arles

A vibrant town that feels a little more like Spain than Provence, Arles boasts a great mix of pedestrian *places*, Roman ruins and modern art. Vincent Van Gogh painted almost 200 canvases here between 1888-89. Today, the arty feeling continues with Arles' annual photography festival, **Les Rencontres d'Arles** (rencontres-arles.com, adult prices vary, under 18s free), making Arles an appealing place to visit with teens.

Get your bearings
On the banks of the Rhône River, much of Arles' picturesque Old Town is pedestrianized. If you've arrived by car, follow signs for the **Tourist Office** (bd des Lices, T04 90 18 41 20, arlestourisme. com, Apr-Sep daily 0900-1845, Oct-Mar Mon-Sat 0900-1645, Sun 1000-1300), then park your wheels one block eastwards at **Parking du Centre** (also bd des Lices). The free **Starlette shuttle bus** (laboutiquedestransports. com) runs between the train station (av Paulin Talabot, T36 35),

a 10-minute walk from the city centre, and the **Tourist Office**.

Note that all museums and monuments in Arles are free for under 18s. For adults, the city offers three different multi-entrance passes, of which the most useful is the **Passeport Liberté** (€9, allows entry to five sights, including at least one museum and no more than four monuments).

Ancient ruins
Rising sharply from the narrow alleys of Arles' Old Town, the **Amphithéâtre** (rond-point des Arènes, T04 90 49 59 05, arenes-arles.com, daily May-Sep 0900-1900 (Wed Jul-Aug until 1500), Mar-Apr and Oct 0900-1800, Nov-Feb 1000-1700, ticket desk closes 30 mins earlier; €6 adult, under 18s free, ticket also allows entrance to the Théâtre Antique) was constructed around AD 90, and inspired by Rome's Coliseum. During its heyday, audiences of 20,000 poured into the colossal structure to watch gladiator swordfights, violent battles and staged hunts.

Today, the amphitheatre continues to draw crowds by the thousand. Poke around the *cavea* (tiers of benched seating), then clamber up to the tower to check out the precipitous rooftop views. During July and August, you can watch **Camargue bull races** (Wed 1730, €9, €4 child (6-12), under 6s free). In 2010, the amphitheatre launched its new summertime **Roman Olympics** revival (Jul-Aug Tue and Thu 0930); on the same days, **gladiator fights** are staged from 1630 until closing. Both of these performances are included in the ticket price.

Arles' 2000-year-old **Théâtre Antique** (rue du Cloître, T04 90 49 59 05, daily May-Sep 0900-1900, Oct 0900-1200 and 1400-1800, Nov-Feb 1000-1200 and 1400-1700, Mar-Apr 0900-1800, ticket desk closes 30 mins earlier; entrance free with Amphithéâtre ticket) is just a short hop south of here. It may not woo the little ones, but it was here in 1651 that the instantly recognizable, apple-holding Venus sculpture

(first century BC, now in the Louvre) was discovered during construction of a well. The theatre's ground-floor stage and inclined seating makes a great pit stop for an impromptu performance or two.

Sunflower city

It's impossible to visit Arles without running into Van Gogh. He lived here, painted here, is believed to have loved here and definitely cut off his ear here. If you're in the company of equally tormented artists, head to the **Van Gogh Café** in place du Forum (which featured in *Le Café de Nuit*) and **Espace Van Gogh** (place Docteur Félix Rey, T04 90 49 39 39, mediatheque.ville-arles. fr; free access to the courtyard). The latter was formerly the hospital Hôtel-Dieu, where Van Gogh was rushed for emergency treatment after taking a razor to his ear. It's now a multimedia

library and exhibition centre. For the more adventurous, **'Van Gogh's bridge'** (which he painted in *Le Pont de Langlois*) is a half-hour's walk south of town, following the pretty Canal d'Arles.

To learn more about the post-Impressionist painter, the Tourist Office organizes a weekly **Vincent Van Gogh Walking Tour** (2 hrs, Jul-Sep Sat 1700, €6 adult, €3 child (12-18), under 12s free).

Grab a bite

For lunch on the go, **Comptoir du Sud** (2 rue Jean Jaurès, T04 90 96 22 17, Tue-Fri 1000-1800) has piles of top-notch sandwiches for around €4 apiece. On a tiny terrace in the shadow of the Amphithéâtre, **La Maison des Gourmands** (28 rond-point des Arènes, T04 90 93 19 38, lamaisondesgourmands.fr, Jul-Aug daily 0830-2200, Apr-Jun and Sep-Oct Fri-Wed 0930-1830, Nov-Mar Sat-Wed 1100-1800) dishes up crêpes, ice cream sundaes, pots of tea and 37 types of hot chocolate. Looking to splash out? Head to **A Coté** (21 rue des Carmes, T04 90 47 61 13, bistro-acote.com, daily 1200-2400, cold plates only from 1500-1930), the low-key bistro owned by Michelin-starred chef Jean-Luc Rabanel. Try his tasty tapas, *menu du jour* or opt for a glass of local wine (from €2.50). And for picky eaters, the menu features a range of sandwiches, including plain old ham.

Clockwise starting top right: little pockets of life and colour line the streets everywhere in Arles; Le Brasserie in the old part of town; the town hall sits proudly; find your bearings at the Place Hotel de Ville.

The Camargue

The **Parc Naturel Régional de Camargue** is Western Europe's largest river delta. Squeezed between the triangular embrace of the River Rhône's arms – the Grand and Petit Rhônes – the Camargue encompasses 930 sq km of marshland. It's also one of France's 44 national parks, and home to vast *étangs* (shallow saline lakes), fresh water reed beds and salt marshes, as well as hundreds of bird species (including flamingos), indigenous bulls and whitish-grey horses. It may be teeming with wildlife, but other than *gardians* (Camargue cowboys), humans are the minority here. Its three largest towns, Stes-Maries-de-la-Mer, Aigues-Mortes and Le Grau-du-Roi, count fewer than 15,000 permanent residents among them.

Named for Ste Marie-Jacobé and Ste Marie-Salomé, who arrived here by boat along with Ste Sara during the first century AD, the tiny town of **Stes-Maries-de-la-Mer** is most famous for its annual **Pèlerinage des Gitans** (24-25 May). Two days of festivities celebrate Ste Sara, the Romany gypsies' patron saint: her statue, housed in the town's **Eglise Forteresse**, is paraded from the church down to the sea, coupled with riotous evenings of singing and dancing. If you miss the party, visit Ste Sara in the church's subterranean crypt, or check out the sea views from the **panoramic terrace** (daily 1000-1200 and 1400-sunset,

€2 adult, €1.50 child (6-12), under 6s free).

Sitting on the Camargue's western edge, it would be hard for the 13th-century town of **Aigues-Mortes** to be any prettier. Around 1.6 km of perfectly preserved **ramparts** (T04 66 53 61 55, May-Aug 1000-1900, Sep-Apr 1000-1730, ticket desk closes 45 mins earlier, €7 adult, under 18s free) ring the

Tourist information offices

Aigues-Mortes 30220, place St-Louis, T04 66 53 73 00, ot-aiguesmortes.fr. Jul-Aug Mon-Fri 0900-2000, Sat-Sun 1000-2000, Apr-Jun and Sep Mon-Fri 0900-1900, Sat-Sun 1000-1900, Oct-Mar Mon-Fri 0900-1230 and 1330-1800, Sat-Sun 0900-1300 and 1400-1800.

Le Grau-du-Roi 30240, rue Michel Rédarès, T04 66 51 67 70, vacances-en-camargue.com. Daily Jul-Aug 0900-2100, Jun 0900-2000, May and Sep 0900-1900, Oct-Apr 0900-1215 and 1400-1800.

Stes-Maries-de-la-mer 13460, 5 av Van Gogh, T04 90 97 82 55, saintesmaries.com, daily Jul-Aug 0900-2000, Apr-Jun and Sep 0900-1900, Mar and Oct 0900-1800, Nov-Feb 0900-1700.

town, offering stunning views over the countryside from the top of the **Tour de Constance**. South of the town, coral-coloured salt marshes are dotted with pink flamingos, eventually merging into the seaside resort of **Le Grau-du-Roi**.

Come summertime, the whole of the Camargue is flooded with nature-lovers. Visitors of all ages strike out on foot, bike and horseback to explore the region's inland lagoons or spend long days dipping in and out of the sea from its wild beaches. Relaxed and just a little unkempt, the Camargue makes a welcome antidote to the South of France's more polished urban areas.

Fun & free

With a little advance preparation, it's easy to explore much of the Camargue independently. A **free map** of the region is available in English from any local Tourist Office, and is marked with scenic drives,

plus routes to walk and cycle. Seek out the rosy-hued salt marshes for a stroll, or hike to **Phare de la Gacholle** (Sat-Sun and holidays 1100-1700), a lighthouse built in 1882. Bring your binoculars for a peek at the **Etang du Fangassier**, home to a massive colony of pink flamingos and their only breeding ground in France.

Owned by drinks magnate Paul Ricard, the **Domaine de Méjanes** (13200 Arles, T04 90 97 10 10, mejanes.camargue. fr, free parking) was a pioneer in rice cultivation, planting paddies in 1940 to boost local employment. Today, the 1200-ha estate boasts the *Sentier du Vaccarès*, an easy wildlife walk (2.5 km), plus picnic areas and an on-site restaurant. Willing to spend a little on site? Prolong the fun with a pony ride (€4/15 mins), a pedal around (€4/hr) or a loop on the *petit train* (Mar-Nov, 25 mins, €4 adult, €3 child (5-10), under 5s free) that winds its way around the property.

Best beaches

If the mere thought of squeezing your towel among throngs of beach-goers makes you want to pack up the family and head home, the Camargue's coastline is for you. This Mediterranean-skirting region boasts more than 50 km of beaches, most of them wild, windy and without facilities. Just south of Le Grau-du-Roi, deep, dune-dotted **Plage de l'Espiguette** is a prime example of the region's untamed beauty. East of Stes-Maries, **Plage de Beauduc** is a long, sandy strip backed by salt marshes, requiring more than a little dedication to reach. Be sure to hit either beach with a stash of ample drinking water and plenty of snacks.

Off the beaten track The Camargue

Action stations

The Camargue's terrain is flat, making it a cinch to explore by **bicycle**. Just outside Aigues-Mortes' ramparts, **BV Location** (7 rue du Vidourle, 30220, T06 67 44 78 16, from €7/day) stocks sturdy mountain bikes. A lovely cycle path edges the northwest side of the canal running south, all the way to Le Grau-du-Roi. In Stes-Maries, rent your wheels at **Le Vélo Saintois** (19 rue de la République, T04 90 97 74 56, levelosaintois.camargue.fr, €15/day adult, €13.50/day children's bikes 16 in-24 in). They also provide free flyers detailing five cycle circuits around the area.

Make like the Camargue cowboys and **saddle up** one the region's indigenous pale grey horses and gallop off into the sunset. **Tamaris** (route d'Arles, 13460 Stes-Maries, T04 90 49 67 78, ballades-tamaris. camargue.fr, €20/1½ hrs, €40/half day) offers hour-long beginner's rides, half-day and full day tours, combination boat trips and horse riding with barbequed lunch. **Domaine de Méjanes** (T04 90 97 10 62, €15/hr, €41/half day) runs similar *étang* explorations on horseback. Les **Cabanes de Cacharel** (route de Cacharel, 13460 Stes-Maries, T04 90 97 84 10, camargueacheval.com, €228) organizes two-day, all-inclusive treks, plus shorter jaunts. And for tots, **Les Arnelles** (route d'Arles, 13460 Stes-Maries, T04 90 97

82 86, chevaux-les-arnelles. camargue.fr, 3-7 years) offers pony rides (€5/15 mins, €10/30 mins). For a comprehensive list of dozens of Camargue ranches, visit camargue.fr.

Explore the Petit Rhône from your own **kayak**: Kayak Vert (Mas de Sylvéréal, 30600 Sylvéréal, T04 66 73 57 17, kayakvert-camargue.fr, Mar-Oct daily 0900-1900, life vests provided but ability to swim essential) organizes one-hour tasters (€10), easy half-day paddles (12 km, €20) and combination cycling and canoeing expeditions (24 km total, €32).

For a range of **water sports**, visit Windsurf Park (Base nautique du Ponant, BP 53, 30240 Le Grau-du-Roi, windsurf-park.com), where there are week-long **windsurfing** (five 2-hr lessons €140, minimum age 7) and **sailing** (five 2-hr lessons €120, minimum age 7) courses. Or you can also simply rent the equipment (windsurfers €15-20/hr, sailboats Optimists €15/hr, Lasers €20/hr, Hobie-Cats €35/hr, **sea kayaks** €10-15/hr, **stand-up paddleboards** €12/hr) and hit the sea.

Fluid W (195 allée des Cols Verts, Etang du Ponant, 34280 La Grande Motte, T04 67 60 39 43, fluid-school.com) offers five-day children's courses for **wakeboarding** (€120 4-11 years, €90 12-18 years). Classes for adults start at €65 for two sessions including lunch.

Nature encounters

Set up in 1949 by naturalist André Lamouroux, **Parc Ornithologique de Pont de Gau** (RD 570, 13460 Stes-Maries, T04 90 97 82 62, parcornithologique.com, daily Apr-Sep 0900-sunset, Oct-Mar 1000-sunset, €7 adult, €4 child (4-10), under 4s free) is the Camargue's 60-ha bird sanctuary. The park is dotted with reed-flanked *étangs* and a 7-km discovery trail, and is an ideal place to get up close and personal with hundreds of unusual birds. Climb the two observation towers for a bird's-eye view over clouds of pink flamingos, herons and egrets.

Spot a white mountain on the horizon? It's likely a huge pile of the Camargue's salt. To learn about where salt comes from and how it's harvested, hop aboard Aigues-Mortes' *petit train* for an educational journey through Le Saunier de Camargue's nearby **salt marshes**. (Departure from Porte de la Gardette, T04 66 73 40 24, visitesalinaiguesmortes.fr, Jul-Aug 10 tours daily, Mar-Jun and Sep-Oct 5 tours daily, 75 mins, €8.20 adult, €6 under 13s, €24.20 for 2 adults and 2 under 13s.)

Boat trips are a fantastic way to see the Camargue's bird life, indigenous horses and herds of bulls. From Aigues-Mortes, both **Péniches Isles de Stel** (Port de Commerce, Bassin d'Evolution, 30220, T04 66 53

Visit... Seaquarium

Why? Hugely interactive, the Seaquarium is worth its steep entry fee. Large tanks hold clown fish (à la *Finding Nemo*), jellyfish and bright coral reefs. Its new shark centre, *Le Requinarium*, is home to 25 different species of shark, plus scores of fun and frightening facts about this sea predator. Different pools house sea lions, seals and turtles, and there are sea-themed video games, quizzes and puzzles. **Where?** Avenue du Palais de la Mer, 30240 Le Grau-du-Roi, T04 66 51 57 57, seaquarium.fr. **How?** Daily Jul-Aug 0930-2330, Apr-Jun and Sep 0930-1930, Oct-Mar 0930-1830, ticket desk closes 1 hr earlier. €11.30 adult, €8.30 child (5-15), under 5s free, free parking.

60 70, islesdestel.fr, tours daily Apr-Oct 1½ or 2 hrs, €7-10 adult, €4-6 child (4-13), €26 for 2 adults and 2 children, under 4s free) and **Croisières en Camargue** (14 rue Theaulon 30220, T06 03 91 44 63, croisieres-camargue. com, tours daily Apr-Oct 1½ or 2 hrs, €8-11 adult, €4-6 child (4-13), €20-28 for 2 adults and 2 children, under 4s free) chug along the Camargue's canals, peek at nearby *étangs* and take in a *gardian* cowboy performance. In Stes-Maries, **Tiki III** (D38, 13460 Le Grau d'Orgon, T04 90 97 81 68, tiki3.fr, tours daily Mar-Oct, 1½ hrs, €10 adult, €5 child (4-13), under 4s free) offers similar tours, exploring the banks of the Petit Rhône.

Various companies also offer daily **4x4 safaris** into the Camargue. Departing from either Stes-Maries (13460, T04 90 97 86 93) or Arles (38 av Edouard Herriot, 13200, T04 90 93 60 31), local favourite **Gallon** (tours daily Mar-Oct, safaris 1 hr-day long, €20-95 adult, under 10s half price) scopes out flamingo nesting sites, stampeding bulls and packs of ponies. They can also organize stops for horse riding, cycling or short boat trips.

Grab a bite

On Monday and Friday mornings, stock up with picnic supplies at Stes-Maries' Provençal market (place des Gitans). Over the road from the beach, **Le Bruleur de Loups** (67 av Gilbert Leroy, T04 90 97 83 31, lebruleurdeloups.monsite. wanadoo.fr, Tue 1200-1430, Thu-Mon 1200-1430 and 1930-2130, closed mid-Nov to Christmas) is the best restaurant in town for sampling traditional Camargue cuisine, including local bull.

Express Bar (9 place St-Louis) is pick of the overwhelmingly touristy bars and restaurants in Aigues-Mortes' main square. Stop in here for a cool, fruit-flavoured *sirop* in the shade. Around the corner, **L'Ange Gourmand** (12 grande rue Jean Jaurès, T04 66 53 87 63) is a top spot to pick up speciality sandwiches. **Les Arcades'** (23 bd Gambetta,

T04 66 53 81 13, les-arcades. fr, Wed-Sun 1200-1400 and 1930-2200) dining room may be too formal for little foodies, but the outdoor terrace provides a more relaxed backdrop to chef Jean-Marie Mercier's delicious dishes. Children's menus (€13.50) are a cut above the norm, with delights like pumpkin soup and baked custard.

Tucked into Le Grau-du-Roi's dunes, beachfront **L'Aigo Boulido** (65 bd du Docteur Bastide, 30240, T06 13 24 79 31, Apr-Oct) is decked out in funky furnishings and a sandy terrace, and serves up great seafood.

Getting there

Driving is the easiest way to explore the Camargue, as there's little public transport between major points of interest. Buses run every few hours between Arles and Stes-Maries: under sixes ride free, and it's also free to bring your bike on board. Buses and trains run regularly between Nîmes, Aigues-Mortes and Le Grau-du-Roi.

Sleeping Western Provence

Pick of the pitches

Camping du Pont d'Avignon

10 chemin de la Barthelasse, 84000 Avignon, T04 90 80 63 50, camping-avignon.com. Mid Mar-Oct. €11.55-22.60/pitch (2 people), free-€4.75 child (3-12), under 3s free, 4-person bungalow €335-500/week.

Ⓐ Ⓔ Ⓞ ⊕ ⊕ ⊕ ⊕ ⊜ Wi-Fi
Lively campground on the Ile de la Barthelasse, with a pool, tennis courts and views over Pont St-Bénézet.

Camping Le Clapas

Salavas, 07150 Vallon Pont d'Arc, T04 75 37 14 76, camping-le-clapas.com. Mid-Apr to Sep. €14-20 2 adults, pitch and car, €4.50-6 extra adult, €3-4.50 child (2-12), under 2s free; 6-person mobile home €300-650/week, 4-person mobile home €310-660, 6-person cottage €450-770.

Ⓐ Ⓔ Ⓞ ⊕ ⊕ ⊜ ⊜ Wi-Fi
Near the Gorges de l'Ardèche's Pont d'Arc, Le Clapas boasts its own rocky riverside beach, plus *pétanque*, themed evenings and plenty of kids' activities. Friendly staff can assist in arranging bike rental, or days out canoeing and rafting.

Camping La Coutelière

Route de Fontaine, D24 84800 Lagnes, T04 90 20 33 97, camping-la-couteliere.com. Apr-mid Oct. €14-20.90 2 adults, pitch and car, €4.60-7 extra adult, €2.60-5.50 child (9-12), €2.60-4.50 under 9s; 4-person bungalow €290-585/week, 4-person mobile home €310-660, 6-person cottage €450-770.

Ⓐ Ⓔ Ⓞ ⊕⊕ ⊕ ⊜ ⊜ Wi-Fi
Positioned riverside between L'Isle-sur-la-Sorgue and Fontaine-de-Vaucluse, La Coutelière is equipped with a large pool, tennis courts and a sports court perfect for basketball or five-a-side. During July and August, the campground organizes activities for six- to 12-year-olds three mornings per week, with quizzes and concerts for adults two evenings per week.

Camping Le Clos du Rhône

Route de l'Amarée, BP74, 13460 Stes-Maries-de-la-Mer, T04 90 97 85 99, camping-leclos.fr. Apr-Oct. €14-24 2 adults, pitch and car, €5-8.50 extra adult, €2.10-4.60 child (2-7), under 2s free; 4-person cottage €317-755/week, 6-person cottage €360-800/week.

Ⓐ Ⓔ Ⓞ ⊕ ⊕ ⊜ ⊜ Wi-Fi
West of Stes-Maries' town centre, this campground is steps from the sea, and boasts a pool, kids' club and crazy golf.

Camping Pegomas

Av Jean Moulin, 13210 St-Rémy, T04 90 92 01 21, campingpegomas.com. Mar-Oct. €15-20 2 adults, pitch and car, €4.50-6.50 extra adult, under 2s free; 4-person bungalow €290-585/week, 4-person mobile home €200-500.

Ⓐ Ⓔ Ⓞ ⊕ ⊕ ⊕
On the outskirts of St-Rémy, this calm campground is a favourite with French families. Its 2-ha grounds have an on-site bar, shared barbeque and wonderful swimming pool.

Camping Les Prés

Lavoir route Lagnes, 84800 Fontaine-de-Vaucluse, T04 90 20 32 38. Mar-Oct. €4.30 adult, €3.30 under 7s, €4.30 pitch, €3.30 car.

Ⓐ Ⓔ ⊜
A tiny but tidy campground with 42 pitches, Camping Les Prés sits on the River Sorgue, a 10-minute walk from Fontaine-de-Vaucluse's town centre. There's a pool with a water slide on the basic site.

Family Favourite
Rent La Platane in L'Isle-sur-la-Sorgue, one of three South of France self-catering spots from Baby-Friendly Boltholes. See page 14 for details.

Fleur de Camargue

D46, 30220 St-Laurent-d'Aigouze, T04 66 88 15 42, fleur-de-camargue. com. Apr-Sep. €16-24 2 adults, pitch and car, €3-4 per additional camper; 4-person cottage €220-630/week, 6-person mobile home €250-780.

Basic but charming, this welcoming campground boasts water slides and plenty of sunloungers. Summer-long activities include *pétanque* championships and karaoke evenings.

Best of the rest

Smart Living Apartments

34000 Montpellier, T06 76 20 84 70, smartliving.fr. From €85/night, discounts for longer stays.

These seven contemporary apartments are scattered around Montpellier's city centre, just outside the Old Town. All have been recently refitted: expect brightly painted interiors, flat-screen TVs and Wi-Fi. Minimum rental two nights.

La Maison sur la Sorgue

6 rue Rose Goudard, 84800 L'Isle-sur-la-Sorgue, T06 87 32 58 68, lamaisonsurlasorgue.com. Doubles €220-310, €55 per additional person, €20 per child under 2.

Four unique B&B rooms, owned by L'Isle native Marie-Claude and the gregarious Frédéric, who also mans their *objets d'art-*cum-furnishings shop, *Retour de Voyage*, next door. The delicious breakfast is locally sourced.

Thames Résidences

36 bd St-Roch, 84000 Avignon, T06 82 66 37 54, thames-residences.com. 4-person apartment €159-179/night, €861/week.

Lovely self-catering accommodation, with petite kitchens, satellite television and Wi-Fi. North-facing apartments share a vast terrace overlooking the city walls, while south-facing ones have private balconies. Access is via the Grand Hotel entrance, while the Thames Résidences's office is just a few doors east.

Cool & quirky

Airotel la Sorguette

871 route d'Apt, 84800 L'Isle-sur-la-Sorgue, T04 90 38 05 71, camping-sorguette.com. Mid-Mar to mid-Oct. 2-person yurt €350-497/week, 3-4-person yurt €385-497, 4-6-person yurt €420-532, 2-person tepee €210-315, 3-4-person tepee €280-385.

Wi-Fi Airotel's *Espace Nomad* is home to Mongolian yurts, tepees, hammocks and a kitchen. *Tente-lodges* (canvas-roofed cabins with cooking corners) are also available. The owners organize kayaking on the Sorgue. Mobile homes (€385-644/week, sleeping up to 6) and tent pitches (€16.80-21.10 for 2 adults, pitch and car) are on site.

Canvas Chic

Mas de Serret, 07150 Labastide de Virac, T06 50 81 21 40, canvaschic. com. May-Sep. 4-person yurt €85/night, 3-day minimum stay May-Jun and Sep, 1-week minimum stay Jul-Aug. €11 tent pitches.

Canvas Chic personifies a non-electric, back-to-nature approach to holidaying. The site comprises 12 beautiful wood

Sleeping Western Provence

In business since 1905, the Hostellerie is one of the few spots to snooze inside Les Baux's walled village. Its terrace overlooks the valley below; the excellent on-site restaurant offers half-board options.

Hôtel du Forum
10 place du Forum, 13200 Arles, T04 90 93 48 95, hotelduforum. com. Apr-Oct. Doubles €80-120, triples €120, quadruples €120-130, apartment €160.
Rooms here are a little dated, but come sweltering summertime, the walled swimming pool is a lifesaver.

Hotel Majestic
10 rue Pradier, 30000 Nîmes, T04 66 29 24 14, hotel-majestic-nimes. com. Doubles €60-75, triples €75-85, quadruples €80-95, family room €80-130.
Equidistant from the train station and the Arènes, this welcoming little hotel is bursting with Provençal personality. Charming rooms are decorated with unique stencils, and the courtyard garden walls are painted with murals of the surrounding countryside.

Villa Mazarin
35 bd Gambetta, 30220 Aigues Mortes, T04 66 73 90 48, villamazarin. com. Rooms €120-300, discounts during low season.
A sophisticated yet infinitely family-friendly spot, tucked away on a residential back street

yurts, draped in textiles and set just above the banks of the Ardèche River. Off season, well-being weekends and canoeing trips are organized.

Péniche QI
Chemin Ile Piot, Ile de la Barthelasse, 84000 Avignon, T04 90 25 40 61, chambrepeniche.fr. Doubles €60-90, additional bed €15.
Across the Rhône from Avignon's Old Town, this B&B offers four rooms aboard a quirky houseboat. There's also a small pool on deck, free Wi-Fi and twinkling night-time views over the city.

Splashing out

Country Kids
Le Mas Pandit, 34650 Brenas, T06 77 54 56 00, country-kids.fr. 4-person apartment €5500-6450/week, €550-600 per additional person.

A luxurious mix of self-catering accommodation and brilliant organized activities. Rates include unlimited use of the Mas's free crèche (10 weeks-6 years), two-nights' free babysitting, two days of adventure (such as mountain climbing or horse and carriage rides), on-site petting farm, pool, Wi-Fi and so much more. Highly recommended for parents of babies and toddlers. Note that Le Mas Pandit is located around 75 km west of Montpellier, making your own transport essential for accessing many of the listings in this guide.

Hostellerie de la Reine Jeanne
Rue Porte Mage, 13520 Les-Baux-de-Provence, T04 90 54 32 06, la-reinejeanne.com. Doubles €56-70, 4-person apartment €100.

in Aigues-Mortes' Old Town. The courtyard pool and excellent restaurant make it a challenge to actually leave the premises.

Provence Paradise

16 av Théodore Aubanel, 13210 St-Rémy-de-Provence, T06 07 82 66 63, provenceparadise.com. 2-4 person cottages €1200-2200/week, 4-8 person garden residences €2100-3000, 8-10 person villas €3000-4500. A handful of stunning 17th-century, self-catering cottages and villas, set on the outskirts of St-Rémy. Surprisingly laid-back, there's a shared pool, and guests are provided with a sumptuous full dinner (and drinks) on the night of arrival. Babysitting, local tours, meals and transport available for an additional fee.

Le Vieux Moulin

Rive Gauche, Pont du Gard, T04 66 37 14 35, vieuxmoulinpontdugard. com. Rooms €80-150. This 19th-century flourmill was converted to a hotel and restaurant in the 1950s: today it remains the only spot to overnight on the Pont du Gard site, with a tasty terraced restaurant to boot (see page 154). The 10 rooms are classically furnished; some have large balconies, none have televisions.

Eating Western Provence

Van Gogh café, Arles.

Local goodies

L'Aile ou la Cuisse

5 rue de la Commune, 13210 St-Rémy-de-Provence, T04 32 62 00 25. *Boutique traiteur* Tue-Sat 1000-1900, closed Jan.

Also a restaurant, this spot's quality deli is perfect for stocking up on cooked meats, pâtés and country-style picnic fodder.

Boulangerie Les 7 Epis Bio

2 rue Esquiros, 13150 Tarascon, T04 90 91 14 92, les7episbio.free.fr. Tue-Fri 0700-1230 and 1530-1900, Sat 0730-1230 and 1600-1900.

Nutty organic breads and local pastries, including *croquants aux amandes*, a long, sweet almond

biscuit similar to Italian *biscotti* and sold by the slice.

L'Isle-sur-la-Sorgue Market

Various points around town. Sun 0900-1900.

Head to the streets surrounding Notre Dames des Anges church for organic breads, garlic-marinaded olives, locally produced salami and picnic nibbles galore.

Quick & simple

Café des Baux

Rue Trencat, 13520 Les-Baux-de-Provence, T04 90 54 52 69. Apr-Oct Tue-Sat 1200-1800.

Tucked inside a sunny, sheltered courtyard, this spot is perfect for refuelling after exploring the next-door Château. Big salads are named after artists (the Picasso, or the Matisse), but it's the desserts here, created by master *pâtissier* Pierre Walter, that are truly the stars.

Delecto

3 rue des Ecoles Laïques, 34000 Montpellier, T04 67 02 08 96. Mon-Sat 0930-1900.

Freshly squeezed juices, smoothies, sandwiches, soups and salads. Plus there's a small outdoor terrace, weekend brunch and free Wi-Fi.

Pâtisserie Courtois

Place du Marché, 30000 Nîmes, T04 66 67 20 09. Tue-Sun 0800-1930.

Open since 1892 and with the gorgeous, over-the-top gilt interior to prove it, this café and pastry shop dishes up excellent lunchtime *plats du jour*: try the *tarte nîmois*, pastry topped with sweet Gard onions, potatoes and cod (€12.50). The children's menu (€7) includes quiche, an éclair and a surprise.

Le Pré Vert

10 rue Ste-Anne, T04 67 02 72 81, 34000 Montpellier. Jul-Aug 1000-1830 daily, Sep-Jun Mon-Sat 1000-1930.

A welcoming spot for breakfast (€6.50) or lunch, including big salads (approx €13). Colourful tables and chairs, including a chalkboard and kids' toy area, are tucked into an Old Town square under the shadow of Ste-Anne's church.

Posh nosh

Le Ciel de Nîmes

Place de la Maison Carrée, 30000 Nîmes, T04 66 36 71 70, lecieldenimes.fr. Tue-Sun 1000-1800, Jul-Aug Thu-Sat 1900-2200, Apr-Jun and Sep Fri-Sat 1900-2200.

Bang on top of Norman Foster's Carré d'Art (Nîmes' library and contemporary arts centre), this cool terrace is ringed by glass barricades, and has great views over the city's first-century Maison Carrée in the square

below. Dishes are light and pan-Mediterranean, including chicken and mozzarella salad, pasta and crêpes.

Le Lisita

2 bd des Arènes, 30000 Nîmes, T04 66 67 29 15, lelisita.com. Tue-Sat 1200-1330 and 1900-2200.

Chef Olivier Douet's cuisine may be Michelin-starred wonders – caramelized cherry tomatoes rolled in sesame, or salmon tartare with coriander and carrot puree – but the ambience here is as relaxed as can be. Meals are served on the spacious terrace, under leafy plane trees and across from the Arènes. Two-course set menus from €22, children's menu €15.

Restaurant Philip

Chemin la Fontaine, 84800 Fontaine-de-Vaucluse, T04 90 20 31 81. Apr-Sep 1200-1500.

Along the sun-dappled pathway to the River Sorgue's source, this

family-run restaurant – doing a bustling business since 1926 – makes a sweet lunchtime stop. Pick one of the cheery yellow seats waterside, then order seasonal specialities, like scallop kebabs or chestnut mash. Set menus €25-36.

La Prévôté

4 rue Jean-Jacques Rousseau, 84800 L'Isle-sur-la-Sorgue, T04 90 38 57 29, la-prevote.fr. Wed-Mon 1230-1400 and 1930-2130, closed Wed Sep-Jun.

Chef Jean-Marie Alloin's Provençal cuisine ranges from simple braised lamb to lobster-stuffed ravioli: opt for his three-course lunch menu (€26, except Sun) to sample his seasonal finest. Dine on the canal-side terrace, or come winter, within what used to be a church sacristy.

For places to eat in Avignon and Arles, see pages 159 and 161 respectively.

Dine in luxury at the fabulous Le Lisita.

Grown-ups' stuff South of France

Getting there

By car London to Aix-en-Provence is a 750-km journey, with a drive time of around 10 hours via Reims. Both P&O (poferries.com) and SeaFrance (seafrance.com) operate hourly ferries between Dover and Calais (1½-hr journey, from £25/car). Alternatively, you can cross the Channel via the Folkestone-Calais Eurotunnel (eurotunnel. com, 35-min journey). Single crossings start at £22 per car. The motorways (*autoroutes*) are excellent but pricey: expect to clock up around €80 of tolls on the way. Allow another two hours and an additional €20 to get to Nice.

The speed limit on *autoroutes* is 130 kph, dropping to 110 kph when it's raining. *Péage* motorways are toll routes. Take a ticket on entry and pay by cash or card when you exit a *péage* section. Do not enter the toll lane marked with an orange 't' as these are reserved exclusively for automatic payments under the *télépéage* scheme. You'll look silly if you do, as everyone will have to reverse their cars to let you out! There are rest stops approximately every 40 km along *autoroutes*. Even better, there are spacious *aires* – grassy areas with toilets and vending machines – every 15 km or so.

Both Mappy (fr.mappy.com) and ViaMichelin (viamichelin. co.uk) are helpful for planning your route. The National Centre for Traffic Information Bison Futé (bison-fute.equipement.gouv. fr) website offers drivers current information on all major roads in France in English and in French, including construction, accidents and hazardous weather conditions.

By plane There are two main airports serving the South of France: Nice Côte d'Azur (T08 20 42 33 33, nice.aeroport.fr), France's second largest airport, and Marseille Provence Airport (T04 42 14 14 14, mrsairport. com), between Marseilles and Aix. Three smaller airports also receive limited flights: Toulon-Hyères (T08 25 01 83 87, toulon-hyeres. aeroport.fr), Avignon Provence (T04 90 81 51 51, avignon. aeroport.fr) and Montpellier Méditerrannée (T04 67 20 85 00, montpellier.aeroport.fr).

Nice Côte d'Azur receives over 50 flights a day from nearly 20 airports in the UK and Ireland in summer, and around half that number in winter. EasyJet (easyjet.com) has services from Belfast, Bristol, Edinburgh, Liverpool, London (Gatwick, Luton and Stansted) and Newcastle. BMIbaby (bmibaby.com) has flights from Birmingham and East Midlands. Jet2 (jet2.com) serves Nice from Glasgow, Manchester and Leeds Bradford. British Airways (ba. com) has services from London Heathrow and London City. Flybe (flybe.com) has flights from Southampton. From Ireland, Aer Lingus (aerlingus. com) has routes from Dublin and Cork, while Ryanair (ryanair.com) also flies in from Dublin. From the US, Delta (delta.com) flies from New York direct to Nice.

Marseille Provence Airport's hanger-type budget airline terminal, MP2 (mp2.aeroport.fr), is linked to London Stansted and Edinburgh on Ryanair. EasyJet flies in from London Gatwick and Bristol. BA flies to the main terminal from London Gatwick. There are also direct flights from Nice and Marseilles to almost every country in Europe and North Africa.

Toulon-Hyères receives flights from London Stansted and Bristol on Ryanair. Flybe connects Birmingham, Exeter and Southampton to **Avignon Provence. Montpellier Méditerrannée** is served by easyJet from London Gatwick, and Ryanair from Leeds Bradford.

By train For families who find luggage limits, airport security and airline extras downright annoying, there is another way. **Eurostar** (eurostar.co.uk) services from London St Pancras link seamlessly with France's high-speed **TGV** trains, whizzing passengers between London and Avignon in six hours flat. Journey

times to Aix and Marseille are an additional half hour. All services require a painless platform change in Lille. Printable e-tickets combined with a 30-minute check-in period means travellers can be on their way quickly.

On board both Eurostar and the connecting TGV, there's a lot to do and see (see box above). Standard Class travellers have access to croissants, *café au lait* and a bistro bar down the hall. Some mainland French services offer DVD and PSP hire. Return tickets start from £118 and go on sale precisely three months before departure, shifting upwards in price the later you book.

Standard Premier costs around 50% extra, but includes complimentary dining and drinks at your table (children's meals can

be requested in advance online). Passengers who upgrade also get to snaffle lots of free magazines and doze through France in larger, ultra-comfy seats.

If you fancy something a little more bespoke, the highly recommended hotel and rail booking specialist **Railbookers** (T +44 (0)20 3327 2475, railbookers.com) can arrange a personally tailored journey to Antibes, Arles or anywhere in the South of France, and post your tickets to you.

Getting around
By bicycle The mild weather makes cycling here a joy, particularly along the coast or in rural areas. The South of France has loads of great bike trails, in particular among the lavender-cloaked Luberon hills (see page

124), although the flatlands of the Camargue and car-free Ile de Porquerolles are top spots too. Aix, Avignon and Nice have electronic bike rental stands. See listings within each chapter for bike hire details and cycle websites, and visit our online resources (see page 177) for details of cycling tour companies.

By bus The South of France's bus network ranges from highly efficient to almost non-existent, depending on the season and your destination. Along the Riviera the service is both cheap and brilliant. **Ligne d'Azur** (lignedazur.com) buses radiate outwards from Nice's *gare routière* (main bus station), linking the city with Monaco, Cannes, Grasse, the ski slopes and beyond. **Varlib** (varlib.fr) buses

zip between St-Tropez, Toulon and St-Raphaël. **Aix en Bus** (aixenbus.com) runs buses in and around Aix-en-Provence, while the **Département de Vaucluse** (vaucluse.fr) gives timetables and tariffs for bus travel around Avignon and Arles. As befits a metropolis like Marseilles, **RTM** (rtm.fr) buses, trams and metro lines neatly cover all corners of the city. **SCAL** (scal-amv-voyages.com) connects Marseilles and Aix with Haute-Provence and parts of the Luberon, although note that public transport in these latter two regions is very limited.

By car   Roads in much of inland Provence are relatively quiet, and touring on empty countryside lanes is a pleasure. However, routes all over the South of France get extremely busy in July and August, so set off early or leave the car at home (get the train in and out of Monaco, for example) where appropriate.

There are lots of car hire places dotted around Provence renting everything from a Ferrari to a 50cc scooter. The cheapest method is to book online before you go (try holidayautos.co.uk, hertz.co.uk or easycar.com) and pick it up at the airport or train station upon arrival.

It is compulsory to carry one warning triangle and one reflective jacket when driving in France; the jacket must be in the car, not in the boot. The regulations also apply to hire cars,

so check that they are present when you collect your car.

By ferry   Many locals rely on ferry transportation, especially around the St-Tropez peninsula, where parking and traffic jams can be a nightmare. In summer, departures are so frequent that you can base yourself in Cannes, Nice or St-Tropez and visit much of the surrounding coast by ferry. To visit the Iles d'Or (see page 74) or the Iles de Lérins (see page 40), just pitch up at the appropriate port (see individual chapters for listings), purchase a ticket and jump aboard.

By foot   Grande Randonnée (GR, see box page 135) walking routes connect most of France's historic towns. A *sentier littoral*, or coastal trail, runs almost continuously along the South of France's Mediterranean shoreline: short chunks of the beautiful pathway are easy to access. See page 32 for further details.

By train   The rail network in the South of France is cheap, extensive and efficient. High-speed **TGV** (Train à Grande Vitesse) services link Nice, Marseilles, Avignon and Aix-en-Provence both with each other and all major points north. Tickets must be reserved in advance from the station, at an SNCF boutique or online (voyages-sncf.com). Most local rail journeys are made on comfortable and

affordable **TER** (ter-sncf.fr) regional trains. No reservation is necessary: just buy a ticket at the station and hop on any TER train.

Bikes travel free on TER services but there are restrictions during rush hours and on some TGV services. Disabled passengers will find wheelchair spaces on most trains (clearly marked on the carriage); look for the wheelchair symbol on the timetable. Fares for kids aged four to 11 are half the price of an adult ticket; advance rates for travellers aged 12-25 are often 50% off too, while under threes travel free.

Families can also purchase a **Carte Isabelle Famille** (Jun-Sep, €35, 2 adults plus 2 under 16s), a one-day rail pass that covers unlimited travel between Fréjus and Ventimiglia (on the Italian border), as well as the routes to Grasse and north to Tende for access to the Parc Mercantour. **Carte Bermuda** (Jul-Sep, €5 per person) is a similar pass, valid for one day of unlimited travel along the Côte Bleue's *calanques*, between Marseilles and Miramas.

Remember, all train passengers must *composter* (validate) their tickets in the yellow machines on the platform before boarding a train.

Handy words & phrases

hello *bonjour*
good evening *bonsoir*
please *s'il vous plaît*
thank you *merci*
I'm sorry, excuse me
  pardon, excusez-moi
yes *oui*
no *non*
child *enfant*
kid *gosse*
teen *ado*
family *famille*
bottle *biberon*

car seat *siège-auto*
cot *lit de bébé*
ticket *billet*
where is the toilet? *où est la
toilette?*
do you speak English? *est-ce que
vous parlez anglais? / parlez-vous
anglais?*
I don't speak French *je ne parle pas
français*
I don't understand *je ne comprends
pas*
help! *au secours!*

Online resources

A click around these websites before you go will set the scene for your visit, and provide a bit of background on eating, sleeping and relaxing in the sun.

Holiday ideas & operators

Angloinfo
riviera.angloinfo.com, provence. angloinfo.com. Geared towards expats living in the South of France, covering seasonal activities, longer-term rentals and day-to-day events.

Cycling for Softies
cycling-for-softies.co.uk Recommended biking trips around St-Rémy, where your luggage meets you at your next hotel.

Explore Worldwide
explore.co.uk Teen and family boating trips around the Canal du Midi and cycling tours around Provence

Headwater
headwater.com Family-orientated walking and cycling holidays in southern France.

Inn Travel
inntravel.co.uk Guided walking tours with hotel stays around the Pont du Gard, Canal du Midi and Haute-Provence.

Provence Family
provence-family.co.uk Holiday ideas run by Vaucluse tourist board

Provence Family Holidays
provencefamilyholidays.com, tourismeenfamille.com. Holiday ideas primarily in and around Marseilles and Aix-en-Provence, suggested by a local parent.

Tots to France
totstofrance.co.uk Excellent resource for travel with little ones.

Tourism in Provence, Alps & Cote d'Azur
decouverte-paca.fr. Official tourism site of the Provence-Alpes-Côte d'Azur (PACA), with holiday ideas and suggested accommodation.

Accommodation links

Camping France
campingfrance.com. Details of and links to almost every campsite in the South of France.

Hotel BB
hotel-bb.com Superb value *autoroute* and city centre accommodation, with cheap breakfasts and family rooms.

Etap Hotels
etaphotel.com Well-priced, basic hotel chain, with around 20 branches in Provence.

Eurocamp
eurocamp.co.uk Six family-orientated camping and mobile home sites in Provence.

F1 Hotels
hotelformule1.com You've never been as close to your family as in these cramped, clean and cheap motorway lodges.

FUAJ
fuaj.org France's Hostelling International site with excellent value dormitories and family rooms across Provence.

Gites de France
gites-de-france.com Rural accommodation for rent.

Holiday Rentals
holiday-rentals.co.uk Literally thousands of villas, farmhouses and apartments to let across the region.

James Villas
jamesvillas.co.uk Dozens of villas with pools in all the coastal resorts.

Keycamp
keycamp.co.uk. Operates a dozen campsites in Provence, all near major towns or beach resorts.

Owners Direct
ownersdirect.co.uk. Hundreds of holiday apartments and villas with pools.

Riviera Pebbles
rivierapebbles.com. Upscale holiday rental properties for rent in Nice, Cannes, Antibes and along the coast.

VFB
vfbholidays.co.uk. Rural villas and *gîtes* with swimming pools in deepest Provence.

Grown-ups' stuff South of France

Babies (0-18 months)

For families travelling with babies, renting an apartment or villa will give you the most freedom in terms of space, privacy and mealtimes. Frequently, higher-end accommodation offers parenting respite, either through babysitting services or a crèche. If you're renting a car in the South of France, you may choose to bring your own baby seat, although it's also common to rent child seats on the ground. Baby food, nappies and generic baby supplies are widely available.

Some visitors may find the Riviera too hot at summer's peak, but conversely, the climate allows for long, warm visits in spring and autumn. During July and August, inland lakes, rivers and the Provençal Alps offer respite from the coastal heat.

Toddlers (18 months-4 years)

The French love little ones. Toddlers in particular are coddled, cooed over and spoiled. However, when compared to the UK, health and safety regulations tend to be a little looser: don't feel embarrassed about questioning accommodation or activity specifics. All private and public swimming pools areas are gated, in accordance with France's strict fencing regulations.

Hotels, campgrounds and beaches often have kids' clubs, usually lasting two to three hours per session. Activities range from arts and crafts to gentle games on the sand, and they're a great way for tots to let loose.

If you're heading to the beach *en famille*, a sunlounger and large parasol (around €10-15/day) will provide protection from the strong summertime sun. Alternatively, beach umbrellas (as well as sunhats, inflatable toys and buckets) are widely available from shops along the coast.

Beach safety

Every beach in Provence is either entirely public or has huge non-private areas for families to enjoy. The Mediterranean is non-tidal, which negates the risk of being swept out to sea, or having your picnic inundated by the encroaching tide. Most beaches fly a *Blue Flag* (see page 5), which denotes clean swimming water. From mid-May to mid-September only, a team of lifeguards surveys the majority of southern France's beaches; two blue flags designate the area of surveillance. The lifeguards are backed up by a first-aid tent, which dispenses treatments for heatstroke and jellyfish stings, although the latter are rare. A roped-off swimming area for tots is also common, but again only during summer. In season almost all beaches operate a safety flag system: green means calm seas with monitored bathing; orange means strong winds and potentially dangerous bathing; red means rough seas with no bathing allowed. For minor 'emergencies', most beaches have a café and restaurant selling ice creams and lollies.

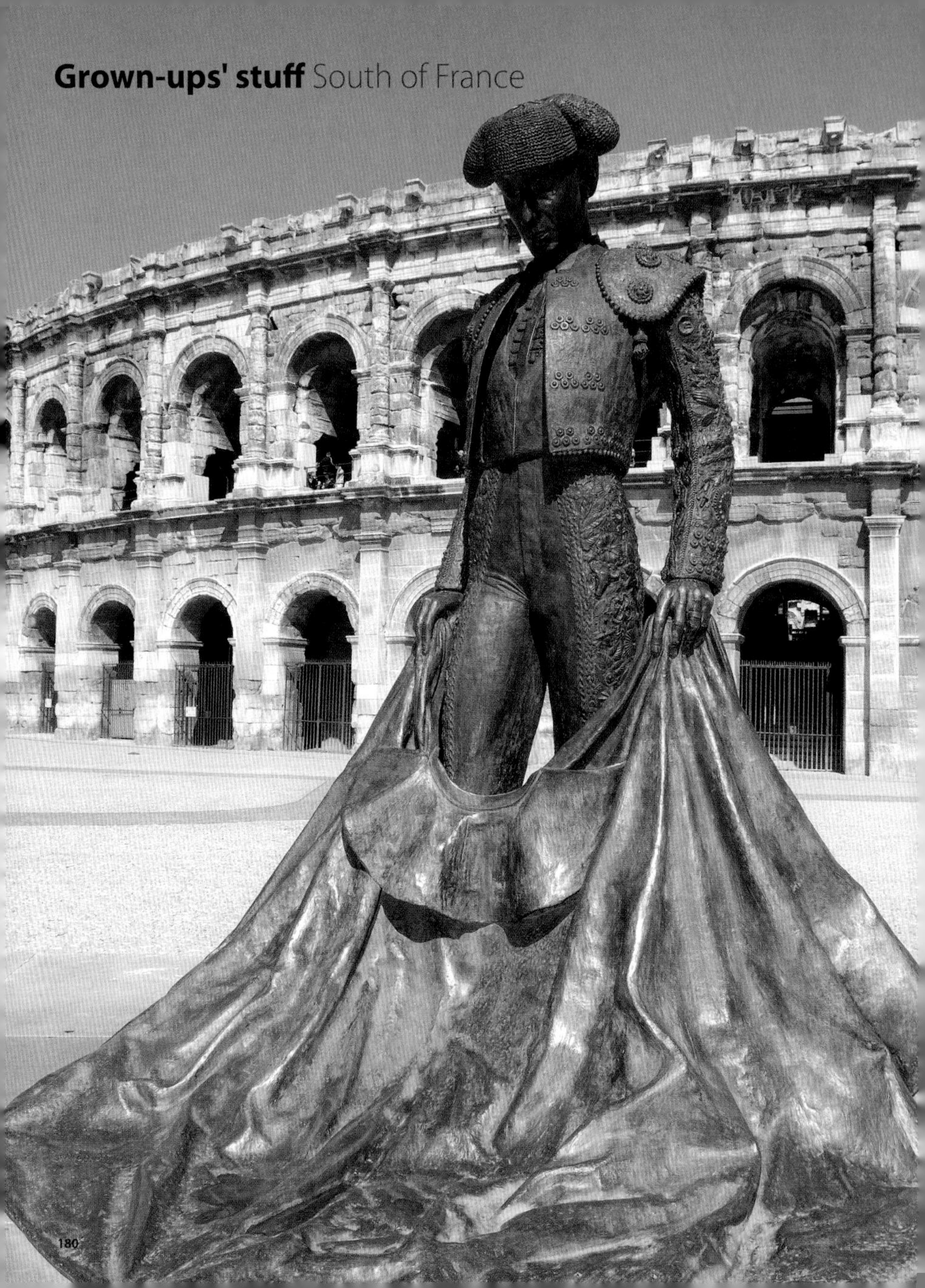

School age (4-12 years)

For most school-aged kids, holidays are all about days on the beach and nights under the stars. Happily, the South of France has both in abundance.

Splash around on one of the coastal beaches, or opt for one of Haute-Provence's cooler lakes. The region's popularity means packs of kids quickly become playmates. And while there's no rock pooling (the Med isn't tidal), there's plenty of shallow snorkelling, lilo floating, pedalo peddling and sandcastle building for hours of non-stop fun. Slap on strong sunscreen (widely available) with abandon, but note that it's best to buy UV-resistant clothing before you travel, as it's more difficult to find in France.

Campgrounds cover the South of France. Some offer organized activities from dawn 'til dusk, others are non-electric, eco-oases, a few even have yurts, treehouses and teepees. All make for memorable family adventures.

Teenagers (13 years +)

A region of car-free piazzas, pavement cafés and chichi shops, the South of France is the country's most appealing region for teens. From St-Tropez's summertime celeb crowd to shopping the backstreet boutiques in Cannes, the Riviera is the epitome of laid-back,

beachside glamour. Teenagers – both local and foreign – roam Nice's promenade des Anglais, and linger over terrace tables in Juan-les-Pins and Cannes.

Conversely, Haute-Provence and Western Provence's plethora of adventure sports are the region's other massive teen attraction. During summer, be sure to book activities like canyoning, white-water rafting, kayaking and horse riding at least three days in advance. Each chapter in this book lists the activities associated with each specific region, along with prices, details and seasonality.

Single-parent families

Accommodation and entrance fees in the South of France are usually calculated per person, rather than at a 'family rate', so single-parent families generally don't lose out. Operators **Acorn Adventures**

(families.acornadventure.co.uk), **Siblu** (siblu.com) and **Eurocamp** (eurocamp.co.uk) can help busy single parents to plan a great holiday; they all also offer discounts for one-parent families.

Special needs

In the UK, **RADAR** (radar.org. uk) can assist you in planning your trip. **Bespoke France** (bespokefrance.co.uk) offers tailored trips for people with disabilities and their families. In France, both **L'Association des Paralysés de France** (apf.asso. fr, French only) and **Tourisme & Handicaps** (tourisme-handicaps. org, also French only) are good sources of local information. **Handiplage** (handiplage.fr) has a detailed map and breakdown of every French beach that offers accessibility to disabled visitors.

Grown-ups' stuff South of France

Baby supplies
Bébé 9 ZI de St-Tronquet, 84130 Le Pontet (Avignon).
Bébé Tendresse Centre Commercial de Fontvieille, 25 av Albert II, 98000 Monaco.
L'Ilot Bébé 3110 route d'Avignon Rn7 Celony, passage à niveau de la Calade, 13090 Aix-en-Provence.
Natalys 4 av Georges Clemenceau, 06000 Nice.
Prémaman Centre Com Grand V - La Valentine, 117 Traverse de la Montre, 13011 Marseilles.

In the Nice and St-Tropez areas, the handy service **Travelling with Baby** (travellingwithbaby.com) rents cleaned and disinfected cots, swings, car seats, high chairs etc by the week. **Petits Nomades** (petitsnomades.com) offers a similar service in Marseilles.

Camping supplies
The sports superstore **Decathlon** (decathlon.fr) is your best stop for reasonably priced camping equipment. There are giant outlets in Aix-en-Provence (13 rue Chabrier, 13100), Antibes (Chemin des Terriers Nord, 06600), Digne-les-Bains (5 route de Marseille, ZI Saint Christophe, 04000), Marseilles (Chemin du Roy d'Espagne, 13009) and Monaco (2 rue de la Lujerneta, Font Vieille, 98000), among many others.

Consulates & embassies
In case of theft, loss of passport or any other emergency, there are UK (24 av du Prado, 13006, T04 91 15 72 10, ukinfrance.fco.gov.uk) and US (place Varian Fry, 13006, T04 91 54 92 00, french.france. usembassy.gov) consulates in Marseilles. Australians (france. embassy.gov.au), Canadians (canadainternational.gc.ca), Irish (dfa.ie) and New Zealanders (nzembassy.com) will need to contact their embassies in Paris.

Emergencies
From a landline: Ambulance T15, Police T17, Fire Service T18. The European emergency number 112 can be dialled free from any phone, including mobiles and call boxes.

Health
EU citizens should obtain a European Health Insurance Card (ehic.org) before travelling to France. This entitles you to emergency medical treatment on the same terms as French nationals. Should you need a doctor, any Tourist Office or hotel reception will be able to assist you in contacting the nearest English-speaking doctor.

Hospitals
Aix-en-Provence Centre Hospitalier du Pays d'Aix, av des Tamaris, 13080, T04 42 33 50 00, ch-aix.fr.

Antibes Centre Hospitalier, av de Nice, by Port Vauban, 06600, T04 97 24 77 77, ch-antibes.fr.
Apt Centre Hospitalier du Pays d'Apt, 225 av Philippe de Girard, 84400, T04 90 04 33 00.
Arles Centre Hospitalier d'Arles, quart Haut de Fourchon, 13200, T04 90 49 29 29.
Avignon Hôpital Général Henri Duffaut, 305 rue Raoul Follereau, 84000, T04 32 75 33 33, ch-avignon.fr.
Cannes Hôpital Les Broussailles, 13 av des Broussailles, 06400, T04 93 69 70 00, ch-cannes.fr.
Digne-les-Bains Quartier St Christophe, 04000, T04 92 30 15 15.
Draguignan Centre Hospitalier, route Montferrat, 83300, T04 94 60 50 00, ch-dracenie.com.
Gassin (St-Tropez) Hôpital du Golfe de St-Tropez, 83580, T04 98 12 50 00, ch-saint-tropez.fr.
Hyères Centre Hospitalier Général, 579 rue Maréchal Juin, 83400, T04 94 00 24 00, ch-hyeres.fr.
Marseilles Hôpital de la Timone, 264 rue St-Pierre, 13000, T04 91 38 60 00, ap-hm.fr.
Menton Centre Hospitalier Universitaire, 7 route du Val de Gorbio, 06500, T04 92 10 13 83.
Monaco Centre Hospitalier Princesse Grace, av Pasteur, 98000, T377 97 98 99 00.
Montpellier Centre Hospitalier Universitaire (CHU Bellevue), place Jean Baumel, 34000, T04 67 33 67 33.

Grown-ups' stuff South of France

Nice Hôpital Saint Roch, 5 rue Pierre Dévoluy, 06000, T04 92 03 33 33, chu-nice.fr.
Toulon Hôpital de Toulon Font-Pré, 83000, T04 94 61 61 61, ch-toulon.fr.

Pharmacies

If you or your children develop a minor ailment while on holiday, visit the nearest pharmacy to discuss your concerns with highly qualified staff, who can give medical advice and recommend treatment.

Aix-en-Provence 17bis cours Mirabeau, 13080, T04 42 93 63 60.
Antibes Pharmacie Centrale, 48 rue de la République, 06600, T04 93 34 00 23.
Arles Pharmacie St Julien, 25 rue Quatre Septembre, 13200, T04 90 96 00 04.
Avignon Pharmacie Tarot, 29 rue Marchands, 84000, T04 90 82 27 91.
Bandol 1 bd Victor Hugo, 83150, T04 94 29 41 06.
Beaulieu-sur-Mer Pharmacie Internationale, 38 bd Marinoni, 06310, 04 93 01 01 39.
Cannes Pharmacie Centrale, 21 rue Félix Faure, 06400, T04 92 59 00 19.
Cassis Pharmacie Trossero, 11 av Victor Hugo, 13260, T04 42 01 70 03.
Digne-les-Bains Gilly, 14 place du Marché, 04000, T04 92 32 32 47.

Draguignan Pharmacie Centrale, 2 place du Marché, 83300, T04 94 68 02 26;
Fayence Pharmacie du Village, place Eglise St-Jean-Baptiste, 83440, T04 94 76 00 61.
Fréjus Pharmacie Provençale, 62 rue Général de Gaulle, 83600, T04 94 51 28 98;
Hyères Pharmacie du Fenouillet, 7 av Gambetta, 83400, T04 94 65 01 15.
Le Lavandou Pharmacie Centrale, 21 av Martyrs de la Résistance, 83980, T04 94 71 03 55.
Les Baux-de-Provence Maussane les Alpilles, 13520, T04 90 54 30 40.
Marseille Pharmacie Tran Nghi, 10 cours Belsunce, 13000, T04 91 90 14 58.
Menton Pharmacie Centrale, 13 place Georges Clemenceau, 06500, T04 93 35 71 52.
Monaco Pharmacie Aslanian, 2 bd d'Italie, 98000, T00 377 93 50 64 77.
Nice Pharmacie de Paris, 60 av Jean Médecin, 06000, T04 93 85 12 81.
St-Martin-Vésubie 50 rue Cagnoli, 06450, T04 93 03 20 02.
St-Rémy-de-Provence Cendre, cours Mirabeau, 13210, T04 90 92 08 05.
St-Tropez Pharmacie du Port, 9 quai Suffren, 83990, T04 94 97 00 06.
Ste-Maxime Pharmacie Bausset, 76 avenue Charles de Gaulle, 83120, T04 94 96 19 56.

Stes-Maries-de-la-Mer 16 rue Victor Hugo, 13460, T04 90 97 83 02.
Vence Pharmacie du Grand Jardin, 30 place Grand Jardin, 06140, T04 93 58 00 39.
Villefranche-sur-Mer Pharmacie de la Paix, 6 place de la Paix, 06320, T04 93 01 70 42.

Supermarkets

Aix-en-Provence Monoprix, 27 cours Mirabeau, 13100; La Vie Claire, 49 rue Italie, 13100.
Apt Intermarché, 368 av Libération, 84400.
Arles Monoprix, 13 place Lamartine, 13200; La Vie Claire, 3 rue Doct. Fanton, 13200.
Avignon Carrefour City, 23 rue République, 84000; Biocoop, 5 rte Lyon, 84000.
Cannes Monoprix, 9 rue Mar Foch, 06400.
Digne-les-Bains Carrefour, ZI St Christophe, 04000.
Fréjus Géant Casino, 911 rue Jean Carrara, 83600.
Hyères Géant Casino, chemin Rocher de St Jean, 83400.
Le Lavandou Champio, av Mar Juin, 83980.
Marseille Monoprix Exploit, 36 La Canebière, 13001; Biocoop Castellane, 87 rue Italie, 13006.
Nice Monoprix, 37 av Jean Médecin, 06000; Biocoop Azur, 59 bd Gén Louis Delfino, 06300.
Nîmes Intermarché, 25 rue Charlemagne, 30000.
St-Tropez Géant Casino, La Foux, 83580.

Tips

During the summer months, be sure to carry sunscreen, and away from the coast, mosquito repellent. Both can be purchased at any French pharmacy or large supermarket.

For rural activities, it's often useful to have some cash to hand. Many places don't take credit cards, for example some woodland adventure courses or kayak excursion agencies.

Note that many self-catering accommodations provide linens, but only at an extra cost – be sure to clarify this point on booking.

Grown-ups' stuff South of France

Tourist information offices

Agay Place Giannetti, 83530 Agay, T04 94 82 01 85, agay.fr.

Aigues-Mortes place St Louis, 30220, T04 66 53 73 00, ot-aiguesmortes.fr.

Aix-en-Provence 2 place du Général de Gaulle, 13080, T04 42 16 11 61, aixenprovencetourism.com.

Antibes 11 place de Gaulle, 06600, T04 97 23 11 11, antibesjuanlespins.com.

Apt 20 av Philippe de Girard, 84400, T04 90 74 03 18, ot-apt.fr.

Arles bd des Lices, 13200, T04 90 18 41 20, arlestourisme.com.

Auron Grange Cossa, 06660, T04 93 23 02 66, auron.com.

Avignon 41 cours Jean Jaurès, 84000, T04 32 74 32 74, ot-avignon.fr.

Bandol Allée Vivien, 83150, T04 94 29 41 35, tourisme.bandol.fr.

Bedoin (Mont Ventoux) Espace Marie-Louis Gravier, 84410, T04 90 65 63 95, bedoin.org.

Bormes-les-Mimosas place Gambetta, 83230, T04 94 01 38 38, bormeslesmimosas.com.

Cannes Palais des Festivals, 1 bd la Croisette, T04 92 99 84 22; **Cannes** train station, T04 93 39 40 19; 06400; cannes.com.

Cassis quai des Moulins, 13260, T08 92 25 98 92, ot-cassis.fr.

Castellane rue Nationale, 04120, T04 92 83 61 14, castellane.org.

Digne-les-Bains place du Tampinet, 04000, T04 92 36 62 62, ot-dignelesbains.fr.

Eze place Général de Gaulle, 06360, T04 93 41 26 00, eze-riviera.com.

Fayence place Léon Roux, 83440, T04 94 76 20 08.

Fréjus 249 rue Jean Jaurès, 83600, T04 94 51 83 83, frejus.fr.

Gordes Le Château, 84220, T04 90 72 02 75, gordes-village.com.

Grasse 22 cours Honoré Cresp, 06130, T04 93 36 66 66, grasse.fr.

Hyères 3 av Ambroise Thomas, 83400, T04 94 01 84 50, hyeres-tourisme.com.

Isola 2000 Immeuble Le Pélevos, 06420, T04 93 23 15 15, isola2000.com.

Juan-les-Pins 51 bd Guillaumont, 06160, T04 97 23 11 10, antibesjuanlespins.com.

L'Isle-sur-la-Sorgue place de la Liberté, 84800, T04 90 38 04 78, oti-delasorgue.fr.

La Croix-Valmer Esplanade de la Gare, 83420, T04 94 55 12 12.

La-Palud-sur-Verdon Le Château, 04120, T04 92 77 32 02, lapaludsurverdon.com.

Le Grau-du-Roi rue Michel Rédarès, 30240, T04 66 51 67 70 30, vacances-en-camargue.com.

Le Lavandou quai Gabriel Peri, 83980, T04 94 00 40 50, ot-lelavandou.fr.

Les Baux-de-Provence Maison du Roy, 13520, T04 90 54 34 39, lesbauxdeprovence.com.

Lourmarin av Philippe de Girard, 84160, T04 90 68 10 77, lourmarin.com.

Mandelieu-La Napoule 806 av de Cannes, 06210, T04 93 93 64 64, ot-mandelieu.fr.

Manosque 16 place du Docteur Joubert, 04100, T04 92 72 16 00, manosque-tourisme.com.

Marseilles 4 La Canebière (Vieux Port), 13000, T04 91 13 89 00, marseille-tourisme.com.

Menton 8 av Boyer, 06500, T04 92 41 76 76, tourisme-menton.fr.

Monaco 2 bd des Moulins, 98000, T377 92 16 61 16, visitmonaco.com.

Mougins 18 bd Georges Courteline, 06250, T04 93 75 87 67, mougins-coteazur.org.

Moustiers-Ste-Marie place de l'Eglise, 04360, T04 92 74 67 84, moustiers.fr.

Nice 5 promenade des Anglais; 3 av Thiers; both 06000, T08 92 70 74 07, nicetourisme.com.

Nîmes 6 rue Auguste, 30020, T04 66 58 38 00, ot-nimes.fr.

Roussillon place de la Poste, 38150, T04 90 05 60 25, roussillon-provence.com.

Ste-Croix-du-Verdon Mairie, 04500, T04 92 77 85 29, saintecroixduverdon.com.

St-Martin-Vésubie place Félix Faure, 06450, T04 93 03 21 28, saintmartinvesubie.fr.

St-Paul-de-Vence 2 rue Grande, 06570, T04 93 32 86 95, saint-pauldevence.com.

St-Rémy-de-Provence place Jean Jaurès, 13210, T04 90 92 05 22, saintremy-de-provence.com.

St-Tropez Le Port, 83990, T08 92 68 48 28, ot-saint-tropez.com.

Stes-Maries-de-la-Mer 5 av Van Gogh, 13460, T04 90 97 82 55, saintesmaries.com.

Tende 103 av 16 Septembre 1947, 06430, T04 93 04 73 71, tendemerveilles.com.

Théoule-sur-Mer 1 corniche d'Or, 06590, T04 93 49 28 28, theoule-sur-mer.org.
Val d'Allos-La Foux Centre Ville, 04260, T04 92 83 80 70, valdallos.com.
Valberg place Ginesy, 06470, T04 93 23 24 25, valberg.com.
Vence place du Grand Jardin, 06140, T04 93 58 06 38, vence.fr.
Villefranche-sur-Mer Jardin François Binon, 06230, T04 93 01 73 68, villefranche-sur-mer.com.

Toys & books
Au Tour de l'Enfant 110 cours Julien, 13006 Marseilles.
Book in bar 4 rue Joseph Cabassol, 13100 Aix-en-Provence.
La carte à Jouer 6 rue Rappe, 84000 Avignon.
L'Atelier des Jouets 1 place de l'Ancien Senat, 06300 Nice.
JouéClub Contesso 36 av Notre Dame, 06000 Nice.
Joupi 17 rue Paul Bert, 13100

Aix-en-Provence.
Rêve d'Enfant 6 rue Henri Seillon, 83990 St-Tropez.

Beach toys and gear can be purchased at the small shops and kiosks that line the seafront at any resort along the coast.

Index

Index

Photo credits

All photos by Kathryn Tomasetti, except: p12-13 – Baby-friendly Boltholes; page 16-17 – Liz Harper; p20-21 – Spacebetween; p39 – Jennifer Boutboul; p43 – Malena Richard; p45 – Rosa Jackson; p53 – Jennifer Boutboul; p70 – Eva Szczesny; p90 – Jean-Charles Grabiaud; p108 – Muriel Giraud; p130 – Alvin West. The following photos were all supplied by Hemis: p16 – MOIRENC Camille, GARDEL Bertrand; p19 – MOIRENC Camille, GARDEL Bertrand WYSOCKI-FRANCES; p20 – GARDEL Bertrand; p21 – LENAIN Hervé; p30 – Romain; p68 – COLIN Matthieu; p76 – MOIRENC Camille; p77 – DOZIER Marc; p88 – MOIRENC Camille; p89 – JACQUES Pierre; p98 – GUIZIOU Franck; p118 - MOIRENC Camille; p 121 – GARDEL Bertrand; p123 – MOIRENC Camille; p139 – GIRAUDOU Laurent; p142 – MOIRENC Camille; p146 – MOIRENC Camille; p162-63 MOIRENC Camille; p 168 – ESCUDERO Patrick; p170 – BOISVIEUX Christophe; Page 162-63 MOIRENC Camille; p179 – LUIDER Emile; p180 – GUIZIOU Franck; p187 – GARDEL Bertrand; p181 – FRANCES Stéphane.

Front Cover

Girl Standing in Field of Sunflowers
Bryan F Peterson/photolibrary.com

Back Cover

1. Harvest of sweet basil 'Grand Vert' at La ferme aux basilics
Frédérique Bidault / photolibrary.com

2. Camargue horses running in water at beach, Camargue, France
Konrad Wothe/LOOK-foto/ photolibrary.com

Inside Front Cover

France, Bouches du Rhone, Marseille, En Vau creek
Camille Moirenc/hemis.fr

Inside Back Cover

1. France, Bouches du Rhone, Marseille, Prado Beaches, the Big Wheel on Escale Borely
Bertrand Gardel / hemis.fr
2. Kathryn Tomasetti

Acknowledgements

Special thanks to Jennifer and Mickael Boutboul, Bruno and Virginie Lang, Rosa Jackson, Eva Szczesny, Alvin and Charlotte West, Malena Richard, Muriel Giraud, Pauline and John Larkin, Delphine, Lisa Fox-Mullen, Aaron Gray, Gianluca Fratantonio, Raoul de Jong and Inga Govasli Nilsen. Thanks also to Alan Murphy, Nicola Gibbs and the staff at Footprint for all the support, enthusiasm and patience, as well as Tamsin Stirk, copy editor extraordinaire.

This guidebook would never have come to fruition without invaluable help from my family. So many thanks go to adventurer and best sis Elizabeth Tomasetti; expert early childhood educator Nancy DiMauro; Daniel Tomasetti and Lucy Parnell and Zoe and Nigel Howorth for having such wonderful children and sharing them; Giuseppe Tomasetti, Susan, Paul and Harvey Rutherford. My husband, Tristan Rutherford, is a star researcher, proofer, creative inspiration and shining beacon of positive energy always.

Credits

Footprint credits

Project editor: Nicola Gibbs
Text editor: Tamsin Stirk
Picture editors: Kathryn Tomasetti,
Davina Rungasamy, Nicola Gibbs
Proofreader: Carol Maxwell
Layout & production: Davina Rungasamy
Maps: Gail Townsley

Managing Director: Andy Riddle
Commercial Director: Patrick Dawson
Publisher: Alan Murphy
Publishing Managers: Felicity Laughton,
Nicola Gibbs
Digital Editors: Jo Williams, Jen Haddington
Marketing: Liz Harper
Advertising: Renu Sibal, Elizabeth Taylor
Finance & administration: Elizabeth Taylor

Print

Printed in India by Replika Press Pvt Ltd

Every effort has been made to ensure that the facts in this guidebook are accurate. However, travellers should still obtain advice from consulates, airlines, etc about travel and visa requirements before travelling. The authors and publishers cannot accept responsibility for any loss, injury or inconvenience however caused.

Footprint Feedback

We try as hard as we can to make each Footprint guide as up to date as possible but, of course, things always change. If you want to let us know about your experiences – good, bad or ugly – then don't delay, go to www.footprintbooks.com and send in your comments.

Publishing information

Footprint South of France with Kids, 1st edition
© Footprint Handbooks Ltd, May 2011

ISBN 978-1-907263-39-2
CIP DATA: A catalogue record for this book is available from the British Library

® Footprint Handbooks and the Footprint mark are a registered trademark of Footprint Handbooks Ltd

Published by Footprint

6 Riverside Court
Lower Bristol Road
Bath BA2 3DZ, UK
T +44 (0)1225 469141
F +44 (0)1225 469461
footprinttravelguides.com

Distributed in North America by

Globe Pequot Press, Guilford, Connecticut